362

Springer Series on
ADULTHOOD and AGING

Series Editors: Lissy F. Jarvik, M.D., Ph.D., and Bernard D. Starr, Ph.D.

Advisory Board:
Paul D. Baltes, Ph.D., Jack Botwinick, Ph.D., Carl Eisdorfer, M.D., Ph.D.,
Robert Kastenbaum, Ph.D., Neil G. McCluskey, Ph.D., K. Warner Schaie,
Ph.D., and Nathan W. Shock, Ph.D.

Donald E. Gelfand, Ph.D., is associate professor at the School of Social Work and Community Planning of the University of Maryland at Baltimore. A sociologist, he has been extensively involved in many applied and basic areas of sociology including mental health, urban sociology, and aging. He has also been actively involved in the formation of the Sociological Practice section within the American Sociological Association. His current research focuses on ethnicity and aging, and changes in the family related to aging. During the 1979–80 academic year he was on leave at the National Council on the Aging.

Jody K. Olsen, Ph.D., is director of the Center on Aging at the University of Maryland. Her activities involve training as well as research programs on all campuses of the university. Formerly director of an Area Agency on Aging, she has a special interest in long-term care and nutrition programs. Her current research interests involve the effects of volunteer service on the aging. She is also still extensively involved in short-term training for practitioners in gerontology.

THE AGING NETWORK
Programs and Services

Donald E. Gelfand
Jody K. Olsen

*with the assistance
of Jules Berman*

SPRINGER PUBLISHING COMPANY
New York

Springer Publishing Company, Inc.
200 Park Avenue South
New York, New York 10003

80 81 82 83 84 / 10 9 8 7 6 5 4 3 2 1

Library of Congress Cataloging in Publication Data

Gelfand, Donald E
    The aging network.

    (Springer series on adulthood and aging; 8)
    Includes bibliographical references and index.
    1. Aged—Services for—United States.   2. Old age
assistance—United States.   I. Olsen, Jody K., joint
author.   II. Title.   III. Series.
HV1461.G44   362.6'0973   80-12563
ISBN 0-8261-3050-X
ISBN 0-8261-3051-8 (pbk.)

Printed in the United States of America

Contents

Preface

Writing this book involved collecting mounds of information and spending days reading pamphlets, government reports, and vertical file materials on programs and services around the country. It is our hope that this effort will save instructors, students, and practitioners the necessity of having to go through the same process individually. We have tried to communicate the enormous variety of programs and services now extant for the aged in the United States. Although it would be impossible to cover all of these programs individually, we have attempted to provide readers with a sense of their breadth and scope. This is important because programs and services in aging have been changing at a dizzying pace. An understanding of the basic premises of these programs and services should help readers integrate future programmatic and funding changes into knowledge obtained from this volume and other sources.

We have provided details on the Older Americans Act and a number of other funding programs, but we have tried not to overwhelm readers with titles and dates. Deciding how much detail is necessary and how much is gratuitous has been difficult. If we have been successful, readers should be able to fill in gaps in areas of their own specific interests by reading publications from the Administration on Aging, the National Council on the Aging, and a variety of other organizations active in the field (see Appendix B).

Anyone digging into this material finds income maintenance one of the most complex social welfare fields. We are grateful to Jules Berman for his willingness to share his many years of expertise in the area of income maintenance by writing the vital Chapters 3 and 4.

We could never have completed our efforts without the invaluable resources of the National Council on the Aging library and staff. Norma Hetricks and Robert Scalaski provided helpful research assistance. Judy Gelfand, Thelma Laing, and Laura Noell provided invaluable editorial assistance; as always, Carol Montgomery contributed flawless manuscript typing. We also thank our respective spouses for their emotional support during the exciting but time-consuming process of developing this volume.

Introduction

Aging has been viewed in the past as a pathological condition with the elderly merely in a final suspended condition awaiting their imminent demise. Growing old was not considered part of any developmental scheme. The problems faced by many elderly were simply attributed to "old age." This pronouncement was used by many professionals as if it were a clinical diagnosis. While aging affects our entire physiology the tendency to view these changes as irreversible has led to the use of labels as a substitute for diagnosis or treatment. Fortunately, this situation has begun to change, and these changes are reflected in new approaches to developing and evaluating programs and services for the aged.

Continuum of Care Approaches

Recent efforts to develop an approach to providing aging services as a continuum of care assume that the elderly have varying degrees of need which must be matched to appropriate services. As is often the case in social welfare programs, the continuum of care model resulted not from a carefully conceived plan but only in retrospect. The increasing numbers of programs and services arising out of the fertile minds of providers in the field of aging ultimately brought about the attempts to sort them into some conceptual framework.

The underlying dimension of the continuum of care is the relative dependency of the older individual. At one end of the continuum is the "independent" person who may have a problem but does not require extensive assistance. Further along the continuum are individuals with some problems that can produce "functional impairment." Increasing levels of dependence follow, ultimately ending with individuals classified as "fully dependent," who require intensive and full-time assistance (McCuan et al., 1975).

The acceptance of a continuum model requires abandoning arguments over whether one service is "better" than another. The major question instead becomes: Is one service more appropriate than another for an individual with specific needs? Defining which services meet a particular need is not always an easy task and is complicated by the overlapping of programs and services and the multiple needs of many older adults.

Matching programs and services to need is most difficult for individuals at intermediate points on the continuum. The types of services that are appropriate can be debated, and alternative models can be considered. Differentiating between services with any clarity requires that goals be explicated and programmatic elements be outlined; unfortunately, this is not always done in health and social services. Throughout the book, we try to clarify the goals, target populations, and important components of specific programs and services. We also outline the background, past and present funding, and major variations in these programs and services as they are delivered to older populations across the country.

Organization of the Book

Part I focuses on the present status of older Americans and the general thrust of programs and services in aging. After a brief glimpse at the characteristics of older adults in Chapter 1, Chapter 2 moves into an extensive examination of federal legislation authorizing programs and services for the aged. The major emphasis is on the provisions of the Older Americans Act.

In Part II, the complex but crucial topic of income maintenance programs is explored, including both the burgeoning private pension plans and the major public programs such as social security, Supplemental Security Income, Medicare, and Medicaid.

Part III provides readers with details on major programs in aging, ranging from information and referral efforts to crime prevention programs throughout the United States.

Part IV moves on to a discussion of the enlarging service delivery systems for the elderly, including senior centers, the growing in-home services, and the relatively recent adult daycare centers. This part concludes with an examination of the always controversial but important nursing homes.

Having discussed the myriad efforts that fall under each of these headings, Chapter 16 provides an opportunity to reflect on the factors that have allowed for such rapid development of these programs and services and their probable future.

Reference

McCuan, E., Lohn, H., Levenson, J., & Hsu, J. *Cost-effectiveness evaluation of the Levindale adult day treatment center.* Baltimore: Levindale Geriatric Research Center, 1975.

Part I
The American Elderly:
Programs and Services

With renewed discussions of aging, stereotypes about the elderly as sick and unable to care for themselves have begun to disappear. Indeed, the danger seems to be that of a new stereotype portraying the older American as full of energy, enjoying every moment of life, spending daytimes jogging and going to college and nights at the local disco. By examining relevant statistical data, Chapter 1 attempts to place the current condition of the aged in the United States in a perspective helpful to the planning and development of programs.

The groundwork having been laid, Chapter 2 plunges into an in-depth examination of the programs and services for the aged. The focus is on program authorizations and funds emanating from the Older Americans Act and on related programs stemming from a variety of federal and state legislation. The complexity of existing legislation will be quickly evident to the reader, but an understanding of the titles and acts discussed is imperative for the student and practitioner planning to work in aging.

1

The Older American

The Elderly Population

Before examining any programs some attention must be paid to the number and characteristics of older Americans. Our aim is to provide a foundation that will enable the reader to critically assess the specific programs and services discussed in the remaining chapters of this book. Rather than viewing characteristics statically, we will focus on how the status of the elderly has changed during the 20th century.

Size of the Population

Many Americans seem surprised when they first become acquainted with the significant increase in the numbers of older adults in the United States. This increase is occurring in every major industrialized country in the world. The ratio of older Americans to the general population will continue to increase during the next century. In 1900, individuals over 60 comprised only 6.4% of the population and individuals over 65, only 2.9%. These figures had tripled by 1977, with adults over 60 making up 15% and those over 65, 10.8% of the nation's citizens. By 2000, these groups will number 16% and 12%, respectively; and by 2035, 23% and 18% of the population (Fowles, 1978).

These figures should be accurate barring any major medical advances, major wars, or substantial changes in the birth or death rates. In 1978, the National Center for Health Statistics reported that

3

the death rate was at an all-time low. The decline in mortality rates has increased life expectancies for men and women. White females born in 1978 could expect to live 77.7 years; nonwhite females, 73.8 years; white males, 69.9 years; and nonwhite males 65 years (Washinton Post, 1978). These figures represent a reduction in the life expectancy gap between males and females. They also indicate an important reduction in the differentials in life expectancies between whites and blacks.

Family Structure

A larger population surviving into their 70s and 80s will create some important shifts in the structure of American families. More families will have surviving elderly parents, and many of these families will be composed of *four* rather than *three* generations. Thus, it is likely that many families will consist of an adult in their 80s, adult children in their 60s, a third generation of adult children in their 30s, and a fourth generation under 10 years of age. Statistical support for this projection can be found in the rapid increase in the over-75 population. Now 25% of the elderly are over 75, and this will increase to 33% by 2035. The over-85 group will comprise 10% of the elderly by 2035 (Fowles, 1978).

Health Status

The service implications of these figures are extensive. First, we can assume that without a major breakthrough in treatment of chronic diseases, there will be increasing numbers of elderly who will need assistance with the activities of daily living (dressing, cooking, bathing, etc.). Second, families that have two generations of individuals entering or in "old age" may find it extremely difficult to provide the necessary psychological, social, and economic supports. Recent estimates are that approximately 15–20% of the elderly population is incapacitated to some degree by chronic conditions. A population evidencing rapid increases in the number of its oldest members may also have larger numbers of individuals with serious chronic conditions.

It is important not to overstate the negative picture of the physical condition of the elderly population. While 80% of the older population has reported a chronic condition, only 18% of these individuals noted that their condition limited mobility, and only 5% were confined to their home. The most commonly noted chronic conditions affecting older Americans are arthritis, hearing and vision problems, hypertension, and heart conditions (U.S. Senate, 1979).

The fact that 69% of the elderly have reported their health as good or excellent when compared with individuals of the same age indicates that these conditions are not seen as an overwhelming burden. Only 9% of these respondents reported their health as poor. Poor health was most notable among those with low-incomes, members of minority groups, and elderly living in rural and southern parts of the U.S.

Living Patterns

One million elderly (over 60) are now residents of long-term care facilities, but this large figure still represents only 5% of the total number of older American adults. The vast majority of older Americans want, and will continue to maintain, their residence in the community.

One of the most striking statistics of recent years is, not the number of older people living in the community, but the increasing proportion of older individuals who are maintaining their own households. In 1960, only one-sixth of the noninstitutionalized elderly lived alone. By 1976 that figure had risen to one-quarter. This growth represents substantial numbers of women surviving for longer periods of time without spouses; 48% of the women over 75 now live alone (Fowles, 1978).

While longevity accounts for much of this increase, living alone requires reasonably stable financial resources. In part these resources can be provided by a combination of increased social security benefits, Supplemental Security Income (SSI), or private pensions. The increased number of elderly living alone also reflects the dispersal of families over a wide area. Poorer families consistently live closer to their elderly relatives. It has been shown that family income is positively related to the use of long-term care residences for elderly parents. Poorer families who cannot afford to provide financial assistance to their parents and cannot afford nursing home care are thus more likely to have an older family member living with them.

During the 1970s, rural states such as Iowa, Arkansas, and Missouri had high proportions of elderly (U.S. Senate, 1979). In these states younger families have moved to more urbanized regions and were not replaced by any significant numbers of new residents. Because of the substantial numbers of elderly who have grown older in rural areas, only 52% of individuals over 65 were living in metropolitan areas in 1978 as compared to 67% of the under-65 population (U.S. Senate, 1979).

The elderly living in metropolitan areas are concentrated in inner-city neighborhoods although Kennedy and DeJong's (1977) analysis of 10 cities indicated that a proportion of the elderly have joined in the migration to the suburbs. The percentage of older adults living in the central city decreased in 8 of the 10 cities between 1960 and 1970. This change is not as apparent among blacks as it is among whites. Concentrations of elderly blacks in the central city may continue to increase as black families continue to find themselves blocked from many residential areas because of discrimination.

Cultural Backgrounds

Although many senior advocacy groups speak out against stereotyping, there is a continued tendency to discuss the elderly as a homogenous group whose values and beliefs are defined by their age. In reality the cultural backgrounds among the present generation of individuals over 60 are enormously varied. In 1960, 4.2 million of the American elderly had been born overseas. This group had declined to 3.7 million in 1970, comprising approximately one-seventh of the population over 60. In 1975, the Bureau of the Census reported that 5% of the over-65 population still primarily relied on a language other than English (Fowles, 1978). Differences in cultural attitudes toward aging and utilization of services, as well as a lack of fluency in English among foreign-born elderly, may create problems for providers attempting to implement aging programs.

Education

The minimal educational background of many present-day elderly also creates problems for service providers. In 1960, the elderly had a median of 8.3 years of education. This had risen to 10.3 years by 1978. Although this increase is impressive, the service provider must understand that the majority of the present-day older adults have not completed high school and possess limited verbal, writing, and reading skills. Programs that involve extensive reading and discussion may thus not be practical for many elderly. At a more basic level, many elderly will have difficulty understanding and following instructions on medication and may utilize their medication improperly.

Employment and Income

Recent changes in American work patterns have not been of major benefit to many American and foreign-born elderly. The inability of these older adults to obtain higher education during the early 1900s relegated them to careers as blue-collar workers. Only 20% of the individuals between 60 and 70 in 1977 were employed in white-collar jobs. Men and women whose work has centered around low-paying jobs have meager financial resources for their old age. Low wages have meant low social security benefits and inadequate or nonexistent pensions. Part-time and intermittent work has prevented many women from accumulating enough quarters to qualify for social security.

Many of the elderly being served by present-day programs are individuals with limited ability to pay for costly programs. Income maintenance programs such as Supplemental Security Income (SSI), Medicare, food stamps, and housing subsidies have helped to raise the income floor of the elderly. Improvements in the income of the elderly during the past 20 years can be documented. The median income for individuals over 65 rose by 33% (taking inflation into account) between 1960 and 1970, and the number of individuals over 60 below the federally determined "poverty" level dropped from 5.9 million in 1969 to 4.3 million in 1976 (Fowles, 1978). Unfortunately, compenstion for long-term employment in low-paying occupations can never be totally achieved. Women and minority groups have had concentrated employments in low-paying industries. The slowest decline in poverty rates during the 1970s were thus women, minorities, and individuals living alone. It is thus doubtful that efforts by the private sector, to expand services available to the elderly will meet the needs of present-day older citizens unless these services are included under government reimbursables (Medicare, etc.).

Although their status has been improving on many fronts, the elderly still suffer from a variety of deficits which require the assistance of formal and informal services. After examining the existing programs we will return in Chapter 16 to a discussion of the anticipated effects of economic, social, and health changes among the elderly on contemporary service delivery systems.

References

Fowles, D. Some prospects for the future elderly population. Washington, D.C.: Administration on Aging, 1978.

Kennedy, J. and De Jong, G. Aged in cities: Residential segregation in 10 USA central cities. *Journal of Gerontology,* 1977, *32,* 97–102.

U.S. Senate, Special Committee on Aging. *Developments in aging, 1978: Part I.* Washington, D.C.: U.S. Government Printing Office, 1979.

Washington Post. U.S. mortality rate dips to record low. *Washington Post,* November 12, 1978, p. A-8.

2

Legislative Bases for Programs and Services

The present generation of elderly benefit from both "categorical" programs designed to serve all individuals who fall into a specifically defined group (in this case older adults), and generic programs that benefit all age groups. In this chapter we will intensively review the legislation underlying existing aging programs. After highlighting the important legislation we will examine other sources of programs and services for the aged and the major funding mechanisms underlying these services. Our attention will focus on the legislative initiatives and programs formulated at the federal level and implemented by state and local governmental units.

The major influence on programs for older adults has been the Older Americans Act (OAA) initially passed by Congress in 1965. Many of the features of the act were influenced by the 1961 White House Conference on Aging. The act has been amended seven times, and the 1971 White House Conference on Aging influenced the 1974 and 1975 amendments. On October 18, 1978, PL 95-478, the eighth amending of the Older Americans Act, was signed into law by President Carter. PL 95-478 reauthorized the OAA until fiscal 1981.

The 1978 amendments indicated a desire to streamline and coordinate services to the aged and to clarify the responsibility of the major organizations providing services to the aging, especially the rural aged. The 1978 amendments also continued the process of emphasizing service priorities, a step first taken in the 1975 amendments. In this chapter we will compare the major thrust of the 1978 amendments with previous versions and examine the funding of aging programs. The complete text of the OAA can be found in Appendix A. The specifics of individual programs are provided in subsequent chapters.

The Older Americans Act in 1978

Purpose of the Act

The basic purpose of the Older Americans Act is to "help older persons" by providing funds to the states for services, training, and research. All three of these activities are to be coordinated through the Administration on Aging (AoA). While the most effective linkage for AoA with the Department of Health, Education, and Welfare has always been a matter of contention in Washington circles, the agency is now formally under the Office of Human Development, a branch of HEW.

Title I: Objectives

In 1965, the goals of the OAA were couched in sweeping language which encompassed 10 difficult but laudable objectives:

1. An adequate income
2. The best possible physical and mental health
3. Suitable housing
4. Full restorative services
5. Opportunity for employment without age discrimination
6. Retirement in health, honor, and dignity
7. Pursuit of meaningful dignity
8. Efficient community services when needed
9. Immediate benefit from proven research knowledge
10. Freedom, independence, and the free exercise of individual initiative. (Butler, 1975, p. 329)

In 1978, a new stress was placed on the provision of community services that enable the older person to make a choice among a variety of subsidized living arrangements. The target population of the OAA was originally individuals over the age of 65. In 1973, this was changed to 60 without extensive opposition in Congress. Part of the logic in the reduction of the eligible age was that the programs and services developed under the act's provisions would assist older individuals in preretirement planning.

Title II: Administration on Aging

A direct outcome of the enactment of the OAA was the organization of the Administration on Aging. Directed by the Commissioner of Aging, AoA is charged with carrying out the provisions of the OAA. The Commissioner is appointed by the President and confirmed by the U.S. Senate.

As can be seen by even a quick perusal of the OAA, the responsibilities of the AoA are extensive. They range from providing information on problems of the aging to planning, gathering statistics, setting policies, and coordinating ongoing efforts in aging at federal and local levels. The 1973 amendments to the OAA also authorized the Federal Council on the Aging, appointed by the President to provide advice to the President on concerns of the elderly.

The 1978 OAA amendments outlined a role for the AoA as an advocate of aging programs throughout the federal government (Section 202a). Section 202 and 203 also stressed the importance of the Commissioner's intervention in a variety of planning, regulatory, and coordinating activities. Initially, the House of Representatives had proposed that the Commissioner be directly responsible to the Secretary of HEW, but the Conference Committee of the House and Senate rejected this in favor of the provision that the Commissioner on Aging report to the Office of the Secretary rather than to the Secretary. By stressing the Commissioner's role, the OAA emphasized the importance of having a federal official responsible for the coordinating of aging programs across such diverse agencies as the Social Security Administration, Housing and Urban Development, and the Department of Transportation.

Parallel to an expansion of the Commissioner's responsibilities, the 1978 OAA increased the responsibilities of the Federal Council on Aging. In 1973, the council was mandated to study the "interrelationships of benefit programs for the elderly, the impact of taxes on the elderly and the effects of funding allotments." In 1978, Section 205 authorized the council to undertake evaluative studies of programs conducted under provisions of the OAA, with special emphasis on the numbers of low-income and minority participants in aging programs.

Title III: Grants for State and Community Programs in Aging

Title III is the most important component of the Older Americans Act. This title outlines the types of services that should be provided at the local level in order to develop "coordinated and comprehensive services" enabling older adults to maintain "maximum independence" (Section 301). The basic foundation for providing these services is an agency designated by the governor of each state with responsibility for aging services. In many states this agency has been a newly formed office on aging. State offices on aging are not always provided with a mandate to oversee all aging programs, some remaining within already established departments. In 1972, Massachusetts opted for a coordinated approach to state services for the elderly with the creation of the cabinet-level Department of Elder Affairs which controlled aging programs and services, licensing of nursing homes, elderly housing, and transportation services.

The agency designated by the governor is responsible for the development of a 3-year statewide plan for serving the elderly. Geographic service areas must be designated by the agency and local Area Agencies on Aging (AAAs) must be established. Within each of these areas the state agency has latitude in outlining geographic service areas. In many states these areas have coincided with health and mental health planning units.

The AAA develops its own 3-year service plan, which must be submitted for approval by the state agency. An area agency can be a unit of county, city, or town government or even a private nonprofit agency. Preference must be given to an already established office on aging. In 1979 approximately 650 AAAs were already in existence across the country.

The service requirements for an AAA in the OAA have been written in fairly unspecified terminology. As can be seen in Appendix A, these services included coordination of plans, improvement of existing social services, information and referral services, evaluation activities, technical assistance, legal services "where necessary and feasible," and an organized advisory council.

In 1978, Title III also stressed the AAA's seeking opportunities for the elderly to further their education. This emphasis continues the effort by Congress in 1975 to increase the specificity of service requirements for AAAs. In the 1975 amendments, four priority areas were noted: transportation, in-home services, legal services, and home repair and renovation programs. In 1978, the three priority areas were access services (transportation, outreach, information, and referral), "in-home services" (homemakers, home health aides, visiting, and telephone reassurance efforts), and legal services.

Social services. Social services as defined in the act include a wide range of programs ranging from health care efforts to transportation, housing assistance, residential repairs, homemaker services, and tax counseling (Section 321). One of the most important new social services is the ombudsman program designed to "receive, investigate and act on complaints by older individuals who are residents of long-term care facilities. . . ." The inclusion of the ombudsman program represents a culmination of 1972 and 1973 demonstration programs and an AoA grant program in 1975 which offered states the opportunity to develop an ombudsman service. The specifics of this new program (Section 307) are discussed in Chapter 15.

At the local level, the AAA must carry through the state's emphasis on serving the elderly with the greatest economic or social needs. An active outreach program aimed at developing contact with underserved and rural elderly should be a vital component of the AAA program. Outreach can also be accomplished through an effective information and referral system developed by the AAA in areas where this service does not yet exist. In all of these efforts a local advisory council composed of elderly, local political officials and nonelderly public members would be utilized to assist in program planning.

Nutrition programs. Until 1978, nutrition programs comprised Title VII of the Older Americans Act. In 1978, Title VII was deleted and reclassified as Section C of Title III. In contrast to previous years, the 1978 amendments placed nutrition programs under administrative control of the AAA as part of its consolidation of social service programs. This provision became effective in September 1980. While the 1978 amendments were an obvious effort to bring some consolidation and coordination to service areas such as nutrition, the framers of the amendment fortunately recognized the upheaval and loss of services that might result if attempts were made to precipitously transfer control and operation of nutrition programs from a variety of local auspices to the AAAs. Because of these concerns, consolidation of nutrition programs under the AAA could be waived in fiscal 1979 and 1980. It was also expected that the consolidation requirements would encourage many nutrition programs to become transformed into AAAs, expanding their service delivery capacity to meet the requirements of the OAA. This transformation will be necessary in communities in which no AAA exists, because only AAAs are authorized to allocate funds for nutrition services in fiscal 1981.

At congregate meal sites the emphasis is on one hot meal available at least 5 days a week. The major new emphasis in nutrition services is the authorization of the expenditure of funds for Home

Delivered Meals (Meals-on-Wheels). These services are required to provide delivery of a balanced meal at least once a day.

The report from the House-Senate conference committee stressed the Congress's intention that

> every effort be made for participants to take part in a congregate setting unless homebound by reasons of illness, an incapacitating disability, or extreme transportation problems. The conferees expect the Administration to follow carefully the development of this new program and discourage its use unless necessary because of the aforementioned reasons. (U.S. House of Representatives, 1978, p. 62)

Guidelines for charges for meals are to be determined by the Commissioner on Aging and income realized from the purchase of meals poured back in an effort to increase the number of meals served as more elderly become aware of the program through outreach efforts.

Senior centers. In 1978, Title V (first included in the 1973 amendments) dealing with multipurpose senior centers also became part of Title III. The 1978 amendments again recognize that the multipurpose senior center is not a separate service entity but rather a "community facility" for organizing and providing the gamut of social and nutritional services authorized by the OAA. In 1978, the House-Senate conferees were unwilling to authorize separate funding for multipurpose senior centers. This unwillingness represents the viewpoint that centers are part of the social services delivery network of the state and its AAAs (U.S. House of Representatives, 1978). In fact, Title III stresses that "where feasible, a focal point for comprehensive service delivery" should be designated with "special consideration" given to "designating multipurpose senior centers as such focal point" [Section 306(a) (3)]. The AoA is authorized to make grants to the states for construction, acquisition, and renovation of buildings usable as senior centers. Mortgages for these centers can be insured by HEW and social service funds can be used for the centers' operating costs.

Title IV: Training, Research, Discretionary Projects and Programs

Title IV has been a mainstay of training and research efforts in the field of aging. This includes efforts of state and local governments as well as a variety of public and private organizations. Under Title IVA diverse training projects have been funded including short-term training courses, in-service institutes, and seminars and conferences.

Concern about a shortage of trained personnel to serve the aging is growing in Congress, and the 1978 amendments encouraged a coordinated approach to expanded training activities, especially training directed at serving minority elderly.

Since 1965, Title IVB research priorities have reflected changing concerns in the field of aging. In 1973, sections were added to IVB calling for special research emphases on transportation problems affecting older adults. This section (412) was repealed in 1978. In 1978, the amendments to Title IVB indicated new emphases rather than any startling new approaches. The emphasis on transportation in IVB in 1978 was not on innovative approaches to transportation services discussed in Chapter 7 but rather on the recent problems of insurance costs, duplicative services, and eligibility.

Title IV authorizes demonstrations (Part C) on social and nutrition services, especially projects concerning rural homebound, blind, and disabled elderly [Section 412(a) and (b)]. Demonstration projects on long-term care, legal services, and model projects aimed at reducing energy costs of the elderly were also authorized. The previous Part C of Title IV was a major support in the development of multidisciplinary centers on aging at 13 universities in the United States. In 1978, the authorization for these centers (now Part E) was broadened by allowing centers with a variety of special emphases to be funded.

Title V: Community Service Employment

Title V of the 1978 OAA was formerly Title IX. Title IX had originally been added to the OAA in 1973. As true of other titles in the 1978 amendments, the stress in Title V in 1978 was on coordination of projects underway in a variety of state, federal, and private agencies. The title also attempted to delineate the role of groups that contract to provide community service employment for older adults. As in the past, the priority recipients of community employment services are individuals over 55 who are unemployed or whose prospects for employment are limited. In 1978, however, the income requirement for eligibility for community service programs was raised from the federally designated poverty level to 125% of the poverty level. The title also attempted to expand the employment opportunities open to part-time elderly workers by authorizing the Senior Environmental Employment Corps [Section 505(c)]. A number of new technical requirements can also be noted in Title V.

Developing special employment programs for the elderly does

not relieve the government from attempting to eliminate age discrimination in the workplace. Section 302 of the OAA reasserts some of the provisions of the Age Discrimination Act of 1975. The section prohibits "discrimination on the basis of age in programs or activities receiving federal financial assistance," rather than outlawing only "unreasonable" discrimination as was true in the 1975 version. The question of exemptions from this provision remains unclear in the law and open to administrative judgments.

Title VI: Grants for Indian Tribes

This new title authorized funds for Indian tribes to develop social and nutritional services for the aged if Title III programs were not already providing adequate services. Congress specified that the provisions of the title would not come into effect unless $5 million was appropriated for this title. The enactment of a separate title on Indian elderly represents an enlargement of the 1975 amendments to the OAA, which encourage states to directly fund Indian tribes interested in providing services to the elderly if these services are not already available.

Additional Programs

As can be seen in Figure 2.1, the number of programs benefiting older Americans that do not come under the OAA is extensive. It is this extensiveness and the large number of federal agencies involved that has encouraged the emphasis on consolidation and coordination in the 1978 amendments to the OAA. The programs included in Figure 2.1 are detailed in the chapters describing specific program areas.

Funding of Aging Programs

Prior to 1973, funding for aging programs and services was minimal. Gold (1974) has characterized the programs and services supported in the 1960s as community demonstrations. The passage of the Nutrition Services Act in 1972 was thus a major breakthrough in its focus on large-scale direct services for the elderly. Since 1973 Congressional appropriations for activities under the OAA have increased dramatically, enabling the implementation of a wide range of programs and services.

Because of the late date on which the 1978 Older Americans Act

Figure 2.1

MAJOR FEDERAL PROGRAMS BENEFITING THE ELDERLY
By Category and by Agency

Program	EXECUTIVE DEPARTMENTS — AGRICULTURE: Farmers Home Administration	Food and Nutrition Service	HEALTH, EDUCATION, AND WELFARE: Health Services Administration	Social Security Administration	Office of Education	Administration on Aging	Social and Rehabilitation Service	Office of Nursing Home Affairs	National Institute on Aging	H.U.D.: Housing Production and Mortgage Credit *	Housing Management	Community Planning and Development	LABOR: Office of Fair Labor Standards	Employment and Training Administration **	D.O.T.: Urban Mass Transportation Administration	Federal Highway Administration	TREASURY: Office of Revenue Sharing	INDEPENDENT AGENCIES: ACTION	COMMUNITY SERVICES ADMINISTRATION	LEGAL SERVICES CORPORATION	RAILROAD RETIREMENT BOARD	SMALL BUSINESS ADMINISTRATION	U.S. CIVIL SERVICE COMMISSION	VETERANS ADMINISTRATION
EMPLOYMENT																								
AGE DISCRIMINATION IN EMPLOYMENT ***													●											
EMPLOYMENT PROGRAMS FOR SPECIAL GROUPS														●										
FOSTER GRANDPARENT PROGRAM																		●						
OLDER AMERICANS COMMUNITY SERVICE EMPLOYMENT PROGRAM														●										
RETIRED SENIOR VOLUNTEER PROGRAM (RSVP)																		●						
SERVICE CORPS OF RETIRED EXECUTIVES (SCORE)																						●		
VOLUNTEERS IN SERVICE TO AMERICA (VISTA)																		●						
HEALTH CARE																								
HEALTH RESOURCES DEVELOPMENT CONSTRUCTION AND MODERNIZATION OF FACILITIES (Hill-Burton Prog)			●																					
CONSTRUCTION OF NURSING HOMES AND INTERMEDIATE CARE FACILITIES										●														
GRANTS TO STATES FOR MEDICAL ASSISTANCE PROGRAMS (MEDICAID)							●																	
PROGRAM OF HEALTH INSURANCE FOR THE AGED AND DISABLED (MEDICARE)				●																				
VETERANS DOMICILIARY CARE PROGRAM																								●
VETERANS NURSING HOME CARE PROGRAM																								●

* Formerly Federal Housing Administration   ** Formerly Manpower Administration   *** In 1978, this was transferred to the Equal Employment Opportunities Commission

MAJOR FEDERAL PROGRAMS BENEFITING THE ELDERLY

By Category and by Agency

Figure 2.1 (Continued)

Column headings (by agency):

EXECUTIVE DEPARTMENTS

- AGRICULTURE: Farmers Home Administration; Food and Nutrition Service
- HEALTH, EDUCATION, AND WELFARE: Health Services Administration; Social Security Administration; Office of Education; Administration on Aging; Social and Rehabilitation Service; Office of Nursing Home Affairs; National Institute on Aging
- H.U.D.: Housing Production and Mortgage Credit; Community Planning and Development
- LABOR: Office of Fair Labor Standards; Employment and Training
- D.O.T.: Urban Mass Transportation Administration; Federal Highway Administration
- TREASURY: Office of Revenue Sharing
- ACTION
- COMMUNITY SERVICES ADMINISTRATION
- LEGAL SERVICES CORPORATION

INDEPENDENT AGENCIES

- RAILROAD RETIREMENT BOARD
- SMALL BUSINESS ADMINISTRATION
- U.S. CIVIL SERVICE COMMISSION
- VETERANS ADMINISTRATION

HOUSING

Program	Agency / Administration
HOUSING FOR THE ELDERLY (sec. 202)	H.U.D. — Housing Production and Mortgage Credit
LOW AND MODERATE INCOME HOUSING (sec. 8)	H.U.D. — Housing Production and Mortgage Credit; Community Planning and Development
MORTGAGE INSURANCE ON RENTAL HOUSING FOR THE ELDERLY (sec. 231)	H.U.D. — Housing Production and Mortgage Credit; Community Planning and Development
RURAL RENTAL HOUSING LOANS	Agriculture — Farmers Home Administration
COMMUNITY DEVELOPMENT	H.U.D. — Community Planning and Development
RENTAL AND CO-OPERATIVE HOUSING FOR LOWER AND MODERATE INCOME FAMILIES (sec. 236)	H.U.D. — Housing Production and Mortgage Credit; Community Planning and Development
LOW RENT PUBLIC HOUSING	H.U.D. — Housing Production and Mortgage Credit; Community Planning and Development

INCOME MAINTENANCE

Program	Agency / Administration
CIVIL SERVICE RETIREMENT	U.S. Civil Service Commission
OLD-AGE, SURVIVORS INSURANCE PROGRAM (Social Security)	Health, Education, and Welfare — Social Security Administration
RAILROAD RETIREMENT PROGRAM	Railroad Retirement Board
SUPPLEMENTAL SECURITY INCOME PROGRAM	Health, Education, and Welfare — Social Security Administration
VETERANS PENSION PROGRAM	Veterans Administration

SOCIAL SERVICE PROGRAMS

- EDUCATION PROGRAMS FOR NON-ENGLISH SPEAKING ELDERLY
- FOOD STAMP PROGRAM
- LEGAL SERVICES CORPORATION
- MODEL PROJECTS
- MULTIPURPOSE SENIOR CENTERS
- NUTRITION PROGRAM FOR THE ELDERLY
- OLDER READER SERVICES
- REVENUE SHARING
- SENIOR OPPORTUNITIES AND SERVICES
- SOCIAL SERVICES FOR LOW-INCOME PERSONS AND PUBLIC ASSISTANCE RECIPIENTS
- STATE AND COMMUNITY PROGRAMS

TRAINING AND RESEARCH PROGRAMS

- MULTI-DISCIPLINARY CENTERS OF GERONTOLOGY
- NURSING HOME CARE, TRAINING AND RESEARCH PROGRAMS
- PERSONNEL TRAINING
- RESEARCH AND DEMONSTRATION PROGRAM
- RESEARCH ON AGING PROCESS AND HEALTH PROBLEMS
- RESEARCH ON PROBLEMS OF THE ELDERLY

TRANSPORTATION

- CAPITAL ASSISTANCE GRANTS FOR USE BY PUBLIC AGENCIES
- CAPITAL ASSISTANCE GRANTS FOR USE BY PRIVATE NON-PROFIT GROUPS
- REDUCED FARES
- RURAL HIGHWAY PUBLIC TRANSPORTATION DEMONSTRATION PROJECT

*Formerly Federal Housing Administration

**Formerly Manpower Administration

Source: U.S. House of Representatives, Select Committee on Aging, *Federal Responsibility to the Elderly*, 1976.

19

was enacted, constituent programs were funded under a "continuing resolution" until the end of September 1979, when fiscal 1980 officially began. Table 2.1 shows the 1979 appropriations for the OAA, which continued the FY 1978 levels. Unfortunately, funding requests of the Carter administration for FY 1980 did not substantially exceed those of 1979. As Table 2.1 indicates, the requests were substantially below the authorization of the act. With an 8.5% inflation rate taken into account, the discrepancy between funding levels and program needs is even greater.

Geographic Funds

The state must allocate its Title III funds according to the geographic distribution of the elderly within the state, providing maximal resources to older individuals with the greatest "economic or social needs." As the conference committee noted, many of the elderly with economic resources have a great social need for resources. The specification of need on two major dimensions may produce a reallocation of funds by state agencies from areas with large populations of poor elderly to areas with large but more affluent populations of elderly residents. This may approximate a redistribution of funding from urban to suburban and rural areas. The formula for allocation of Title III funds determined by the state aging office must be submitted and approved by the AoA.

Program Allocations

Senate-House conferees also stressed their belief that AAAs should continue to fund senior centers at present or higher levels. This laudable goal may face competition from other funding requirements placed on AAAs, especially in regard to nutrition programs. Although the consolidation of nutrition programs under AAAs takes effect in 1980, funding cannot be terminated from existing sites unless these centers are shown to be "ineffective."

Many nutrition programs have also developed extensive supportive services for their clients. The Congressional conference committee continued a regulation allowing the state to spend up to 20% of its nutrition allotment for recreational and informational activities and health and welfare counseling. When nutrition programs come under control of the AAA, funds for these services will then have to be allocated from social service budgets, a step which may create problems for AAAs now attempting to maintain extensive social ser-

Table 2.1. Older Americans Act Service Appropriations and Authorizations (In Thousands of Dollars)

Services	FY 1978 Appropriation	FY 1979 Appropriation (Authorized)	FY 1978 Appropriation +8.5 Inflation	FY 1979 Appropriation +8.5 Inflation	FY 1980 Appropriation (Authorized)	FY 1981 Authorization
Title II:						
Clearinghouse on Aging	2,000	2,000 (SS)[a]	2,170	2,354	2,000	SS[a]
Federal Council on the Aging	450	450 (SS)	490	530	450 (SS)[a]	SS[a]
Title III:						
State administration	19,000	22,500	N/A	N/A	22,500	
Social services	193,000[b]	196,970 (300,000)	209,900	227,200	246,970 (360,000)	480,000
Nutrition	250,000	272,500 (440,000)	271,000	295,663	320,000 (475,000)	520,000
Title IV:						
Training	17,000	17,000 (SS)[a]	18,400	20,000	17,000 (SS)[a]	SS[a]
Research	8,500	8,500 (SS)[a]	9,200	9,900	8,500 (SS)[a]	SS[a]
Multidisciplinary centers	3,800	3,800 (SS)[a]	4,100	4,500	3,800 (SS)[a]	9,900[a]
Model projects and demonstrations	18,000	15,000 (SS)	16,300	17,700	25,000[c] (SS)[a]	SS
Title V:	200,900	209,800 (350)	217,977	227,633	266,900 (400,000)	450,000
Title VI:						
Direct grants to Indian tribes	N/A	(SS)[a]	N/A	N/A	600,000 (SS)[a]	SS[a]
White House Conference on Aging 1981	N/A	300,000 (SS)	N/A	N/A	(SS)[a]	SS[a]

[a]Such sums as may be necessary.
[b]Social services represents $153 million for social services and $40 million for senior centers under previous Title V.
[c]Includes $10 million for a 10-state demonstration program in long-term care services for the homebound, blind, and disabled.

vice programs. Also placing pressure on AAAs' funds is the requirement that expenditures for services to the rural elderly must be 5%
above the previous year's.

Social Services Allocations

The distribution of funds within the broad "social service" category
was not left to the discretion of AAAs' planners in the 1978 OAA
amendments. This continues the trend begun in 1976 when Congress specified that 50% of any increased funds for that fiscal year or
one-third of the states' fiscal 1976 allotment had to be earmarked for
services specified as priorities. In 1978, the OAA specified that area
agencies must spend at least 50% of their social services budget on
the priorities of access, in-home, and legal services. Exact amounts to
be spent in each of these categories are unspecified, but some money
must be expended on each of these three program areas. If funds
from non-Title III sources were already meeting needs for any of
these three service areas, the AAA could apply for a waiver from the
state. The state could also reduce the percentage of funds the AAA
needed to allocate for the two remaining areas being funded through
Title III.

Administrative Costs

The unwillingness of the federal government to increase funding for
aging programs at a pace consistent with past years is evident. It is
also clear that the state and local communities will have to take on
added responsibilities for the costs of administering these programs
as well as contributing funds to the programs themselves. The 1978
OAA amendments specify that only 8.5% of Title III funds may be
used by an AAA to cover administrative costs. Until FY 1981, the
state and local areas will only be expected to contribute 10% of the
costs of services. In 1981, the state and local "match" will rise to 15%.
Fortunately, "in-kind" services will still be allowed as part of this
15%, but the "in-kind" services must be important to AAA programs
and be valued at a reasonable rate by the AAAs (U.S. House of Representatives, 1978). As pressures for increased state and local contributions of both actual funds and "in-kind" services increase, advocates
of aging programs will have to concentrate their efforts on convinc-
ing state legislators and city and county councils that aging services
should remain a top priority.

Additional Funding Sources

The reader will quickly realize that the majority of the programs listed in Figure 2.1 are primarily funding mechanisms. Many of these funding mechanisms are not specifically targeted for elderly groups but allow the elderly to be considered as an eligible population.

Decisions on allocation of many of these programs are made at the local level. This is characteristic of Title XX of the Social Security Act, General Revenue Sharing, and the Community Development Block Grants of the Department of Housing and Urban Development.

In 1974, Title XX was included in the Social Service Amendments to the Social Security Act, replacing Titles IVA and VI. Title XX funds are distributed according to the size of the state's population. The state must design a package of services and define the eligible population. In Maryland, 25 services were included in the FY 1979 Title XX plan (State of Maryland, 1978). Aging services to receive funding included adult daycare, foster care, homemaker services, nutrition programs, multipurpose senior centers, protective services, services in long-term care institutions, and funds for comprehensive community mental health centers.

Despite the seeming extensiveness of this list, the number of programs and services for the elderly that can be adequately funded under Title XX is limited. This limitation results from the federal requirements that states at least fund a specific group of "mandated services" and the ceiling that Congress has placed on Title XX allocations.

The federally "mandated services" include: adoption, daycare for children, early periodic screening, diagnosis and treatment of chronic and potential illnesses, employment counseling; family planning; foster care for children; information and referral; protective services for abused and neglected spouses and children; and services to the disabled, elderly, and blind.

As the cost of funding these and other services rises because of increased clientele and inflation, the total amount of money available through Title XX remains basically constant. When it was authorized in 1975, Congress attached a ceiling of $2.5 billion to Title XX. This ceiling has since been raised to $2.9 billion and was expected to reach $3.1 billion in FY 1980 or 1981. As a result of the funding limitations, social services in individual states must compete for moneys from the same limited pool of Title XX funds. States that have declining populations are placed in an even more difficult position since the amount of money allocated to any state is based on population rather than on social service needs. Faced with all of these problems, the state must develop a Title XX plan.

After an initial plan outlining services and target populations is drafted, 45 days must be allowed for public comments. Based on these comments a final plan is developed and submitted to HEW for approval. The state must also designate the agency responsible for delivery of the services and contribute a share of the funding for these services based on a 75-25% federal-local matching formula.

All of the services funded under Title XX must contribute toward realization of five major goals:

1. To help people become or remain economically self-supporting

2. To help people become or remain self-sufficient

3. To protect children and adults who cannot protect themselves

4. To prevent and reduce inappropriate institutional care as much as possible by making home and community services available

5. To arrange for appropriate placement and services in an institution when this is in an individual's best interest (State of Maryland, 1978)

General Revenue Sharing and Block Grants

General Revenue Sharing (GRS) was created under the State and Local Fiscal Assistance Act of 1972. GRS returns money to state and local governments based on a formula which takes into consideration the population size, the proportion of the population below the poverty level, and the local tax rate. The actual usage of this money is determined by the local areas. In 1972, "social services for the poor and elderly" were one of the eight priority areas, but these priorities were eliminated from the 1976 amendments to the act. The 1976 amendments added two requirements to the GRS program that strengthened the opportunities for public participation: requirements for publicity and public hearings about usage of revenue sharing funds by local and state governments and opportunities for citizens and organizations to give testimony on proposed GRS expenditures. Local municipalities were also permitted to use revenue sharing funds as "matching funds" in federal programs (National Institute of Senior Centers, 1977).

The majority of GRS funds have been utilized for physical improvements and property tax relief, but some funds have gone into operating programs for the elderly. In Niles, Illinois, a senior center used revenue sharing money to acquire and renovate a building. In Montpelier, Vermont, a senior center has supported the bulk of its programs through GRS funds (National Institute of Senior Centers, 1978). Local hearings are also characteristic of the Community Development Block Grants (CDBG).

Community Development Block Grants are also earmarked for improvement of substandard physical facilities and housing. Of these funds, 75% must be spent by the local community in low- or moderate-income deteriorated areas. CDBG funds are being used to rehabilitate housing, set up community centers, or build storm drains and sewers.

Flexibility and Change in Programming

The 1978 OAA amendments authorized the third White House Conference on Aging. In contrast to the situation at the first conference in 1961, the third White House conference can be expected to assess the effectiveness and approach of a complex set of programs already in existence. As our discussion has indicated, important shifts have taken place between 1975 and 1978 that affect the scope of services; the administrative authority under which they are conducted; and the responsibility of federal, state, and local providers for funding. The White House conferees will need to critically assess these changes while keeping in mind the need to maintain flexibility in programs and services. As the bureaucratic regulations in which aging programs and services are enmeshed become more stringent, the emphasis on coordination in the 1978 OAA amendments has to be counterbalanced by an equal emphasis on allowing opportunities for innovative service providers and researchers to test new ideas and reassess old methods of meeting needs.

References

Butler, R. *Why survive? Being old in America*. New York: Harper and Row, 1975.

Gold, B. The role of the federal government in the provision of social services to older persons. In F. Eisele (Ed.), Political consequences of aging. *Annals*, 1974, *415*, 55–69.

National Institute of Senior Centers. Funding. *Senior Center Report,* 1978, *1*(9), 3.

National Institute of Senior Centers. GRS public participation requirements strengthened. *Memo,* 1977, *5*(5), 1-2.

State of Maryland, Department of Human Resources. *Proposed FY 1979 Title XX Comprehensive Annual Services Plan.* Annapolis: Md., 1978.

U.S. House of Representatives. *Conference report No. 95-1618: Comprehensive Older Americans Act Amendments of 1978.* Washington, D.C.: U.S. Government Printing Office, 1978.

U.S. House of Representatives, Select Committee on Aging. *Federal responsibility to the elderly.* Washington, D.C.: U.S. Government Printing Office, 1976.

Part II
Income Maintenance
Programs

The system of income maintenance in the United States is a complex, fragmented one. Responsibility is divided among all the units of government and the private sector. The system—if it can be called one—was created step by step over a period of many years. Programs were created or modified and occasionally abandoned, as circumstances arose or changed. A prime example of incrementalism, the system is an illustration of block-by-block building to meet recognized need, often without careful consideration of the impact of the new developments upon existing programs.

A complete inventory of the existing U.S. system of income maintenance has rarely been attempted. The inventory list becomes long and includes a large variety of programs that provide some degree of income or other support, often as incidentals to other program objectives. Although these inventories are useful as a reminder of what is encompassed in the total system and of what a fragmented system it is, they wander too far astray from the narrow concept of income support to be helpful here.

The present system of income maintenance is characterized by program distinctions made on the basis of:

• *Governmental responsibility.* Some programs are federally operated, others by the states, and some are privately operated.

• *Financing.* Appropriations from the general revenues of government, both federal and state, finance some programs. Others are financed out of reserve funds created by insurance premiums.

• *Relationship to the work force.* Some programs are limited to those who have an attachment to the work force, while others are available without such connection.

• *Eligibility.* There are some universal programs with no means test. Others are limited to those who pass a means test and the test varies from program to program.

• *Participant contribution.* Some income maintenance programs are financed in part from contributions or taxes imposed upon the individual. Others are financed by payments made by the employer or from governmental tax revenue.

The consequences of the interplay of these factors are not only confusion in grasping what the system includes but also revelation of the weaknesses in the system. There is some duplication of coverage, and there are also gaps and omissions. There are serious variations in the level of adequacy of payments among the programs. Although some elements in the overall system are well financed, others are less securely financed. A number of programs operate in obscurity, thus limiting their utilization by many potential clients.

Elements in the U.S. income maintenance system will be reviewed in this part from the point of view of the resources available to help older people. The programs will be considered in terms of governmental response to the risks to which people—especially older people—are exposed, which are:

• Growing old without adequate income
• Being unemployed and without income
• Being ill and unable to work in order to support oneself and dependents
• Being ill and unable to pay for medical care.

In Chapter 3, the risks of inadequate income will be the focus. The role of income maintenance programs in periods of illness and existing medical care coverage programs will be the focus of Chapter 4.

3*

Age, Employment, and Income Maintenance

Growing Old without Adequate Income

The risk of becoming old and being unable to work is one of the most serious situations that people face. While many older people retire from employment voluntarily, the tendency is for people to remain employed for as long as possible. Older workers who become unemployed because of obsolete skills or because companies go out of business or consolidate very often do not find another job. These workers are thus less able to plan their entry into retirement than those who have been steadily employed.

Historically, the aged have been recognized as in need of help, as evidenced very early by the enactment of poor laws. In the 1920s the impact of the rigorous poor law was eased by the introduction of the Old-Age Pension, a means-tested program of aid usually available at age 70. These programs were liberalized and incorporated into the Social Security Act (SSA) of 1935 in the form of grants to the states for old-age assistance. The SSA also established the Old-Age Benefit Program. Since it was apparent that it would be several years before that program would actually provide benefits, the means-tested program was the major source of income for the elderly.

Progressive liberalizations in the retirement provisions of the Social Security Act have resulted in that being, since 1951, the pri-

*This chapter and chapter 4 were written by Jules Berman, Professor Emeritus, School of Social Work & Community Planning, University of Maryland. He previously worked at the Department of Health, Education and Welfare in a variety of legislative and policy positions.

mary source of income for the aged. The old-age assistance program gradually diminished in size, to the point that it provided assistance for only a small proportion of the aged. In 1974, the old-age assistance program was federalized and merged with similar programs for the blind and disabled as part of the SSI program.

Even though pension programs of private industry have, over the years, contributed to the provision of retirement income, a succession of favorable actions by the Congress combined with the growing interest of industry, have resulted in an enormous growth in private pensions. Today they play a significant part in the retirement plans of a large number of people.

Before these programs are examined in greater depth, it is important to view them in relationship to each other. The old-age benefit program under the SSA is generally considered the basic program. By now, nearly every employed person is covered and will eventually receive social security benefits. Not only is the program broad in its coverage, but the rights that are accumulated under the program are "portable." That is, the rights are cumulative throughout one's lifetime and are carried from one employer to another. Social security has become the cornerstone of protection in old age. Although benefits are increasing in adequacy and will assure future beneficiaries of about 43% of their preretirement income (based upon earnings which are subject to tax—a point which is discussed later), the amount will inevitably fall short of what many people will need or want in their retirement years. It is at this point that the private pension system enters the picture.

The government has acted to encourage the growth of private pensions with a view toward provision of income in addition to social security benefits. Social security was never intended to provide benefits which were measurable against a specific standard of adequacy. The adequacy of social security income is obviously improved when combined with private pensions. Employers are now encouraged to establish private pension programs. Workers are given an opportunity to negotiate with employers in the establishment of such plans. Indeed, under rulings of the National Labor Relations Board, employers are required to bargain in good faith with their employees, not only over hours and wages, but also in regard to the pension plan.

In recent years, further steps have been taken by the Congress to encourage the growth of private pensions. In those instances where the employer does not have a plan, individual employees may set up an Individual Retirement Account (IRA) which provides income in the future and is a tax shelter in the present. Self-employed persons can establish Keogh plans—similar to the IRA—in which the self-employed individual can be both the employer and the employee, so far as the pension is concerned. In addition, Keogh or IRA plans can be set up to include the individual's spouse. The principle for these programs is that everyone in retirement should have a source of income in addition to social security benefits.

This principle is further broadened by the establishment of the SSI program—a program in which the federal government has finally tackled the difficult problem of minimum adequacy. In 1979, the federal government assured the aged of $189.40 income per month ($284.10 for a couple living together). This amount could consist of an SSI supplement to social security or other income, or it could all be the SSI payment. The figures given above are indexed to the cost of living and are adjusted annually as are basic social security benefits.

In summary, social security remains the basic retirement plan. The private pension programs add to that benefit at the top, and the SSI program adds to social security or other income to create a floor. Thus there is some coherency to the retirement income planning of the federal government.

Old-age Benefits

The entire social security program is work related. That is, individuals are eligible for benefits only if they have been in employment (or self-employment) or are dependent upon one who has been so employed. There are specific requirements concerning the length of employment and the kind of work in order to qualify for benefits.[1] The basic requirement involves 40 quarters, or 10 years, of work in "covered employment." Until 1979, the law provided that in order to receive credit for a quarter of work, individuals had to earn at least $50 in 1 quarter. Self-employed persons had to earn at least $400 in

1. The basic requirements for social security are the same for all programs—old-age benefits, survivor's benefits, and disability benefits—and are only slightly modified for medical benefits. When these additional programs are discussed in this chapter, basic eligibility information will not be repeated.

Social security is a highly complex program with numerous detailed eligibility and benefit provisions, which are only summarized in this chapter, as is the content of other programs discussed. For technical details or the need to apply these provisions against a particular situation, consult with the nearest District Social Security Office, or the state offices which deal with unemployment insurance, welfare programs, workmen's compensation, and medical assistance.

a year in order to receive a year's credit. Effective January 1979, employers are required to report earnings on an annual basis, and $400 income earns an employee a year's credit under social security. Employers must still identify the quarters in which the work occurred. This will make it slightly more difficult to obtain credit for work performed at low wages.

The 40 quarters that are needed in order to be eligible can be accumulated over a period of a lifetime. "Covered employment" has been broadly defined to include all work as an employee in commerce or industry or in self-employment. Work in certain government operations or nonprofit organizations is also included, if a particular agreement has been made between the federal government and these other levels of government or the nonprofit employers.

Coverage of employees of state and local governments and nonprofit organizations requires between the employer and the Social Security Administration an agreement which accepts the notion of a federal tax; the employees must also agree. This agreement can be terminated upon 2 years' notice. In recent years, such a termination has occurred in a few instances.

The eligibility requirement of 40 quarters was written into the law as a minimum period of time in order to qualify and assumes that the individual entered the labor force after the social security system was established. Millions of Americans were already well into their work life when social security was established in 1935, or before it became inclusive in coverage. Because of this situation, older people can qualify for benefits with fewer than 40 quarters of coverage. An individual who became age 62 in 1978 was eligible with only 27 quarters of covered employment. This eligibility minimum has increased gradually, and by 1991, everyone will be required to meet the 40 quarters of employment.

Workers covered by social security pay a tax on their earnings, and employers add a like amount. The size of the ultimate benefit is based upon a calculation which takes into account the total of such taxable earnings. When the system was first initiated in 1936, the maximum earnings subject to tax was $3,000 a year. Over the years, this amount has gradually been increased. In 1979, the taxable earnings base was $22,900. The ceiling on earnings subject to tax will be $25,900 in 1980 and will rise to $31,800 in 1982. People whose annual incomes are in excess of these amounts pay taxes only on that portion of their annual earnings as specified in the law for that year.

When the taxable base is increased, it affects only those workers who have been earning more than the previous year's taxable base.

The tax rate is also fixed by law, and it too has been steadily moving upward. In 1979, the tax rate was 6.13% of the taxable income base; this will rise to 6.7% in 1982 and ultimately to 7.65% by 1990. The tax rate for the self-employed is somewhere between the tax on employees and the total tax on the employer and the employee. For 1979, the self-employment tax was 8.1% which will also rise, ultimately reaching 10.75% in 1990. Self-employed persons pay their social security tax each year at the same time they pay federal income tax.

Veterans receive gratuitous credit for military service between September 1940 and December 1957. When veterans apply for benefits, it is assumed that they earned $160 per month during the years of military service. After 1957, servicemen paid the social security tax on their military earnings and therefore are eligible for benefits the same as any other employed person.

The size of the benefits reflects the level of earnings during the wage earner's working years. Upon application for benefits, lifetime earnings, that is, earnings from age 21 until the time of application, are totaled. The 5 lowest years of earnings are excluded, and the number of months—less the excluded 5 years—is divided into the total earnings. The resulting amount—the Average Monthly Earnings—is then used against a table provided in the law to determine the monthly benefit which will be received. The table of benefits reflects some favorable treatment for low-paid workers in that they receive more in benefits as a proportion of previous earnings than higher paid workers. In 1979, the law also incorporated a new principle, which is to adjust previous earnings to upgrade them to more nearly reflect current wage levels. Wages paid 25 or 30 years ago seem completely unrealistic by today's scale; yet their small amounts depress the Average Monthly Earnings figure, which is crucial to the size of the benefit to be paid. The goal has been included in the law of having benefits replace, for average earners, about 43% of previous earnings, that is, that portion of earnings which had been subject to the social security tax. This provision has the effect of increasing the size of some benefits while keeping new awards from exceeding this level of replacement.

Benefits are automatically adjusted annually, without any action by the Congress, to reflect changes in the cost of living. Inasmuch as social security benefits are not subject to income tax, this adjustment enables beneficiaries to maintain their purchasing power under pressures of upward movement of prices. Until this procedure became automatic, an act of Congress was necessary to adjust benefits. This adjustment procedure was carried out on a regular basis, but some of the increases voted by the Congress exceeded the cost of living figures. Since this is now accomplished automatically, beneficiaries will be assured of maintaining the purchase power of their benefits but will not receive any upward adjustment in their living standards.

A minimum benefit of $122 per month is provided for by the law for wage earners whose lifetime earnings which were covered by social security were low. No matter what the formula would yield in the way of benefits, no less than $122 a month will be payable as a primary insurance amount. There is another form of minimum benefits which helps persons who have worked many years in covered employment, yet at wages so low that they will enter retirement with very small benefits. The law now provides that long-term low-paid workers will receive benefits larger than they would under the normal formula incorporated in the law. This provision, introduced in 1972, allows individuals to receive benefits of $230 a month in 1979, if they worked a minimum of 10 years at low earnings. This provision was added to the law because the minimum benefit discussed earlier was found to be aiding many persons who were not long-term workers but who had been in other retirement systems and for whom the social security benefits were only supplementary. Even so, the workers who were in real need of some protection against a low benefit were not being sufficiently aided by the old minimum benefit.

The normal age for retirement is 65. Provision is made, however, for workers who have the required number of quarters of coverage to retire at an age as low as 62. The benefits for these earners are reduced on an actuarial basis so that their early retirement does not cost the system any money. This reduction is 20% for those retiring at age 62, proportionately less as the individual is nearer age 65 when applying for benefits. More than half of current applications for retirement benefits are being made by persons who are below 65 years of age.

The benefits of a retired wage earner may be increased if his or her spouse is of the appropriate age. This provision was added to the law in 1939 at a time when the pattern of family living was for the husband to be in gainful employment and to support his spouse and children. Thus the increase in the wage earner's benefits—usually the husband—of 50% was in behalf of a wife who had not been employed outside of the home. That addendum is paid in the instances of wives who have no earning records of their own, or if a wife's earning record would yield a benefit of a lesser amount than she would receive as a dependent spouse. The Social Security Administration will make a comparison at the time of application for benefits and award the larger of the two amounts. While the addendum is added to the wage earner's monthly check, the wife can receive a separate check if she requests it. An addendum is also allowable if the retired wage earner has dependent children living at home. In this instance, benefits are payable on behalf of such children up to the age of 18, through age 22 if the children are attending school.

The addendum covering the spouse of a retired worker is available for both a husband and wife. That is, the wife can be the wage earner to whom a 50% increase will be granted in behalf of her husband, if the husband had no wage earning record or if his wage record will yield benefits smaller than 50% of his wife's. The law provides, however, that if the husband or wife who is claiming benefits on the basis of the earnings of the other is also receiving benefits from any governmental program, the spouse's benefits will be reduced by the amount of the additional benefit being received. The purpose of this provision is to disallow the social security benefits claimed by a spouse who is covered by the U.S. Civil Service retirement system or a comparable state system and who consequently is not in any way dependent upon the spouse who is covered by social security.

Benefits are payable to retired wage earners if they meet the retirement test as stated in the law. The test of retirement is put in terms of annual earnings. An individual receiving social security benefits but also earning an annual amount higher than the amount stated in the law may lose part, or if the earnings are sufficiently large, all of her or his benefit. This is an often misunderstood provision. Strictly speaking, the social security program is not an annuity program but a wage replacement benefit program. At age 72, the retirement test no longer applies and wage earners can earn without limit and still receive full benefits. Income other than earnings is not counted for the retirement test, which means that individuals may have unlimited income from investments, rents, and the like without any impact on their social security benefits. The earnings limit for the retirement test has been raised considerably in recent years. For 1979, it was $4,500 for persons age 65 and over and $3,480 for those under age 65. These amounts will be further increased to $5,000 and $3,720 for 1980; $5,500 and $3,960 for 1981; and $6,000 and $4,300 in 1982. Thereafter these amounts will automatically increase as average wages in the United States increase. Earnings above the amounts stated reduce the monthly benefits on the basis of a $1 reduction for every $2 in earnings. The point at which an individual's benefits are phased out because of earnings varies and depends upon the size of the benefits and the amount of earnings.

Legislation passed in 1977 provided that the age at which the retirement test will not apply will drop to age 70 in 1981. There is an incentive in the law for wage earners to remain in the work force by increasing benefits by a small percentage for the period an individual would have received benefits but instead remained in the work force.

The retirement test is the most unpopular provision in the Social Security Act. It has been criticized as a discouragement to work and a denial of essential supplementary income to people whose basic benefits are insufficient. Counter to this are the arguments that social security is not designed as a pension but as a wage replacement benefit and that the elimination of the retirement test would increase the cost of the system, with the additional money going to people who are the least needy—those who are working and earning well above the $5,000 level.

A common problem experienced by older people concerns the death of a spouse and the remarriage of the surviving spouse, who receives social security benefits. Often the remarriage is to a person who also receives benefits. A spouse who receives survivor's benefits could lose them upon remarriage. As a result of amendments in the law which became effective in 1979, the remarriage of a surviving spouse after age 60 will not reduce the amount of benefits.

Another problem occurs in the breakup of a marriage which leaves a divorced mate without any marriage ties to a retired worker and thus unable to claim the spouse's 50% addendum. Other recent changes in the law, also effective in 1979, state that a divorced spouse who was married for 10 years may claim benefits based upon the former spouse's earning record at the time of retirement. The fact that the wage earner may have remarried does not affect the benefits to the divorced spouse. Unfortunately, the divorced spouse is in a difficult position if she or he has no income and no social security benefit rights in her or his own name and the former spouse chooses to continue working and consequently does not apply for benefits.

The system also includes a death benefit of $225, which is payable to the estate of the deceased wage earner. For those who do not retire—although eligible—and who have no dependents, such as spouse, children, or dependent parents, the death benefit may be the only payment out of the system.

Financing Social Security

The financial integrity of the social security system is of crucial importance to the 34 million beneficiaries. All costs of the program, including the cost of administering it, come from a tax imposed on employers and employees. This tax money is identified separately in the U.S. Treasury and is available for appropriation to pay benefits and the cost of administration. Although most wage earners believe the social security tax is a single figure—6.13% for 1979—it is actually a series of smaller tax sums designed to reflect the cost of the various elements of the system. These include the retirement program, disability, survivors, and health insurance. In recent years, it has become apparent that some of these so-called trust funds for individual program purposes were running short and soon would be in deficit. The disability fund was in the deepest trouble and, were it not for the Social Security Amendments of 1977, would have already run out of money. The basic retirement fund was also heading for a deficit. The 1977 amendments, which increased both the tax base and the tax rate (as discussed earlier), rescued the social security system from imminent deficit. The amendments increased the flow of money into the Treasury from wage earners and employers and thus gave assurance that, for at least a time, the income would equal the outgo.

Since the social security system is financed solely by the tax on employers and employees, there is no other money from the Treasury going into the basic system. Unless the nation should decide to allocate some general revenue funds to pay at least part of the cost, the benefits will continue to be paid for by the payroll tax. It is a pay-as-you-go system. That is, there is no vast accumulation of money in Treasury trust funds for social security purposes; the trust funds are small and are more of a contingency fund to help smooth out any changes that might occur in the income and outgo.

Under pay-as-you-go funding, the system will continue to be reasonably self-supporting until around the year 2010. At that point it is likely that the financing will again approach a near-deficit status and that further increases in taxes will be necessary. The alternative, of course, would be funding assistance from the general revenue— an issue that promises to be an active one for years to come. Another alternative for consideration in dealing with the financing problem would be to curtail benefits. People may think that they have a "contract" to pay in certain taxes and in turn to receive certain benefits from social security; in fact the SSA can be modified by the Congress at any time. Changes, especially those which would reduce benefits, are not readily enacted by Congress, but some curtailment of benefits is possible in the future. Both Presidents Ford and Carter proposed some minor curtailments. While the Congress has thus far not responded vigorously to these proposals, the financial pressures looming in the future could change the Congressional stance.

It is extremely difficult to finance benefit increases to take into account the rising cost of living. Beneficiaries are assured of annual adjustments in payments to reflect fully the cost of living increases that have occurred. Theoretically the cost of these increases is covered by additional taxes paid by workers who are receiving higher earnings by virtue of inflation. Problems arise, however, when wage increases lag behind the rate of inflation. One possible, but unpopular, step that would deal with this financial stress on the system would be to put a cap on the upward adjustment in benefits.

Another possibility for getting the social security system on a firmer financial basis without using general revenue money is to shift some of the benefits to a means-tested basis. Certain provisions in social security are expressly designed to aid particularly vulnerable groups such as low-paid workers or dependent spouses. It has been proposed that these so-called welfare provisions be transferred from social security to the SSI program and financed out of general revenue. The cost would be less than it is as part of the social security system because some of the currently eligible people would not qualify on the basis of a means test. This point of view is effectively stated by Alicia H. Mannell (1977). Some evidence of this point of view is also apparent in the recommendations concerning social security made by President Carter to the Congress in 1979.

Survivor's Insurance

Benefits for survivors of deceased wage earners under the social security system are available to the survivors (wife or husband and young children) of a prematurely deceased wage earner. These benefits are also available to the surviving spouse (age 60 or older and young children if any) of a wage earner who was either retired or had been eligible for retirement. For purposes of this chapter, only the latter group of survivors—the older people—will be discussed.

As explained earlier, an addendum will be added to the benefit of a spouse if he or she is at least 60 years of age. (As noted earlier, this benefit can be reduced by the receipt of a public pension.) This benefit is paid, not only in behalf of spouses who have had no employment record of their own that would qualify them, but also to those who have a record of work in covered employment but for whom the earned benefit is less than 50% of the wage earner's Primary Insurance Amount (PIA). The survivor's benefit will be 100% of the wage earner's PIA. Thus it is possible that a woman whose earned benefit was less than 50% of her husband's will, upon the death of her husband, receive a larger benefit—her husband's PIA—not an uncommon occurrence.

A benefit of the same size will also be paid to the widow or widower of a wage earner who had been eligible for a retirement benefit but who had not claimed it because of continuing employment, assuming the survivor meets the usual age requirement. In the event the aged survivor also has responsibility for young children of the deceased, the benefit will be 75% of the PIA plus a payment made in behalf of each child equal to 75% of the PIA. Benefits are also payable to dependent parents of deceased wage earners.

Beneficiaries of survivor's benefits are subject to the same earnings test as are retired people. Therefore if a widower or widow is employed and receiving an income, the survivor's benefit might be reduced and even eliminated, depending upon the amount of the survivor's earnings.

Supplementary Security Income

The SSI program was established in 1974 on the basis of legislation enacted in 1972. It provides for federalizing the former grants-in-aid programs of old-age assistance, aid to the blind, and aid to the permanently and totally disabled. These programs—except the disability program—had been administered by the states since 1935, with states administering grants for the disabled since 1950. Under the 1972 legislation, the federal government provides assistance to the aged, blind, and disabled who qualify under the specific provisions of the law. National standards are used both for eligibility and for payment. The payment level in 1979 was $189.40 for an eligible individual living alone and $284.10 for two eligible individuals—husband and wife. The odd amounts derive from a provision added to the original law that indexes the payment level to the cost of living, which is adjusted annually as with social security.

There are several major differences between the SSI program and the comparable programs in the social security system. (Comparable programs would be old-age and disability benefits.) The major difference is that the SSI program is means tested, while social security benefits are not. Funds for the SSI program come from the general revenue of the Treasury, while social security is financed by a payroll tax on employers and employees. The SSI program is available to anyone who meets the proper qualifications—age, blindness, and disability—without regard to their participation in the work force. The social security program is directly related to employment, either by the beneficiary or by his or her dependents. Although both social security and SSI are administered by the Social Security Administration of HEW, a distinction is maintained between the two programs by printing the checks on a different color of paper.

National eligibility requirements for SSI are:

• No one is eligible who is an inmate of a public institution.

• If an otherwise eligible person is in a medical institution (public or private), the payment to that individual is greatly reduced.

• No one is to receive an SSI payment if she or he is eligible for, but has not applied for, another kind of benefit payment, such as workmen's compensation or social security.

• Anyone who is otherwise eligible but who has been medically established to be a drug addict or an alcoholic will receive payment only if undergoing appropriate treatment for the condition at an institution approved by the Secretary of HEW and if she or he demonstrated compliance with the outlined treatment.

• Payment to eligible persons under SSI will not be made if those persons are outside the continental United States. If such persons have been so removed from the country and later return, they are required to wait 30 days before being reinstated for SSI payment.

• A disabled person under the age of 65 must accept a referral to the state vocational rehabilitation agency for a study of her or his condition and must accept a proposed plan of treatment in order to continue eligibility for SSI.

• The resources of an eligible individual may not exceed $1,500; however, the value of a home owned by the individual or certain other possessions are not counted.

• Applicants must be either citizens or legally admitted aliens in order to be eligible for SSI.

• Persons who are age 65, or blind, or disabled are eligible. If the eligibility is blindness or disability, the individual must meet the test used in the social security program of disability insurance.

The system promises a certain level of income, which consists of SSI alone, if the individual has no other income, or a combination of SSI and other income to reach the established payment level. In determining the amount an individual or a couple will receive, some modifications are made in the treatment of income:

• Only net income from employment is counted.

• The first $240 per year of income such as from social security is not counted, but all income paid on the basis of need is fully counted.

• Earned income of eligible persons up to $780 per year is not counted.

• Casual and inconsquential income not to exceed $60 in a quarter is not counted.

• If the eligible individual is living in another person's household and is receiving support or maintenance in kind, the SSI payment is reduced by one-third.

A state may establish a higher payment level at its own expense but may not add eligibility requirements. The federal government will administer that payment at no administrative cost to the state. Many states have chosen to provide a state supplement, with some states administering it themselves. This means that the payment level varies around the country as individual states decide whether to add to the federal payment, how much to add, and to what extent these supplements should be increased as living costs rise.

State General Assistance Programs

All the states have a program of general assistance which is the direct linear descendant of the old poor law relief programs. Like the earlier programs, they are largely local in character. Some states, however, help finance the program and may even set state standards. The primary eligibility provision is need, which often is severely tested. The program is available to persons who do not qualify for other programs such as social security, SSI, and the like. A likely candidate is a needy person age 60, for example. Unless such persons are disabled or blind, they would not be eligible for social security or SSI and could very well be in need. Inasmuch as there is no federal financial help in the state programs, the availability of benefits depends upon state eligibility requirements and often some local requirements.

Private Pension Plans

Private pensions are becoming an increasingly large part of the national income support system. As noted earlier, the federal government has encouraged and facilitated their development. Although the government has looked favorably on these programs, it is difficult for the federal government to impose effective controls over them. The reason is that, fundamentally, these are private programs, and the federal government cannot readily make demands about what industry and commerce do with their private programs. By 1974, however, several situations had developed in private pension plans which forced the federal government to take action. Evidence was accumulating that there was gross inequity in the benefits being paid. There were indications of corruption by managers of the plans. Plans were being set up which were poorly funded and which, in all probability, would not be able to pay benefits. Meanwhile workers were making retirement plans on expectation of receiving benefits from their private pension plan to supplement what they knew would be inadequate social security benefits.

Although the action Congress took in 1974 was relatively strong —especially in light of its hesitation over the years to act decisively —one important characteristic of the system was not changed. That is, the private sector has a choice of whether or not it wants to provide a pension plan; and it retains the choice of discontinuing a plan, once one is set up. Further, it was impossible for the Congressional action to correct a major weakness in private plans. That is, the benefit rights of an individual are only rarely transferable—or portable, which is the technical word—when the worker moves from one employer to another. Thus, social security remains the only income support insurance program with that feature.

The main objective of the federal legislation was to assure the receipt of benefits upon retirement after a period of service for an employer. A further assurance is provided by setting up a reinsurance fund, similar to the Federal Deposit Insurance Corporation, which insures bank deposits. The reinsurance fund collects a small fee from all pension funds and maintains a reserve to pay off accumulated obligations to beneficiaries of any bankrupt fund.

The standards imposed by federal law on the private pensions operate separately for funds in which the employee has contributed as compared to those in which the employer makes all the contributions. There are more severe requirements for vesting (that is, the rights to a benefit) for the former than the latter. The employee-contributed funds are in a small minority, however. For the employer-financed funds, vesting the benefits takes place following 5 years of service. After that time, the size of the benefit payment to which the employee is entitled grows in size as the number of years employed, when added to the employee's age, becomes larger. Conceivably an employee could work for several companies, working the minimum number of years for each in order to have vested rights and, upon retirement, receive several benefit checks, although each would be a small one.

It was impossible to make requirements for all pension plans specific and uniform because of the immediate impact on the cost of the system to the employer. Since the pension system is voluntary on the part of the employer, the government does not impose requirements that might add considerably to the cost. Even so, the impact of the pension reform legislation has been that many hundreds of small pension plans have gone out of existence. The employers felt they could not meet the financial cost requirements, nor the reporting requirements which became more extensive with the legislation. However, larger plans are not as severely affected, and the total number of covered individuals has not diminished appreciably.

There are several important characteristics of the private pension system:

• The payments are growing in adequacy although they do not equal social security. An exception is benefits to high-level executives, who often have a generous pension plan built into their remuneration.

• Benefits are payable to survivors of deceased plan members in a small but slowly growing number of plans.

• Few plans provide for adjustment to the cost of living, and if they do, it is not usually the full increase.

• The plans tend to favor the long-term employee who, by virtue of continuous employment by one employer, can become eligible for a more significant payment.

• In a few instances, an employee may carry over benefit rights to another employer in the same industry. An example is the trucker's pension fund, which operates across the industry.

Private pension funds share the same problem of nearly all retirement plans in the United States—that of being marginally secure financially. The insurance fund accumulates reserves very slowly and could be wiped out by a few large claims made simultaneously. The actuarially determined obligation for pension payments on some (even large) corporations is excessive. An issue which will gradually have to be faced is the extent of the corporate obligation for payment under terms of the plan versus the shareholder's rights to the assets of the company. While it is likely that this will be resolved without reaching a crunch, it does suggest that the private pension system has to face the reality of financing troubles.

Unemployment and Inadequate Income

The distinction between unemployment of an older person and retirement is often a thin one. An older person who loses his or her job may be vigorously looking for another one yet, since he or she needs income, may be forced to apply for and accept some income transfer benefits. Before moving on to the social security program—if he or she is eligible—the person may wish to exhaust his or her unemployment compensation rights. Many older persons receive unemployment compensation either before moving on to social security or simultaneously. It is possible for a person to receive both unemployment compensation and old-age benefits at the same time.

Unemployment compensation is a program of benefits for persons who were employed in specified fields of work but who have, not of their own choosing, lost their jobs. The program is administered by the states, who have considerable latitude in establishing eligibility standards, including the amount of the weekly benefit. Unemployment compensation is financed by a federally imposed tax, most of which is returned to the states by the federal government to pay the cost of the benefits granted and the cost of administering the program, which includes the operation of an employment service. States may add to the amount of the tax, making more funds available to support more generous benefits, both in dollar amounts and in duration of receipts of benefits, as well as to pay the cost of less onerous provisions for eligibility. Many states do this.

The number of workers covered by unemployment compensation has been increasing in recent years, until most workers in commerce and industry and many people in public employment and in teaching professions are now covered. Some progress has been made in incorporating casual employment into the system, such as domestic work and farm work. Even so, most people engaged in these kinds of jobs are still not covered, nor are self-employed persons.

Benefits are payable only after a worker has been in employment for a specified period of time set by the states and therefore varying from state to state. There is no doubt, however, that too short a period of employment will disqualify one for benefits. The duration of benefits is also set by the states, with 26 weeks emerging as the general pattern. Extended benefits are available for another 13 weeks in instances of high unemployment in a state.

The trend has been for the Congress to provide extended benefits in the course of an economic recession. The receipt of benefits has extended for as long as 15 months in recent years. Many people question the wisdom of these extensions on the grounds that the availability of benefits tends to discourage diligent search for work. Also such a long period of unemployment strongly indicates that a work program is needed rather than an income transfer program. If benefits are to be extended, many observers contend that the recipients of such benefits ought to be means tested, which they are not now. All benefits payable are exempt from income tax. Some states include an addendum for dependents, but generally benefits are awarded to the worker without regard for family circumstances.

Eligibility for benefits hinges upon the unemployed individual being ready, willing, and able to work. Presumedly illness or disability should exclude a worker, although in practice the unavailability of the worker for a job often is not known to the state. An unemployed person is not expected to take the first job that materializes without regard to experience or training; the system allows the worker to hold off accepting employment until a job becomes available in her or his line of work that uses her or his skills. As time passes, however, the unemployed worker is expected to lower his or her job expectations and accept less ideal work. Workers are not expected to take strike-breaking jobs nor ones that are below the usual wages paid.

Workers who wish to receive unemployment compensation are required to register for work with the employment service. If that office is successful in finding a job for the receipient of unemployment compensation, the unemployed person is expected to accept it unless she or he can show good cause for not doing so. Inasmuch as the employment service has few job openings for older workers, it is unlikely that an older person's willingness to work will be put to a test. Even if the employment office should refer the unemployment compensation beneficiary to a job, the employer may reject him or her, and of course this would not affect continued eligibility for benefits.

It has been a practice for older persons to apply for unemployment compensation as a prelude to retirement. Since the likelihood is very slight that they will be faced with a decision of whether or not to accept suitable employment which may be found by the employment service, the unemployment compensation program offers some additional tax-free income for the almost-retired person. While this appears to be legal, it is not within the spirit of the law and there have been discussions about making such persons ineligible for unemployment benefits.

The basic program of unemployment compensation benefits is sometimes supplemented by private funds created as a consequence of labor-management agreements. In the automobile, steel, and some of the other highly organized industries, management contributes toward a fund used to supplement the basic unemployment compensation program whenever needed. This supplement can take the form of continuing benefits after the regular program ends or more likely can supplement the size of the basic benefit. These funds are relatively new, having only been established in recent years. When put to a test, they were proven to be insufficient to last the duration of the unemployment period in the industries, although they were helpful to the workers who received them. These supplementary funds tend to provide more help to those with the greatest seniority.

Reference

Mannell, A. *The future of social security.* Washington, D.C.: Brookings Institution, 1977.

4
Illness, Medical Care, and Income Maintenance

Becoming ill or disabled creates two major problems for those affected. If inability to work cuts off income, the unemployed need some income transfers to support themselves and their dependents. The primary problem of the sick or disabled is providing income. The other major problem is paying for medical care.

Risks of Illness, Disability, and Inadequate Income

Several programs, all of which depend on the particular status of the individual, address the need for income. The social security program includes benefits available to persons disabled on a long-term basis. Some states provide short-term disability benefits as an element in their unemployment compensation program. Workmen's compensation is available for those who have become ill or disabled on the job; this includes wage replacement and medical expenses. Many employers provide sick leave, which is a form of short-term disability benefits. The SSI program is available for the disabled who, for one reason or another, are not eligible for social security or any other income-producing programs.

Social Security Disability Benefits

Eligibility for these benefits follows along the lines of eligibility for social security in general, as described earlier. The major difference in eligibility, say, for old-age or survivor's benefits and disability benefits, is a requirement for a longer attachment to the labor force. Although disability benefits are available to younger workers who meet the test of severity of disability, the law requires that disabled persons have worked under covered employment for a proportionately longer period of time than is required of deceased wage earners who die prematurely and leave survivors. The intention is to emphasize that the worker to be covered has made a significant financial contribution to the system before becoming eligible.

For purposes of determining the amount of benefits after disabled workers establish eligibility on the basis of severity of disability and length of time in the work force, they are considered retired. That is, their lifetime wages in covered employment are totaled and divided by the number of months of work. For younger workers, the number of months of covered employment may be small, certainly when compared to the retired person. However, the average monthly earnings of the younger worker could be as high as those of a retired worker. Indeed, the monthly average might well be higher since the younger worker's wage history is more recent and during the time when wages have been higher than those of a retired person whose wage history may go back 40 years. This peculiarity of the system has resulted in disability benefits generally running higher than those granted for retired persons.

Benefits for disabled workers are increased if they have spouses and even more if they have dependent children. The procedure for determining the amount of these awards is similar to that used for retired workers, their spouses, and young children if any. Inasmuch as disabled workers are generally younger, very possibly with young children as well as spouse, the total benefits awarded have been higher than for other parts of the social security system. This has caused criticism, and efforts are being made to bring these benefits into line with survivor's benefits by limiting benefits to a fixed family maximum.

For claiming benefits, the definition of disability is a severe one. It attempts to limit the program to those persons with severe and long-lasting disabilities, mental or physical. The words in the definition, "inability to engage in any substantial gainful activity," suggest that a test is to be made of the individual's ability to engage in "any gainful activity," not just a test of whether or not there is employment in the community in which the individual lives. This definition could conceivably result in the denial of benefits to people who might be able to do certain kinds of work even if there is no possibility of any work of that nature showing up.

The individual applicant is responsible for presenting proof of disability and, if medical examination or testing are involved, must pay for that cost. If the Social Security Administration is not satisfied with the proof offered, it will pay for additionally required examinations and reports. When the program began in the 1950s, it was small and grew very slowly. In recent years it has expanded broadly, with some disagreement over the reasons for the growth. Some observers feel that the administrators of the program have relaxed some of the standards. Others feel that applicants have become more knowledgeable about the various benefit programs and that they have been helped by experienced lawyers and encouraged by recipient advocate groups. Many instances of denial by the Social Security Administration have gone to appeal within the organization and, if that failed, to the courts. A surprisingly large number of adverse administrators' decisions have been reversed by the courts.

Although the definition speaks in terms of long and severe disability, from the very beginning the assumption was that some beneficiaries might be rehabilitated. For this reason, provision is made for the state vocational rehabilitation agency to review all applications with a view toward identification of potential cases for vocational rehabilitation. The applicant who is recommended by the vocational rehabilitation agency for rehabilitation must accept the plan of that agency or forfeit rights to disability benefits. The rehabilitation plan is financed by the Social Security Administration as a charge against the social security funds. Those who are rehabilitated and who go off the program save the program a great deal of money over the years. Thus the cost of rehabilitation is regarded as a prudent investment. The actual record of rehabilitation cases shows that comparatively few are able to be fully rehabilitated and return to work. Legislation under consideration would encourage beneficiaries to undertake work by assuring them of quick reentry to the program if the work does not prove feasible.

Supplementary Security Income

The SSI program provides assistance to persons who are disabled or blind, which is the federalization of the old grant-in-aid program for the needy disabled or blind which was adopted by the Congress in 1972 and became effective in 1974. When the program was operated by the states with federal financial support, each state set its own definition of disability and blindness within the broad guidelines of the federal law. When the program was taken over by the federal

government, a national definition was introduced for both disabilities
—a definition which follows along the concepts of the disability insurance program under social security. A grandfather clause was included to make it possible for those already certified by the states in
1974 to continue eligibility. Since the definition is now similar to that
for the social security program, the SSI program qualifies only the
long-term, severely disabled.

At the time the program was federalized, the minimum age of
18 was eliminated, thus allowing young children to qualify for benefits if they are severely disabled and, of course, if they are needy. The
benefit payment for the disabled is the same as for the over-age 65
group, as noted earlier. The eligibility requirements relating to resources, citizenship, or legal status and the like are the same as under
SSI old-age assistance provisions.

Sick Leave

Important but often overlooked resources for providing income to
people who are temporarily sick or disabled are the provisions many
employers make for sick leave. Employers that provide sick leave
tend to be those which employ white-collar workers—office, sales,
and similar work—however, manufacturing companies have begun
to provide this benefit as well. Government work of all kinds includes
this form of illness protection.

Workmen's Compensation

Programs of workmen's compensation are operated by the states or
private insurance companies under state supervision. Typically, benefits include both financial assistance in lieu of lost wages and payment for medical bills. The illnesses and disabilities covered by this
program are those incurred on the job, under the concept of *no fault;*
that is, no test is made to determine whether employees were care-
less or otherwise contributed to their own accidents. Benefits are
often time limited and are usually related to the severity of the
disability. For the severely disabled, benefits include some form of
rehabilitation, often in conjunction with the state vocational rehabilitation agency.

Not all employees are covered by workmen's compensation.
Since these are state programs, eligibility provisions differ around the
country. In some states there are exemptions of small employers,
those with five or so employees. Typically, others not covered are
domestic, casual, and farm workers. Because of these variations

among the states and omissions from the program, there is some interest in enacting a federal law which would establish uniform standards for the nation.

Temporary Disability Insurance

Short-term disability benefits are available in about six states as an offshoot of the unemployment insurance program. These states include some of the large industrial states, such as New York and California, with the program providing coverage for approximately 25% of the national labor force in commerce and industry.

Benefits are available for workers who are covered by the state unemployment insurance law and who are absent from work because of illness or disability. These would be people whose illness or disability are unrelated to their work (otherwise they would be eligible for workmen's compensation) and whose absence from work will be temporary as contrasted with long-term absences as defined in the social security program. Workers covered by an employer's sick leave may not be excluded in some states; in others, disability benefits may be reduced or denied. Temporary disability benefits are not permitted to overlap unemployment insurance benefit payments.

All of the laws have minimum requirements for days absent or loss of wages before benefits will begin and, of course, limits on the duration of benefits being paid. Benefits are related to the size of previous earnings, as in unemployment compensation. The plans are financed by a state-imposed tax on employees and, in some states, on the employers. There is no federal financial support for these programs.

Risks of Aging, Medical Bills, and Inadequate Income

Medical costs for the aged are increasing each year. This reflects not only the growing proportion of the gross national product devoted to medical care (rising annually, to in excess of 8% in 1978) but also the proportionately higher medical costs of the aged as compared with the population as a whole. The aged represent about 11% of the nation's total population; yet expenditures made by and for the aged represent just under 30% of all medical expenditures. The aged become sick more frequently than others, are hospitalized more often, and stay there longer. Hospital care as an element in the overall medical cost has been accelerating at the greatest pace, and the aged require hospital care more often than others. In addition, long-term care—a type of medical care needed almost exclusively by the aged—is costly and, by definition, long lasting. For these reasons, provisions to help the aged meet medical costs have been in the law for many years. From the earliest history of government and through the years, welfare programs have provided some medical care and some payment for medical care for poor people, especially the aged. That practice is now being carried out through the Medicaid program (Title XIX of the SSA).

Private insurance for health care costs has been available for decades but has been especially prominent since World War II. The Blue Cross plan for hospital insurance was begun during the Depression and has had many individual subscribers as well as group subscribers. Private health insurance has become a fringe benefit of employment. While Blue Cross—as a nonprofit community plan—had a large number of older persons as subscribers, other private plans (especially the profit-making ones) shunned the elderly because of their poor risk record and conducted all of their business through employers. Thus, if older persons remained in employment, they would have some financial help for medical expenses in this manner. There have always been questions about the extent to which private health insurance continues to be available to workers once they leave the work force and whether this form of insurance help is equitably available to people of all income groups—not just the aged, but all people.

It became obvious over time that private health insurance could not be depended upon to provide protection for the aged. Indeed, there was doubt that private profit-making health insurance companies wanted a major role in insuring the aged. The high incidence of illness among the aged made them a poor risk for private health insurance. Although private Blue Cross plans have been an exception to this rule, even this group of nonprofit private insurers began to be concerned about the stability of their financial position, especially as the cost of hospital care began to escalate dramatically in the 1960s. Even though the private health insurance industry and private medical practitioners were opposed to further government involvement, the public interest and demand for hospital insurance for the aged prevailed, and Medicare was enacted in 1965.

There are now three broad protective devices for the aged in meeting their medical costs, one being private health insurance, which is a major factor in payment of medical bills. Private programs vary widely in the protection offered, provisions for coverage, and circumstances of enrollment but provide considerable protection for many elderly persons, especially those under the age of 65. For those over age 65, private health insurance is widely available to supplement the Medicare program.

Medicare—a second element—covers nearly all persons age 65 and over, those receiving disability benefits under social security, and a few other small and highly exceptional groups. Eligibility and benefits will be discussed below. Although this program is universally available and at low cost to the aged, the result of exceptions and omissions is that Medicare is meeting only about 40% of the medical costs of the aged.

The third element in this fabric of protection is the Medicaid program. This is a grant-in-aid program which is operated by the states and provides protection for some of the poor population. Coverage varies from state to state, and benefits also vary but are broader than those of Medicare. Each of these programs will be discussed.

Medicare

The Medicare program (Title XVIII of the SSA) is an integral part of the social security program. Generally speaking, eligibility for Medicare is determined by eligibility for social security; that is, Medicare benefits will be provided to persons who have established eligibility for old-age benefits or disability benefits. No separate eligibility determination is made except for disabled beneficiaries, who must have been in receipt of cash benefits for a period of time prior to Medicare eligibility. However, individuals are eligible for Medicare who, although eligible, are not actually receiving old-age benefits because they are earning more than the retirement income level, as discussed earlier. Medicare is not available to persons who are below the age of 65, which eliminates from eligibility those persons who receive cash benefits on an actuarially reduced basis at an age below 65.

The Medicare program is divided into two parts: Part A—hospital insurance—and Part B—medical insurance. All persons eligible for Medicare receive Part A benefits without any additional cost to them. Part B benefits are available only to persons who "join," that is, agree to pay a certain amount each month. This monthly fee is deducted from the check of persons who receive social security cash benefits. For persons who are eligible for social security benefits but who do not receive a check because they are earning above the retirement level, a bill from the Health Care Financing Administration is sent for subsequent payment. In both parts, deductibles and coinsurance payments are required (discussed below).

Part A. Under Part A, persons with medically established need for hospitalization are entitled to 60 days of hospitalization. As a condition of eligibility, they must pay for the first day of that care. That amount is raised annually as the cost of hospitalization increases. It was $160 in 1979. If additional days of hospital care are needed, 30 more days are available upon the payment of a daily coinsurance fee, which in 1979 was $40. This is also raised annually. There must be a short period of time between hospitalizations before the 60-day and 30-day periods become applicable again. If additional hospitalization is needed beyond the 60- and 30-day limits, an individual can draw upon a lifetime reserve allowable for each eligible person. That lifetime reserve is 60 days, with a daily coinsurance fee of $80 (in 1979). The services provided by the hospital are those usually included within a hospital's per diem charges but not including the services of the anesthesiologist, pathologist, and radiologist. These services are charged separately by the doctors and are considered a Part B expense.

When patients have been hospitalized for at least 3 days and are found to be in need of medical care which cannot be provided in the home but which is not as medically sophisticated as that offered in the hospital setting, they may receive care in an extended care facility (ECF). These facilities are high-quality nursing homes which must be closely related to or have working agreements with a hospital and be able to provide the kind of care the patient needs. Without additional charge, patients may receive up to 20 days of care in an ECF. An additional 80 days of care will be provided upon payment of a daily fee of $21 (in 1979). The service of an extended care facility shortens the stay of patients in hospitals; it is not intended to be long-term nursing home care. Indeed, the Medicare program as a whole does not respond to the need for long-term care.

For patients being dismissed from either the hospital or the extended care facility, home health care is available, up to 100 visits in a year, if needed, and at no additional charge. Home health care must be medically ordered and must be of a medical nature, not homemaker service.

Part B. Part B of Medicare is called Supplementary Medical Insurance. As mentioned earlier, Medicare-eligible persons do not automatically participate in Part B. They agree to this insurance and pay $8.20 per month (in 1979) or accept that deduction being made from their social security checks. Nearly everyone receiving social security belongs to Part B. This plan provides partial payment for physicians for medical services. There is an annual deductible amount which, in 1979, was $60. That is, in order to be eligible for help from Part B, participants must first pay at least $60 for the kinds of medical services covered by Part B. Expenditures for drugs, dental services, and the like are not included in Part B. Individuals who have joined Part B, have paid their deductible amount of medical expenses, and have maintained monthly payments into the Part B fund will then be able to receive 80% reimbursement for reasonable charges for medical services received.

Physicians can be paid in either of two ways. They can agree to make a direct charge to the Health Care Financing Administration, through a system of intermediaries which have been set up to deal directly with doctors. If they follow this route, they will receive 80% of the fee which the intermediary has set, following the rules and directives of the Health Care Financing Administration. These rules, reflecting the concern in the Congress over the rise in medical costs in general and physicians' charges specifically, are directed toward keeping the Medicare payment in the general range of average payments and not the higher charges made by some doctors. The doctor must look to the patient for the remaining 20% of his charges.

The other route doctors can follow is to submit a bill to the patient who, in turn, sends it to the intermediary for payment— again, equal to 80% of the reasonable charges. If the doctor's bill is in excess of the reasonable charges which the Medicare plan recognizes, then the patient is responsible for the excess amount, plus the 20% of the charges which are paid by Medicare. Although the proportion of Medicare billings which go directly to the Health Care Financing Administration (through intermediaries) has been slowly declining in recent years, it still remains about 50%.

As noted earlier, more than approximately 40% of medical care costs of the aged are not being covered by the Medicare program. The remaining 60% represents the various deductibles and coinsurance charges in Medicare (as described above) and payments for services not covered. Notable among these are drugs and dental services, although other services are also excluded. A major element in excluded costs is long-term care. As stated earlier, the Medicare provisions for institutional care are all time limited and, in the case of intermediate care facilities (ICFs), relatively short. Medicaid (discussed below) picks up some of these charges.

Long-term care is not included under Medicare because of its large costs but also because it is a combination of both medical and domiciliary costs. The growth of expenditures for these services nationally reflects not only the rising cost of medical care in general but the fact that intergenerational families have diminished in number. Provisions are not always available in the homes of children for older parents who need custodial-medical care. Planners of medical insurance programs hesitate to assume a cost under the heading of medical care which is only partially medical care in nature and which is a reflection of societal changes. Framers of national health insurance legislation almost uniformly leave out provisions for long-term care.

Medicaid

This program, known officially as Medical Assistance, is authorized by Title XIX of the SSA. Given all of its complications, Medicare is much easier to understand than Medicaid. The reason is that Medicaid is a grant-in-aid to the states and is not a national program like Medicare. The federal law offers states the choice of, first, whether they wish to have a Medicaid program and, second, a variety of options on the breadth of eligibility and services covered as well as the fees to be paid. The result is considerable variation in the kinds of programs which have evolved in the states. All but one state had the Medicaid program in 1979.

Once a state decides to have a Medicaid program, it must first decide whether the program is to be available only to people receiving money payments from welfare programs or whether the program will also include some of the medically needy. The welfare group are those recipients of Aid to Families with Dependent Children (AFDC) and SSI. With the expansion of eligibility in 1974 through the inauguration of SSI, states were given a further option of excluding persons eligible under the expanded SSI program or including them. The medically needy are those people who would qualify for the money payments programs except that their incomes or resources exceed the stated limits for eligibility. This is a very important distinction to understand because it accounts for the large number of medically needy people who are not included in the Medicaid program. Among the excluded groups are those below the age of 65 who are not disabled. Those over age 65 would qualify for SSI, as would those who are under 65 and disabled. The lack these people have of a tie to the SSI program, in these examples, accounts for their exclusion from Medicaid. Another example is the intact family in which the father is employed but earns very little. Since such a family is not eligible for AFDC, the family is also not eligible for Medicaid.

About half of the states include some medically needy. In each of these states, a decision had to be made concerning the income level to be regarded as qualifying. Although federal law prevents states from being too liberal in making this decision, most states that include the medically needy have eligible points below the federal maximum.

The federal law sets up the classifications of services which states must, and can, offer to pay for. States must offer some institutional and some noninstitutional services. In addition, states must offer:

• Inpatient hospital services.
• Outpatient hospital services and other X-ray and laboratory services.
• Skilled nursing home services for adults.
• Early periodic screening services for children.
• Physicians' services in the home, office, or hospital.

For the medically needy, the states may offer a smaller range of services. In addition to those required services, there is a long list of other optional services, which includes drugs, home health care, dental services, and the like. A major optional service which the states may offer is intermediate care facility (ICF) care. An ICF provides services that range somewhere between those of a domiciliary facility and a nursing home. This obviously includes many nursing homes which offer only minimal services and often charge fees which, although hard pressed, the state Medicaid agency will pay.

The federal law imposes a series of requirements on the states, most of which are designed to ensure efficient administration and continuous effort to weed out overutilization and ineligibility and also to make sure that applicants and recipients receive fair consideration by the state agency.

The federal share of Medicaid cost ranges from 50% in states with per capita income equal to or greater than the national average, to 83% for the state with the lowest per capita income in the United States. For those states with below-average per capita income, the federal medical percentage will range from 50–83%, depending on their rank in the states by per capita income.

By far the largest sums expended by the states for Medicaid are for hospitals, skilled nursing homes, and ICFs. Medicaid is the major source of public funds for long-term care. Inasmuch as all Medicare institutional services have time limits and the institutional services under Medicaid generally do not, many older persons find themselves receiving care in various kinds of nursing homes which are Medicaid eligible. The federal law prohibits states from requiring that children be responsible for supporting parents. Even if older persons have resources in their own names—even considerable resources—many months of care in a nursing home will exhaust them. Thus when the resources of the older persons diminish to the eligibility level for such resources as set by the state, they then become eligible for Medicaid.

Provisions for financing long-term care are greatly deficient. Medicare is weak in this regard; private health insurance policies rarely cover this need; and individual resources are—except for the very rich—inadequate to cover this care. Families who feel responsible for older members and their resources can, often at personal sacrifice, provide such care, if needed. Proof that these resources are inadequate is suggested by the fact that over half of all nursing home patients are recipients of Medicaid.

The Medicaid program has been engulfed in the rapidly rising cost of medical care. States have taken some steps to protect themselves, but even these measures have not been sufficiently effective to prevent the costs from becoming burdensome. In response to this, states have tended to trim services as best they can and have attempted to keep fees which they pay from rising too rapidly. The consequence is that many medical practitioners have refused to treat Medicaid patients and the level of ICF service has diminished as states have been unable to raise the amount of payments they will make for this care.

To some observers, the only answer to this problem of providing medical care for low-income people is national health insurance. To some degree, all national decisions made around Medicaid have been regarded as temporary, made in the belief that national health insurance will surely come to be and will help solve the problems. Even as proposals continue, the prospects of such a national health plan still seem to be in the future.

Private Health Insurance

A major force for paying medical costs in the United States is private health insurance. Public policy has supported the notion of a strong private sector for paying for medical care. Medical practitioners have encouraged it; industry has looked to the private sector to provide help to employees with their medical bills; and tax laws have encouraged the development of private health insurance plans. Consequently, private health insurance pays about 27% of the medical costs in the nation, while government—mainly through Medicare and Medicaid—pays about 42%. Direct payments made by individuals amount to about 27%. (Philanthropy accounts for the remainder.)

Significant as private health insurance is, its impact is much less for the aged than for younger workers. Since so few of the aged are employed, they tend to have less private health insurance than do younger people. With the advent of Medicare in 1965, the private health insurance industry was pleased to assume a smaller role for the aged for obvious reasons. There is great risk that the aged will become ill and will need costly medical services. Private insurance provides policies that supplement Medicare. These policies pay for some of the deductibles and coinsurance charges (discussed earlier) and may provide payment for some additional hospital days, but they rarely cover long-term care. Thus even the combination of Medicare and supplemental private health insurance does not provide the aged with full coverage. No insurance plan will provide full coverage because of the open-ended nature of the obligations it would be assuming. Moreover, long-term care is very costly, and were it to be included in insurance policies, the increased premium cost would make the policy prohibitive.

The long-term care part of the medical care industry is largely in the hands of private profit-making business. If new sources of funding should become available—through extended private or public insurance—rates would surely move upward without necessarily providing better service.

Part III
Programs for the Aged

Existing programs and services can be classified according to the dependence of the individuals assisted. Programs and services can also be classified in a format utilized by the Government Accounting Office (Comptroller General of the United States, 1977): home help, medical, financial, assessment, referral, social-recreational, and transportation.

Many of the programs and services included in this list have common elements. Adult daycare centers and multipurpose senior centers both utilize transportation and have major social components. Although we often discuss providing "services" or "serving" the elderly in this volume, we have attempted to differentiate between *programs* and *services,* terms often used synonymously. As we have defined them, *programs* contain individual elements; *services* include many of these same elements combined under a larger umbrella. We attempt to discuss these programs and services as they are most commonly organized, but the existence of state-by-state variations means that our descriptions of a program or service may be more applicable to one area than another.

In this part, will be discussed individual programs vital to the well-being of the elderly: information and referral, health and mental health programs, transportation, crime prevention and legal assistance programs, employment and volunteer programs, and nutrition programs.

Reference

Comptroller General of the United States. *Report to the Congress: The well-being of older people in Cleveland, Ohio.* Washington, D.C., 1977.

5
Information and Referral

Goals

Creating an extensive network of services has no benefits for the older person unless they are informed about the availability of these services and how to make use of them. Information and referral programs are thus a natural outgrowth of the tremendous increase in public and private programs for the general population and specifically for the elderly. The size of the agencies giving services, the size of the population being served in a given geographic area, and the number of different services available determine the extent of need for an information exchange system that can both identify appropriate services for those expressing a given need and collect and identify information on services being given.

> For the population at large, including the elderly, information and referral is a social service in its own right: an activity by which a person in need is made aware of, and connected to, a service or resource which can meet the need. However, the simple concept of establishing a link between need and resource becomes complex as one takes a closer look. It is a means to an end—an intermediate service which is determined by the final outcomes it attempts to facilitate. (Schmandt et al., 1979, p. 22)

The functions of information and referral for the elderly are essentially the same as the functions for the general population except for the focus on the specific needs of the elderly:

1. The assemblage and provision of information to link older persons with the opportunities, services, and resources designed to help them meet their particular problems

2. The collection and reporting of information about the needs of older people and the adequacy of resources available to them as aids to the evaluation, planning, coordination, and resource development efforts required of state and local agencies

Information and referral systems thus link individuals to services and services to each other in an effort to provide the individual with greater access to programs and services that can meet their needs.

History

Information and referral programs began in the 1960s when moneys were increasing for social programs. Some large federal and state agencies offered information and referral to the public in response to an expressed need. Information was provided in booklets and over the telephone as the need arose.

Official federal interest in information and referral began in 1971, with the passage of legislation authorizing the Social Security Administration to provide information to wage earners who would soon be retiring. In 1973, under the Comprehensive Service Amendments to the Older Americans Act (OAA), priority was to be given to the development of information and referral programs for the elderly. Similarly, the information and referral needs of the general welfare population, including the elderly, were addressed under the 1974/1975 Title XX social services regulations, which made these optional services that states could elect to provide. However, information and referral services were mandatory for SSI recipients. Title II of the Community Services Act of 1974 provided for urban and rural community action programs. Under a special section for senior opportunities and services, provisions were made for information and referral programs. Information and referral programs could also be operated under the National Health Planning and Resources Development Act of 1974 and the Community Mental Health Centers Amendments of 1975. In addition, a series of interagency agreements have been developed at the federal level to promote coordination of information and referral services through joint efforts at the federal, state, and local levels. The most recent agreement was signed in 1975 and included 17 different federal agencies.

Operation and Functions

A truly productive information and referral system not only will be able to generate and respond to questions of need but will be constantly testing the degree to which the belief that adequate services exist is based on fact. Information and referral systems thus appear to have the potential for generating beneficial changes in the service system. An effective information and referral system cannot work outside the service system.

> The best service system will be of little use if people do not know how to enter the system or to receive a package of services addressed to their particular needs. And the best information and referral service amounts to little if it does not lead to delivery of services beyond information and referral itself. (Schmandt et al., 1979, p. 23)

The success of an information and referral program is dependent, at least in part, on the extent and quality of the service system to which it refers.

Not only does information and referral provide information, acquired both formally and informally, about the service system; it must generate that information through active and relatively frequent contact with the services available. Information and referral programs can only be helpful to clients if the service agencies have a clear understanding of what they are actually providing. Because the information given by agencies is not always an accurate rendition of what is really available, some information and referral programs use client-supplied data to regenerate their descriptions. In addition, once the information about the agencies is in storage, it can be used as important data for planning and development purposes. Follow-up on clients receiving information from the information and referral program can indicate how effective the service response has been —information important for future service planning.

Organization

Scope

The diversity of information and referral programs almost matches the number of information and referral services available throughout the country, a number difficult to identify because information sharing takes many forms. In order to identify a minimum requirement for an adequate information and referral program, the Administration on Aging (1977) prepared policy guidelines to state agencies administering plans under the provisions of the OAA. Issued in August 1974, these guidelines also discussed long-range goals for the development of comprehensive information and referral programs. The nine service components were designed to build uniformity and comprehensiveness into the information and referral programs and to give some measurability of adequacy. The service components emphasized (1) having an adequate facility to serve those seeking information, (2) making continuously updated resource files available to agencies needing service information, (3) making the service easily available to older persons, (4) providing outreach to those not familiar with using such a service, (5) following up on referrals, and (6) providing transportation when necessary to help the older person reach a service identified through information and referral. The individual who calls or walks into an information and referral service is assured of anonymity, and usually no names are recorded on data forms. A casework approach is often utilized in which the information and referral worker explores the individual's problem and the alternative services available. As needed, the older person is referred to a specific service.

Schmandt et al. (1979) have attempted to bring some clarity to the wide range of efforts that fall under the information and referral label. Their attempt again indicates the complexity of the seemingly simple function of information and referral. An information and referral program may define its clientele on the basis of age, income, or specific problems. The program may confine itself to telephone assistance or move into extensive outreach including contact with individuals in their own homes. Limited research on the needs of the population within the community may also be undertaken. Within a defined city or metropolitan area, the agency offering the information and referral program may adopt a posture which emphasizes a personal type of relationship with clients or a relatively impersonal and highly professional one.

One of the difficulties in identifying and maintaining a minimum standard for information and referral programs is the pressure to have these programs reflect the style, service system, and needs of the locale in which they are located. Schmandt et al. (1979) argue for both the standardized and localized programs. This would include a centralized telephone center as well as decentralized walk-in centers in local neighborhoods. A two-part system of this type can effectively respond to the multifaceted needs of a variety of clients in the local community.

Because of their diversity, there are a wide range of institutions involved in the planning and delivery of information and referral programs. As indicated earlier, at the federal level, information and referral responsibilities for the elderly are shared among the Administration on Aging, the Social Security Administration, and the Community Services Administration. State and county social service departments represent a second layer of organizations responsible for information and referral functions. At the community level, a variety of public and private organizations dispense information and referral, generally to populations that include the elderly as well as other groups.

Types of Programs Available

An extensive study by Battle and Associates (1977) for the Administration on Aging found that 85% of information and referral programs were part of public agencies, about half of which were operated by state or area agencies on aging. In addition, the geographic area covered by the programs ranged from small communities to entire states. Age-segregated information and referral programs tended to have more linkages to a variety of programs and services including nutrition, recreation, health, transportation, and counseling. Information and referral programs under the auspices of area agencies on aging were also more likely to have linkages to a greater variety of programs and services than independently operated programs.

The type of information generation, storage, and retrieval systems used are essential to determining the success of information and referral. When local structures and community needs are taken into consideration when choosing a type of system, the system has a greater chance of success. A local walk-in information and referral program has different information needs than one that serves a large region and supplies data for planning. The service, then, that can clarify its informational goals can be more effectively evaluated.

According to Battle and Associates (1977) regardless of size, most of the information and referral programs maintain an inventory of opportunities, resources, services, and providers.

While the level of sophistication of the information and referrals varied, the degree of detail and the number of resources were usually related to the availability of services within the area and did not necessarily reflect any laxness on the part of the information and referrals in identifying and including services for older persons. (p. 42)

Although information was basically classified by type of service, provider, need or problem, geographic location, and segment of population served, the use of standardized classification systems has not produced more effective information and referral systems, nor has there been much incentive for such uniformity. Funding is not yet available for highly sophisticated systems; and the primary purpose of information and referral systems, namely responding to individual inquiry, does not require a highly interrelated systems approach. Unfortunately, information and referral programs have not been generally recognized for their full potential as resources in building better programs and services for the aged (Battle and Associates 1977). Trying to achieve a sophisticated information system while presenting the intimacy of one-to-one informal responses that encourages public use of the program creates a difficult situation for many information and referral systems. Of the 62 information and referral programs reviewed, only 8 used a computer for any part of their work. Most of the requests from individuals required information that was readily at hand and did not require computer capabilities.

Although it has been suggested that the availability of late-hour and toll-free telephone lines would increase the success of information and referral efforts, very few programs have instituted these options or even indicated a need for them. Many information and referral programs do not consider using toll-free numbers because of the small geographic area they serve. Of the information and referral programs studied by Battle and Associates (1977), 65% were large enough to effectively use a toll-free telephone service. However, before toll-free lines are mandated for any program, more knowledge is needed on their utilization. Telephone exchanges identify certain geographic locations, and unusual exchanges can be intimidating to potential users. In the Central Maryland program, it was found that local exchanges were more likely to be called than a central toll-free exchange serving the entire area.

The basic purpose of information and referral programs is to provide information to individuals. The ability of these services to fulfill this function is difficult to evaluate from the perspective of users because "many users do not conceptually separate the information and referral service from the actual service provider" (Burkhardt, 1979, p. 30). Individuals tend to call an information and referral service when faced with an immediate problem. In the vast majority of cases they are referred to an agency or specialized service for assistance. Thus clients' perceptions of the effectiveness of information and referral may be intertwined with how well they felt the agency to which they were referred dealt with their needs.

Information and referral programs can, however, increase their perceived effectiveness by taking the necessary measures to insure that those clients calling information and referral programs actually make contact with appropriate services; that is, those who call an information and referral program would have a better chance of getting the services they need if the information and referral plays a linkage and advocacy role. To facilitate referral, information and referrals can refer a client directly to one or more agencies; arrange for transportation or escort to insure that the client can reach the referred service; go to the client's home to provide direct assistance; call the service provider directly, giving information about the client, and then tell the client that the necessary contact has been made; or persuade a provider to handle a unique or difficult problem.

According to the information and referral program, the problems of the elderly most often requiring referral include the following individual and related problems: income– money–social security, transportation, health problems and care–home health care, housing–home maintenance–repair, food-nutrition, homemaker services, employment, consumer needs-problems, legal problems, companionship, and nursing home care (Battle and Associates 1977).

One of the big problems of information and referral programs, as with any program available to the elderly, is accessibility to anyone who needs the service. The information and referral program has the potential of being the most widely available of any service for the elderly because by nature of its service it is relatively inexpensive and equally accessible to everyone. However, despite their relative accessibility, information and referral programs are used by a disproportionate number of people who are already connected into the system in some way. The isolated and unattached remain unattached to this service, as they do to most other services that are potentially available to them. According to Battle and Associates (1977) only 66% of the information and referrals tried to solve this problem by providing outreach and case-finding services. Door-to-door canvassing was done by 29%, and 19% conducted outreach through churches, senior citizens' groups, and other community organizations. Unfortunately, direct outreach is expensive, and many such programs do not have the funds. When funds are limited, extensive use of the media appears the best way to reach isolated elderly populations. In Detroit, an ambitious information and referral program begun in the 1960s had to be cut back when it was found that outreach to and follow-up on individual clients were beyond the limited resources the agency (United Community Services, 1965) could make available for the information and referral program. It is thus likely that most information and referral services will not undertake the wide range of follow-up and client-advocacy functions that are possible for an information and referral program.

Funding and Costs

Information and referral programs have a low cost per unit of service. In 1977, the average cost per inquiry was $4.60, with a range of $1.00 to $20.00 per inquiry. The higher costs per inquiry were for those programs with a small number of inquiries, both in small rural and large metropolitan areas. The cost per inquiry does not relate to the number and type of services provided to the elderly. In fact, fewer information and referrals with calculated costs per inquiry of over $10.00 provided more extra services (such as transportation and outreach) than did their lower cost counterparts (Battle and Associates 1977).

Funding for information and referral programs comes from a variety of federal, state, local, and private sources, although state and area agencies contribute a larger percentage of funds to more information and referrals than other types of contributors. Major federal resources available include the Administration on Aging, the Office of Human Development Services under Title XX, and the Community Services Administration (HEW).

Additional sources of funds include state and county taxes; civic and religious groups; private, nonprofit sources such as United Way and Community Chest Agencies; private groups such as local foundations, corporations, and unions; and income from the project itself through the sale of items such as brochures, directories, and planning information.

Importance

Information and referral programs can be the link between the individual needing some type of service and the service that can best meet that person's needs. Many older people are unaware of the kinds of services available and how they can be found and, in many cases, are approaching the thought of professional assistance for the first time in their adult life. A well-implemented information and referral program can make older people aware of services, help them formulate their problem in the context of available services, and assist them in actually making the contact with the appropriate service. Organizing the maze of possible service systems, regulations, and eligibility requirements into a package of information, the information and referral program is essential for responsive service delivery to the elderly, regardless of the size of the community. Just as information and referral cannot be effective without a good service delivery system, service delivery systems cannot be effective without an efficient information and referral program, one that reaches to everyone in need of problem solving.

References

Battle, M., and Associates. *Evaluation of information and referral services for the elderly.* Washington, D.C.: U.S. Government Printing Office, 1977.

Burkhardt, J. Evaluating information and referral services. *Gerontologist,* 1979, *19,* 28–33.

Schmandt, J., Bach, V., & Radin, B. Information and referral services for the elderly welfare recipients. *Gerontologist,* 1979, *19,* 21–27.

United Community Services of Metropolitan Detroit. *Information and referral services.* Detroit, 1965.

U.S. Administration on Aging. *Program development handbook for state and area agencies on information and referral services for the elderly.* Washington, D.C.: U.S. Government Printing Office, 1977.

6
Health and Mental Health

As noted in Chapter 1, the elderly suffer from a variety of chronic illnesses. Medical problems of the older adult are not so much the common cold as they are arthritis, the effects of strokes, and vision and hearing problems. Medical care for a population with these types of problems must stress not only efforts to cure but treatment that allows the individual to adjust to living with a condition that may vary in intensity but will always be present.

Attempts to provide medical care for the elderly have met a variety of roadblocks: (1) the lack of interest by physicians in treating individuals whose conditions are not "curable," (2) the high costs of medical care, (3) the inaccessibility of medical treatment. These problems are also endemic in mental health treatment of the elderly.

Medicare and Medicaid have helped to reduce the cost of medical care for many older adults, although the out-of-pocket share of medical expenses incurred by the elderly has been increasing consistently. Specialized transportation programs for older adults have also targeted medical appointments as a top priority. The major problem that remains to be addressed is the recruitment and training of professionals and paraprofessionals dedicated to providing medical care for seniors. Until the mid-1970s, there was little emphasis on geriatrics in American schools of medicine. The curriculum in most medical schools has only recently begun to include any appreciable content on the aging process.

Even if physicians show increased interest in treating the elderly, hospitals are oriented toward acute illnesses, and individuals who remain hospitalized for an extended length of time run up enormous costs. The alternative to acute care hospitals—a long stay in a nursing home—has not been attractive to the elderly or their families. Only the introduction of in-home services and adult daycare centers (discussed in Part IV) have made care possible outside of long-term facilities such as hospitals and nursing homes. The majority of health care programs serving the elderly are part of the extensive range of home care services that are becoming available. In this chapter we will examine health care programs available through clinics, hospitals, and non-home care agencies.

It is ironic that the elderly are among the major consumers of health care in this country but receive less medical attention than other age groups. In 1977, the elderly spent 3.4 times more for health care than individuals under 65. Of these expenditures, 44% went to pay hospital bills, 26% for nursing homes, 17% for physicians, 7% for drugs, and 3% for dentists. Of the funds to pay for these medical expenses, 44% was received from Medicare (U.S. Senate, 1979). In sum, while the elderly comprise only 11% of the population, they account for 29% of the health care expenditures.

With the elderly spending such vast amounts of money on health care, the question has arisen whether separate services oriented to older adults should be developed. Separate services may require duplication of facilities and equipment already available. These facilities may be avoided by older individuals who feel stigmatized by attending special clinics. Alternatively, while encouraging the elderly to utilize existing services may avoid major capital outlays, older patients at large clinics often receive less attention from health professionals attracted to younger, more "curable" clients. With younger clients being assertive about the health care to which they feel entitled, the net result is that the elderly are relegated to long waits and poor care.

Health Care Programs

Geriatric Clinics

A geriatric health clinic in a medical center is a compromise service delivery system that avoids setting up new facilities but guarantees the elderly that their medical needs will receive attention. At Syracuse University, a geriatric clinic was integrated with other community health facilities. The clinic planners hoped that this integration would help to avoid ostracization of the elderly. Patients were assisted in establishing a relationship with a physician, but the clinic also maintained a referral service for specialized medical problems not treatable at the clinic (Syracuse University School of Social Work, 1971).

A similar model was utilized at the geriatric clinic opened in 1970 at Worcester State Hospital in Massachusetts. Patients were referred to the clinic by neighborhood workers. At the clinic, medical histories, physicals, and laboratory tests were undertaken. Based on the results of these tests, a decision was made by clinical medical personnel either to treat or to refer the client to other medical services. Clients with no regular physician were referred to an outpatient clinic or a local hospital, or they remained as patients of the geriatric clinic (Worcester State Hospital, 1972).

The Worcester clinic provided treatment, but other programs have been primarily oriented to either screening, publicizing medical needs of the elderly, or encouraging the elderly to obtain adequate medical care. In Hawaii, difficulties in reaching facilities and psychological fears resulting from limited fluency in English or low education resulted in underutilization of health services by the elderly. To meet this problem, a senior center health screening program was instituted. Conducted on a bimonthly basis in Honolulu, the program was able to screen 100 individuals in 3–4 hours. Counseling was provided to the individual about existing medical conditions and abnormal test results. Abnormal results were also reported to the individual's primary care physician. In some cases where serious conditions were noted, the screening program instituted follow-up to insure that the individual obtained the necessary medical treatment (Hawaii Senior Services, 1975).

Health Fairs

The Worcester and Hawaii programs contain elements of both primary and secondary prevention. Local primary prevention programs have been built around educational programs informing the elderly about nutrition, care of chronic illnesses, correct drug usage and a variety of other medical issues. These educational programs have been run at senior centers, nutrition sites, and adult daycare centers. Short television and radio announcements have also been utilized in efforts to alert the elderly to potential health problems and appropriate treatment.

In many localities health fairs have been inaugurated. These one-day fairs provide information on a variety of health conditions and programs and also conduct basic screening of blood pressure, vision, and hearing. In 1979, the Administration on Aging (AoA) provided funds for health fairs throughout the country.

Exercise Programs

In recent years it has become evident that regular exercise is an important element of health prevention for individuals of all ages. Increasing numbers of senior centers as well as daycare programs are offering exercise classes and activities for their clients. The President's Council on Physical Fitness and Sports has received funding from the AoA to develop and promote an "Active People Over 60" program. This program utilizes workshops and demonstrations to promote the goal of exercise for older adults (National Institute on Senior Centers, 1978). In West Virginia the Preventicare program offers 3-day-a-week exercise sessions at senior centers, nutrition sites, churches, mental health centers, hospitals, and nursing homes in 51 of the 55 West Virginia counties (National Institute on Senior Centers, 1978).

The Adults Health & Development clinic at the University of Maryland offers older adults regular Saturday morning exercises and physical activities in which they are assisted by individual students. The relationships developed through this one-to-one contact often extend into close friendships between students and older persons. Similarly, the Senior Actualizations and Growth Exploration (SAGE) program begun in California works with small groups of older persons, who join together for an extended involvement. A variety of techniques are used including exercise, meditation, yoga, massage, and gestalt therapy. SAGE's efforts show that many of the newer growth and therapy techniques can be effective with any age group given the individuals' willingness to undertake the intensive commitment required.

Dental Care

Dental problems increase with age. The lack of adequate dental treatment for older people is reflected in the fact that only half of the individuals between 55 and 74 have any natural teeth remaining (National Council on the Aging, 1978). Although this figure of 50% represents an improvement from past years, dental care for the aged demands considerably more attention than it has received. In some states, the dental societies are beginning to work with senior centers and area agencies on aging to offer dental care to elderly clients at reduced rates. This reduced-rate dental care may be provided at the dentists' offices, but some senior centers are incorporating dental suites into their facilities. These dental facilities also serve as training sites for dental students.

Drugs

As major consumers of both prescription and over-the-counter drugs, the elderly are faced with the problems of absorbing the enormous costs of these medications, even when assisted by Medicare and Medicaid. The shift in many states to utilization of generic rather than brand name drugs is helping to lower costs. Nonprofit pharmacies for the elderly are now being discussed by many senior centers. Since 1958, the American Association of Retired Persons (AARP) has operated direct-mail pharmacies for its elderly members. In 1978, AARP pharmacies were located in eight cities and offered a full line of over-the-counter and prescription drugs.

All of these diverse efforts will need to be greatly expanded in the future if the requisite health care for the elderly is to be provided. As Shanas (1978) has noted, the proportion of elderly living in long-term facilities has not increased greatly since 1966. As the proportion of community-based elderly increases, a larger complement of health care programs will be needed to prevent and treat acute and chronic illnesses prevalent among older adults.

Mental Health Programs

In the United States, mental hospitals have often functioned as quasi-homes for the aged. Although the number of patients in state mental hospitals has lessened dramatically in the past thirty years, many of the elderly released from the hospitals had been patients for 20 years or more. Community-based treatment programs, psychotropic drugs (Bloom, 1975), the tightening of legal grounds for commitment, and the growth of nursing homes should guarantee that the numbers of elderly in state hospitals will never even rise to the 29% figure of 1969 (Gottesman & Hutchinson, 1974).

Community Mental Health

The community mental health programs took root in 1963 with the passage of the Community Mental Health Centers Act. The intention of the act's supporters was to enlarge mental health expenditures at all levels and develop a network of community-based treatment facilities. These treatment facilities would be located in geographic areas that had a maximum population of 175,000. Each state, however, had to determine appropriate catchment-area boundaries. In each catchment area an organization was to be designated as responsible for providing community mental health services.

As originally specified in 1963, the services included 5 major components. At present, however, this list has been enlarged to a total of 12 different services:

1. Inpatient care
2. Outpatient care
3. Partial hospitalization (daycare)
4. Emergency services
5. Consultation and education
6. Specialized services for children
7. Specialized services for the elderly
8. Screening of individuals considered for referral to a state mental hospital
9. Follow-up services for discharged inpatients
10. Transitional halfway houses for former mental patients
11. Programs for prevention and treatment of alcoholism if not already in existence in the catchment area
12. Programs for the prevention and treatment of drug addiction if not already available in the catchment area.

To reduce the pressures on new mental health centers attempting to implement all 12 of these services immediately, the Health Services Amendments of 1978 allowed centers to concentrate on 5 services, phasing in the additional 7 services over a 3-year period. The 5 services required initially from federally funded centers are emergency care, outpatient services, screening of individuals for mental hospital referrals, follow-up care for discharged inpatients, and consultation and education (*Hospital and Community Psychiatry*, 1978). The actual proportion of effort and funds allocated by a mental health center to any one of these components would be determined by the needs of the community. While 675 centers were in operation by 1979, the goals of having a center in all 1,500 catchment areas in the country remains a long way from being realized.

Primary prevention as embodied in the consultation and education programs was one of the major assumptions of this "bold new approach" (Kennedy, 1963) to mental health services. Treatments for individual mental health problems were supposed to be supplemented by primary prevention programs that located the sources of stress in the environment and worked with community groups to alleviate these negative influences. Primary prevention efforts focused on at-risk populations would include the elderly in many communities.

Mental Health Prevention Programs

Unfortunately, adequate appropriations to replace federal funding have not been forthcoming, and cutbacks in programming have been made at many centers. These cutbacks have often been at the expense of primary prevention programs. Primary prevention programs are often seen by traditionally trained mental health professionals as irrelevant to therapeutic intervention with individuals.

Tertiary prevention programs aimed at reintegrating discharged patients into family and community life have also encountered difficulty in becoming well established and accepted. Part of this difficulty can be traced to the methods used by advocates of these programs in obtaining support for deinstitutionalization. During the 1960s, mental hospitals were derided not only for their effects on individuals and the lack of adequate treatment but for their supposedly high costs.

Deinstitutionalization

Proponents of community-based programs argued that individuals could be treated outside the state mental hospital without creating an "institutional personality" and at a lower cost. Actual experiences have not always shown these cost claims to be true. While state mental hospital costs are evident upon careful auditing, accounting for the costs of a community-based program are more difficult.

Mrs. S. provides a good example. A woman in her early 70s, she had been in the state hospital for 20 years. Discharged under the new community approach of the 1960s, Mrs. S. has been living in an old hotel in a beachfront community in New York. Because of her lack of any other means of support, she receives financial aid from the state as well as casework services from the Department of Social Services. The mental health services she obtains are provided through the Department of Mental Hygiene. If any vocational training is included in the supports she receives, these will be provided by the Department of Vocational Rehabilitation.

Mrs. S. is thus receiving a variety of services, most of which are not provided under mental health auspices. Unless this is taken into account when cost-effectiveness studies of institutionally based versus community-based programs are compared, the figures will show that the costs of the community services are considerably cheaper. This may not be true given the number of paid professionals involved in assisting Mrs. S. remain in the community. As the reality of the costs involved in providing quality aftercare services in mental health has become evident, claims about cost effectiveness have become muted. The opening of new programs to serve released patients has also been retarded.

Discharged mental patients living in old hotels and domiciliary facilities operated by state mental health departments continue to make headlines as many communities protest these problems being "dumped" in their neighborhoods. As some communities pass zoning regulations making it difficult to open new facilities, the discharged mental patients become concentrated in areas such as Long Beach, New York; South Miami; or parts of Chicago. If the ex-patients themselves do not create problems, their assumed vulnerability attracts individuals who attempt to prey on them. In the 1980s, the emphasis of the National Institute of Mental Health will be on the development of "community support systems" with specific agencies becoming responsible for obtaining and coordinating services for discharged individuals involved in mental health deinstitutionalization programs.

Elderly in the Mental Health System

There are now three major groups of elderly involved in the mental health system: (1) elderly who have been long-term residents of state hospitals and are attempting to live outside the controlled hospital environment, (2) elderly who have been utilizing mental health services for a period of time, and (3) elderly who begin to exhibit major mental health problems only as they become older. These problems may include depression, insomnia, hypochondria, paranoia, and organic brain disorders. We will examine the present condition of mental health services for former residents of state hospitals and older persons exhibiting mental health problems often associated with aging.

Discharged Patients

Individuals who have been in a mental hospital for a long period of time may have major difficulties readjusting to any form of independent life in the community. As Kirk and Therrien (1975) have argued, family members are often opposed to long-term mental patients living in their home. An added complication is that mental patients often have few employable skills and minimal financial resources. Watson (1976) has shown, however, that the morale among elderly psychiatric patients being treated on an outpatient basis was significantly higher than among elderly inpatients. For elderly outpatients to function adequately in the community, extensive supportive services are needed, including a means for obtaining regular medications.

Mental Health and Nursing Homes

The hue and cry about the lack of aftercare programs would be even greater if the 1960s had not seen a major growth in the number of nursing homes. Nursing homes have now taken a major share of the burden of caring for the institutionalized elderly. The drop in individuals in state hospitals since 1960 was matched by an equivalent increase in nursing home patients.

The National Center for Health Statistics's 1973 survey of nursing home patients found that the largest percentage were labeled "senile," a label that now appears to be as vague as it is overused (Glasscote et al., 1976). Whatever the mental condition of nursing home patients, few are actively receiving psychiatric care. Glasscote et al. summarized a 1976 investigation of the mental health needs and treatment of nursing home patients:

> Our sample of nursing facilities estimated that about three quarters of their patients are either formally diagnosed with a psychiatric disorder or are "de facto psychiatrically impaired," if this figure can be projected to the 1,100,000 population of all nursing homes, then there are more than three-quarters of a million nursing home patients with psychiatric disability, most of whom have had no contact at all with psychiatrists. (p. 71)

Elderly in Mental Health Centers

Fortunately, only 5% of today's elderly are in long-term institutional settings. For the majority of the over-60 population, mental health services must be obtained from community mental health centers. As already shown, services to the elderly are now a requirement for federally funded mental health centers. Despite this new mandate in 1975, mental health centers have still not shown a major interest in providing extensive mental health services for older adults. For the majority of mental health professionals, the most desirable clients remain youthful, attractive, verbal, intelligent, and successful individuals (Schofield, 1964). In contrast, the elderly are often perceived as depressed individuals whose problems are merely the product of "getting old." Whereas the younger persons have an extensive future ahead of them, mental health professionals may view older persons as having their "best years" behind them and thus as less deserving of attention.

The present generation of elderly may also fail to utilize mental health services because of their limited education and fluency in English. Other more complex reasons are that they may (1) not recognize some behaviors as mental health problems, (2) believe that many mental health problems are the responsibility of the family unless extremely serious (Fandetti & Gelfand, 1978), (3) stigmatize mental illness and be fearful of being labeled "crazy" if it becomes known that they are utilizing mental health services, (4) be unaware of the services available at mental health centers, or (5) have difficulty reaching mental health centers and clinics because of a lack of transportation.

At present the mental health needs of the elderly are much greater than the services provided:

> The prevalence of mental illness and emotional distress is higher among the over age 65 than in the general population. Up to 25% of older persons have been estimated to have significant mental health problems. Yet only 4% of patients seen in public outpatient mental health clinics and 2% of those seen in private psychiatric care are elderly. (President's Commission on Mental Health, 1978, p. 7)

Widowed Persons Programs

The widowed persons programs are important efforts run independently of mental health centers. These programs provide counseling on an individualized basis to men and women who are recently widowed. These widows and widowers are paired with volunteers who provide support on emotional issues relating to the loss of a spouse and practical information about preparing to lead a life as a single person. This practical information may cover finances or even learning to drive for the first time. The AARP runs the largest widowed persons program in the United States. In 1978, there were more than 2,500 volunteers working with more than 10,000 recently widowed older adults (Brickfield, 1979).

Specialized Aging Services

Berkman (1977) found one mental health center in Texas totally oriented to serving the elderly. The center was providing services ranging from crisis counseling through supportive social services. It is doubtful that this approach will be expanded in many other regions. Instead we can expect to find "creative mental health services for the elderly" (Glasscote et al., 1977) integrated with other service delivery systems, including nursing homes and senior centers.

Ross's efforts (1975) to develop a "neighborhood family" of elderly living in trailer parks in an area of Miami illustrates how effective outreach can bring the elderly into a variety of programs including mental health ones. As the President's Commission on Mental Health (1978) emphasized, the lack of outreach to older persons is a major factor in their low representation in mental health services.

Limited Medicare coverage for mental health services remains an even more important obstacle to the expansion of mental health services for the elderly. Medicare provisions emphasize hospital treatment and nursing home care, with only limited coverage for outpatient mental health services. Changes in these provisions to emphasize community-based treatment might provide the transfusion necessary for financially strapped community mental health centers and clinics to turn their attention to the mental health needs of the elderly.

References

Berkman, B. Community mental health services for the elderly. *Community Mental Health Review,* 1977, *3*(2), 1–15.

Bloom, B. *Community mental health.* Monterey, Calif.: Brooks/Cole, 1975.

Brickfield, C. AARP 1979. *Modern Maturity,* 1979, *22*(2), 41–46.

Fandetti, D. & Gelfand. D. Attitudes towards symptoms and services in the ethnic family and neighborhood. *American Journal of Orthopsychiatry,* 1978, *48,* 477–486.

Glasscote, R., et al. *Old folks at homes.* Washington, D.C.: American Psychiatric Association and the National Association for Mental Health, 1976.

Glasscote, R., Gude, J., & Miles, D. *Creative mental health services for the elderly.* Washington, D.C.: American Psychiatric Association and the Mental Health Association, 1977.

Gottesman, L., & Hutchinson, E. Long-term care in the community. In E. Brody (Ed.), *A social work guide for long-term care facilities.* Rockville, Md.: National Institute of Mental Health, 1974.

Hawaii Senior Services. *Health screening for the elderly.* 1975.

Hospital and Community Psychiatry (Special Report), 1978, *29*(5), 320–323.

Kennedy, J. *A message from the President of the United States relative to mental illness and mental retardation.* Washington, D.C., February 5, 1963.

Kirk, S., & Therrien, M. Community mental health myths and the fate of former hospitalized patients. *Psychiatry,* 1975, *38,* 209–217.

National Council on the Aging. *Fact book on aging.* Washington, D.C., 1978.

National Institute on Senior Centers. *Senior Center Report,* 1978, *1*(4), 3.

President's Commission on Mental Health. *Report to the President,* (Vol. 1). Washington, D.C.: U.S. Government Printing Office, 1978.

Reuss, K. *Life time: A new image of aging.* Santa Cruz, Calif.: Unity, 1978.

Ross, H. Low-income elderly in inner-city trailer parks. *Psychiatric Annals,* 1975, *5*(6), 86–90.

Schofield, W. *Psychotherapy: The purchase of friendship.* Englewood Cliffs, N.J.: Prentice-Hall, 1964.

Shanas, E. New directions in health care for the elderly. In I. Brookbank (Ed.), *Improving the quality of health care for the elderly.* Gainesville, Fla.: University Presses of Florida, 1978.

Syracuse University School of Social Work. *Concerns in planning health services for the elderly.* October 1971.

U.S. Senate, Special Committee on Aging. *Developments in aging, 1978: Part I.* Washington, D.C.: U.S. Government Printing Office, 1979.

Watson, C. Inpatient care or outplacement: Which is better for the psychiatrically medically infirm patient? *Journal of Gerontology,* 1976, *31,* 611–616.

Worcester State Hospital. *Two year activities of a geriatric clinic in the Worcester area.* Worcester, Mass. 1972.

7
Transportation

Transportation programs are a necessary support for community-based aging services, including daycare centers, senior centers, mental health centers, and nutritional and educational programs. Transportation is also a crucial factor in the elderly being able to obtain medical care and maintain relationships with family and friends or attend social and cultural events.

Many communities lack any transportation system designed to serve the general public. This lack of public transportation programs will be a more significant problem in the future as the elderly population living in suburban communities increases. Dependence on the automobile is difficult for many older persons, who feel a lessening sense of security behind the driver's wheel as their reflexes slow. Visual problems also preclude many elderly from driving at night, limiting the social events they can attend. For the elderly on fixed incomes, the cost of purchasing and maintaining an automobile may also prove to be too burdensome. At present, reports indicate that the majority of elderly living in urban areas depend on walking to reach their destinations. The mobility problems of the isolated rural elderly are intensified because of inadequate and often poorly maintained road systems.

A variety of approaches to the transportation needs of urban, suburban, and rural elderly are thus required. To place the present thrust of transportation programs in an appropriate framework, we need to examine the goals of these services and the factors that impinge on realization of these goals.

Options

Transportation systems can vary in their extensiveness, their frequency of operation, and their ability to meet the individualized interests of potential consumers. In the language of transportation planning, these systems can be "demand responsive," "need responsive," or "desire responsive." While demand responsive systems respond to call for service on the part of individuals, need responsive systems attempt to service transportation requirements felt to be important to the individual's maintenance of a satisfying life. The demands placed on transportation services by elderly individuals may be less than what they "need" for an independent, healthy life-style. "Need responsive" systems are close to "desire responsive systems," and planners usually confine their analyses to these first two groups.

The optimal transportation system for the elderly and the handicapped would be need responsive, increasing their options for interactions with a range of individuals and programs. In densely populated areas an inexpensive, properly designed mass transit system may enable the older person to reach a variety of important destinations. In suburban and rural areas with low density and dispersed services, a system responsive to the older person's needs is more difficult to implement.

Models

The major variables in transportation systems are routing, schedules, and loading points. Four major combinations of routing and scheduling are possible: (1) fixed-route services with fixed scheduling, a model corresponding to mass transit; (2) fixed routing with varied scheduling; (3) variable routing with fixed scheduling; and (4) variable routing with variable scheduling. As we examine in-place and newly developing transportation systems we will note examples of all four of these alternatives.

Aggregate trips taken by individuals to different sites and the costs or subsidization that must be borne for each trip taken are major factors in choosing transportation models appropriate to a community. As transit authorities around the country have discovered, public transit systems cannot be expected to run at a profit if fares are to be kept at a reasonable level. The growing understanding that public transit of any form needs to be subsidized has retarded its development in many areas. Unfortunately, many transit authorities attempting to stop the rise of deficits have become involved in a cycle of raising fares, resulting in a lower number of riders and subsequent fare increases. With each fare increase the differential between the costs of mass transit and driving decreases, and increasing numbers of individuals therefore turn to their automobiles for commuting and pleasure trips. Transportation systems of all kinds must face the issue of the maximum subsidies that the community will tolerate and optimal methods for financing these subsidies.

Forms of Transportation for the Elderly

Mass Transit

During the 1960s and 1970s, an effort was made to encourage the elderly's use of existing mass transit facilities. Under the 1974 National Mass Transit Assistance Act, the Urban Mass Transit Administration was authorized to allot funds for capital and operating costs of mass transit systems. Communities attempting to qualify for these funds were required to institute programs for the elderly that reduced fares in nonpeak hours to no more than one-half of peak-hour fares. A number of major cities had already instituted this approach before the federal legislation was enacted. By 1974, 145 cities had already instituted half-fare programs (U.S. Administration on Aging, 1975).

Cantor's (1970) interviews with a sample of New York City elderly indicated that they felt they used the subway and bus system more extensively because of the low-fare privileges. This increase in ridership creates some methodological problems in evaluating the costs of this type of program. Half-fare rides are obviously not matching the operating costs for each ride. If, however, the ridership increases at nonpeak hours, even at half-fare, is this increase reducing the subsidization? Alternatively, have some of the individuals now riding at off-peak hours switched their riding patterns from peak hours, reducing the number of full fares collected by the system and thus increasing the number of heavily subsidized rides?

Answers to these questions have been difficult to obtain, but the positive effects of the program for elderly riders have been demonstrated. This includes increased use of the mass transit systems by the elderly to attend social activities and programs and to obtain medical care. Unfortunately, available studies do not reveal the reasons many elderly still refrain from using the transit system. The stress of the elderly on convenience and accessibility rather than costs of transportation may account for reduced ridership among older people who have to walk long distances to reach transit stops or take buses even to reach the subway. Having accomplished this task, they then must surmount the obstacles posed by steps on buses or stairways in subway stations.

The Urban Mass Transportation Act (UMTA) specifies that elderly and handicapped persons have the same rights to utilize mass transportation facilities and services as other individuals. In 1975, regulations were issued requiring recipients of UMTA funds to build their facilities in a manner that would not create physical barriers for the elderly and handicapped. Installation of elevators at all new subway stations has been one major outgrowth of this requirement.

The physical barriers on buses are more difficult to overcome. In East Orange, New Jersey (Rinaldi, 1973), an escort service was provided during the early 1970s to help elderly individuals negotiate the steps of buses and other public transit barriers. In 1973, a negative report on this effort was issued. Despite the assistance made available by the escorts, the costs of this service were prohibitive. Costs were doubled since fares were required for both the elderly person and the escort. The service was also not found to promote new trips by elderly individuals.

A more important innovation is the regulations issued by the Department of Transportation that require all new buses purchased with UMTA funds after September 1979 to have boarding ramps or hydraulic lifts, floor heights not more than 22 inches off the ground, and an ability to "kneel" to 18 inches. While the disputes about the technical effectiveness and added costs of these "transbuses" continue, the regulations have been viewed as an indication of a real commitment by the Department of Transportation to the needs of the elderly and the handicapped. Opposition to the costs of this new bus design threatens to delay introduction of the transbus until the mid-80s.

New Transportation Systems

Building public transportation systems is an extremely costly process, and these systems do not always provide the most direct route to a destination. In some cases a bus trip to a medical center may require 50 minutes, a transfer of buses, and cost $1.00. A taxicab ride to the same destination might occupy 10 minutes, cost $1.50, and be door to door.

The problems involved in creating new transportation systems for the elderly are more complex than reductions in fares on existing mass transit facilities. Critical examinations of the potential of new systems is necessary because of the increasingly decentralized living patterns of Americans. In 1974, it was estimated that 5.5 million of the 54 million rural American residents had mobility problems (McKelvey & Ducker, 1974). The Federal Aid to Highways Act of 1973 emphasized the need to take the mobility needs of rural elderly and handicapped into account in highway planning and improvements (U.S. Department of Transportation, 1976).

Financial assistance for transportation programs is available under Section 16(b)(2) of UMTA grants to assist nonprofit organizations in providing services to the elderly and handicapped when mass transit systems are unavailable, insufficient, or not appropriate (U.S. House of Representatives, 1976). By 1977, over 1,400 organizations had utilized more than $30 million worth of grants distributed by UMTA to purchase 3,000 specialized vehicles (Transportation Projects Face, 1977). Over 75% of these vehicles have been 10–16 passenger vans for the elderly. Under the UMTA program, 20% of these vehicle costs must be contributed by the local agency or transit authority. Supplementing the UMTA funds in many communities are funds from Title III of the OAA (which as noted in Chapter 2 now places a strong emphasis on issues of access), revenue sharing funds, Title XX funds, and purchase of care arrangements among individual social service agencies.

Substantial amounts of Title III funds have been channeled into transportation programs, although testimony in 1977 made it clear that the AoA discourages the use of these moneys for the purchase of vehicles. AoA officials fear that many agencies will not be able to afford the expenses of maintaining and operating these vehicles after using Title III funds to purchase them. The difficulties of meeting operating expenses is a common theme among organizations running extensive transportation efforts and facing mounting repair costs for heavily used vehicles. The costs of repairs plus the steadily increasing gasoline prices continue to make transportation an expensive service.

Obtaining adequate insurance at reasonable rates has become a major headache for agencies attempting to implement transportation services for the elderly. A program in Idaho found it could not obtain insurance for volunteer drivers, especially those who intended to use their own automobiles. Drivers were informed by insurance companies that they would not receive liability coverage for transportation of the elderly. As a result many of the volunteer drivers quit the program. In Dayton, Ohio, a Title III transportation project was unable to obtain any insurance for their program from commercial insurers and was forced into an assigned-risk pool with an increase in insurance premium from $300 to $900 (U.S. Administration on Aging, 1977). In Wisconsin a program found its insurance rates jumping from $200 to $1,500 at renewal time, and in Virginia a minibus program which paid $2,130 for insurance coverage in 1977 had its rates more than doubled in 1978. The program was also informed it would not be covered for any drivers over 65 (U.S. Administration on Aging, 1977).

Although there seems to be no quick solution to this problem, the AoA is advising agencies to take a number of steps to combat this problem, including shopping for the best possible rates among insurance agencies, coordinating efforts with other agencies to obtain alternative insurance coverage, setting high standards for drivers (including tests and certification programs), and gathering statistics for insurance companies to show that the elderly are not more prone to injury when transported than other groups (U.S. Administration on Aging, 1971). It is also expected that "add-ons" to existing insurance policies held by individual counties and municipalities will be increasingly utilized in many areas.

Despite these problems, a large number of diverse transportation systems were begun during the 1970s. The Older American Transportation Service (OATS) in Missouri began in 1971 with $30,000 from Title III. In 1978, 125 vans and buses (25 wheelchair equipped) were being utilized in the program, which serves 89 counties. The OATS budget for 1979 was $125,000. Deficits in grant funding are made up by a variety of dinners and sales. OATS is a variable route, variable schedule program but requires that users send in a postcard or call for a reservation 1 week in advance. Medical trips are given priority (Pierce, 1979). In Nebraska, a similar Senior Handi-Bus program dispatches six passenger vans on 24-hour advance reservation, and similar efforts are underway in St. Petersburg, Florida, and Rhode Island.

In Cape May County, New Jersey, fixed route, fixed schedule dial-a-ride vans with seats reserved a week ahead make weekly trips to Atlantic City and Philadelphia. Trips to Philadelphia, the closest city, are usually in connection with medical treatment. Drivers working in this program must complete a National Safety Council defensive driving course and other safety requirements. All of the vans carry emergency first-aid equipment. The vans are also used during the week to transport seniors to Title III nutrition sites (Jones, et al., 1976).

School Buses

Besides vans and minibuses, school buses would appear to be the vehicle most available for elderly transportation services, since these buses are usually only utilized to transport school children at early-morning and late-afternoon hours. Unfortunately, only 15 states have legislation permitting school buses to be used for nonschool purposes. During summer months when the weather allows many older individuals to attend activities, school buses are often being rotated in and out of repair shops for yearly maintenance. If state legislation permits the utilization of school buses for any purposes, the ultimate decision on their disposition usually rests with local communities. In some localities, parents have opposed additional use of school buses, fearing that this extensive use will create additional wear and tear and make the buses unsafe for their children (U.S. Department of Transportation, 1977). School buses also present the physical obstacles of high steps, making them inaccessible for wheelchair-bound individuals.

In Klamath, Oregon, school buses are being used to transport the elderly on a fixed route and fixed schedule basis. The Cape May County program already mentioned uses school buses to provide extensive services for its 15,000 elderly residents. The county estimates that each ride costs $1.55, of which the county contributes $.43. Running on a fixed route with fixed schedules, four buses travel through each town and village in the county at least once a week and stop at major shopping centers. At the shopping centers the buses wait 1½ hours before returning to their original departure points. On Saturdays the buses are used for recreational trips for the elderly (U.S. Department of Transportation, 1975).

Ridership Problems

Encouraging frequent utilization of these transportation services is important in reducing the average cost per ride. A shuttle system developed in Washington, D.C. in 1978 to transport the elderly to shopping on Thursdays found it difficult to attract new riders to the

13-passenger wheelchair-accessible vans. As the director of the program commented: "So far, I think we haven't been reaching the people. Many of them remain isolated in their apartments, so how can we reach them?" (Bernhard, 1979, p. 15). Cantor (1970) found the same problem in New York, where a sample of elderly indicated a mistaken belief that the available Dial-A-Ride systems were to be used only for medical purposes.

Faced with the problems of financing $15,000 vans and then obtaining sufficient numbers of riders to keep subsidization at a reasonable level, it would appear that taxicab usage would be more economical and more convenient. Taxicab-based systems might also reduce any negative feelings that elderly residents have about riding special buses and would make use of existing dispatching systems.

In the early 1970s, a shared taxicab service was implemented in Arlington, Virginia. By 1975, this system had been abandoned on the basis of excessive costs. Each passenger paid $.15 for the taxicab, but the actual cost per taxi trip was $2.74. Although 45% of the eligible elderly were using this service, it was hard to persuade passengers to share the taxis or that a reservation 2 hours in advance was not an arbitrarily imposed requirement. As the program reached its final stages, only 1.4 passengers were being transported in each taxicab ride (Kast, 1975). Aside from cost problems, many cab drivers may not want to pick up elderly passengers who live in poor inner-city or rural areas. The flexibility and convenience of the taxicab has thus been difficult to match with a program that is economical and efficient.

Coordination of Programs

Many of the transportation programs for special groups are mandated under federal legislation. Title XIX specifies that each state plan must include provisions for assuring the transportation of Medicaid recipients to and from medical services. This provision can be satisfied by reimbursement of recipients for their transportation costs. Title III of the OAA requires the provision of transportation for clients to and from nutrition sites if transportation is otherwise unavailable.

An indication of the proliferation of transportation programs was provided by a study in Chattanooga, Tennessee, where 40 agencies were found to be operating transportation programs in 1975 (U.S. Department of Transportation, 1975). Coordination of these individual agencies' efforts in order to pool resources for capital outlays and operating costs is one step that promises to reduce the constantly increasing financial burdens of these programs. In Roanoke, Virginia, a nonprofit transportation agency was formed in 1975 to pool all the transportation resources and needs of individual agencies. Funds received by the transportation agency (Roanoke Dial-A-Ride) are then distributed to the participating organizations. In California, the local Transportation District provides 64% of the expenses for transportation programs in Marin County. The Transportation District also coordinates transportation programs for senior citizens, a medical transportation program, and a system of transportation for service and charitable organizations. In Delaware, the state legislature has set up the Delaware Authority for Special Transportation, which coordinates all resources for transportation to the elderly and handicapped (U.S. House of Representatives, 1976).

Future Trends

The major thrust of transportation systems in the future will be the purchase and operation of minibus and van systems, many of them equipped for wheelchair passengers. A number of communities will also be making efforts to run both flexible and fixed schedule programs such as are already in place in Cape May County, New Jersey (U.S. Department of Transportation, 1977).

Unanticipated legal issues may be raised as communities attempt to organize separate transportation systems for the elderly and handicapped. Aside from the need to determine eligibility for transportation services based on program guidelines, the inception of new transportation services may be viewed as violating long-standing franchise agreements between the municipality or county and public or private transit authorities.

Buses being utilized by two passengers an hour are more expensive than cabs, especially when the taxes and depreciation are figured into the total cost per ride. The coordination of programs being attempted in Delaware, California, and Virginia, as well as intensive efforts to inform the elderly of transportation services now available, are vital to counteract such high costs.

Aging programs are constantly proclaiming the provision of adequate transportation to be one of their major headaches. The expenses associated with this service will not decrease, although the spiral in insurance premiums noted in the late 1970s can be expected to abate. Transportation will continue to consume a major portion of the budget of service agencies even with proper coordination, and program planners must be aware of the costs and difficulties of providing adequate transportation.

For the elderly we can expect transportation programs to remain demand responsive rather than need responsive. Although flexible schedules and route services may be officially available, priorities of shopping and medical trips may consume most of the van and bus capacity available in many areas. It is thus doubtful that any new public transportation system will be able to open up major new opportunities for elderly individuals to expand their range of activities. The realistic goals of transportation services in the 1980s would appear to be to enable (1) formerly isolated elderly to reach the variety of agencies and programs now available, (2) elderly individuals to obtain the medical and mental health care they require, and (3) the elderly to undertake the necessary shopping trips to avoid doing without important goods or becoming dependent on any local store and its possibly inflated prices. Visiting or attendance at cultural events requires a flexible and individualized service not within the resources of transportation services presently in operation.

The goals mentioned are major, and their fulfillment will not be a simple task. Their attainment promises an improvement in the isolating conditions under which many elderly and handicapped now live, but it will remain an expensive effort. Subsidization of transportation services will always be necessary. Providing adequate transportation services may prove to be a major test of the general public's commitment to maintaining the network of services needed by older individuals.

References

Bernhard, M. Giving a lift to the elderly. *Washington Post,* January 8, 1979, A-15.

Cantor, M. *Elderly ridership and reduced transit fares: The New York City experience.* New York: New York City Office on Aging, 1970.

Jones, P., Rott, E., & Murphy, M. *A report on services to the elderly (Pt. 1). Transportation: A low-cost fair-fare transportation program for the elderly and disadvantaged.* Washington, D.C.: Aging Program, National Association of Counties Research Foundation, 1976.

Kast, S. Arlington elderly about to lose those free rides. *Washington Star-News,* January 2, 1975, B-2.

McKelvey, D., & Ducker, K. *Transportation planning: The urban and rural interface and transit needs of the elderly.* Iowa City: University of Iowa Institute of Urban and Regional Research, 1974.

Pierce, N. Elderly freedom is riding on OATS. *Washington Post,* January 5, 1979, A-16.

Rinaldi, A. *Aid to senior citizens' mobility in East Orange, New Jersey: An escort service.* Millburn, N.J.: National Council of Jewish Women, 1973.

U.S. Administration on Aging. *Coordinating transportation for the elderly and handicapped.* Washington, D.C.: U.S. Government Printing Office, 1971.

U.S. Administration on Aging. *Transportation for the elderly: The state of the art.* Washington, D.C.: U.S. Government Printing Office, 1975.

U.S. Administration on Aging. Transportation projects face insurance coverage problems. *Aging,* September-October 1977, pp.11-12.

U.S. Department of Transportation. *Transportation for the elderly: The state of the art.* Washington, D.C.: U.S. Government Printing Office, 1975.

U.S. Department of Transportation. *Rural passenger transportation: Technology sharing.* Cambridge, Mass.: Transportation Systems Center, 1976.

U.S. Department of Transportation. *Transportation and the elderly: A literature capsule.* Cambridge, Mass.: Transportation Systems Center, 1977.

U.S. House of Representatives, Select Committee on Aging. *Transportation: Improving mobility for older Americans.* Washington, D.C.: U.S. Government Printing Office, 1976.

8
Crime and Legal Assistance Programs

Crime prevention and victim assistance programs serving the elderly increased dramatically in the 1970s. In order to place these services in an appropriate perspective, we will briefly examine factors specific to crimes against the elderly and then review the programs that are now being emphasized throughout the country.

While programs related to crime attempt to protect the older adult from victimization by others, many of the legal services being stressed in aging attempt to protect the elderly from themselves. Legal services have increased since they became the focus of attention at the 1971 White House Conference on Aging and in the 1975 amendments to the OAA. Their appropriateness and the manner in which they are administered remains a point of contention.

Legal programs are diverse in nature. As we shall see, even the laws on guardianship and protective services differ from state to state. While it is impossible to cover all of these rapidly growing and changing programs, this chapter will provide an overview of the types of programs now in existence. It will also outline the legal issues involved in programs designed to protect the elderly from doing harm to themselves, either physically or financially.

The Elderly and Crime

Concerns and Figures

Concern about crimes against the elderly has intensified in recent years. Reports of elderly people being mugged and murdered have made front-page headlines. In 1977, the report of a Brooklyn, New

York, couple who committed suicide after leaving a note stating that death was better than living in continual fear received major coverage throughout the United States. A recent volume on crime and the elderly utilizes a cover made up of headlines and articles describing crimes against the elderly that have occurred throughout the country. In New York State, attempts were made in 1976 to enact legislation that would have mandated treating juveniles as adults if they committed crimes against the elderly. While public outrage against the victimization of the elderly mounts, it remains unclear whether the reality of the crime rate matches this concern.

Data collected on crimes committed against elderly victims are imprecise, as are criminal statistics in general. The FBI compiles its widely relied upon statistics from figures based on reported incidents of crime provided by local police departments which have varied reporting requirements. There is also widespread belief that because older individuals may fear dealing with the police or retaliation by attackers who live in the neighborhood, they often do not report crimes of which they have been the victims. If a crime is reported to the police, the age of the victim is not always recorded.

Patterns of Crime

Besides the FBI crime reports, additional data is now available from major surveys undertaken by the Law Enforcement Assistance Administration (LEAA). Utilizing this data, Antunes et al. (1977) have attempted to provide some definitive answers to the confusion about the rate of crime against the elderly. Their investigation covered a number of issues: the likelihood (1) of an elderly person being a victim of violent crime, (2) that an older person will be in or near home when the crime is committed, (3) that elderly individuals will be attacked by youth gangs, (4) that the attackers will be strangers, and (5) that the attackers will utilize weapons. The researchers found that attacks on the elderly were in proportion to those committed on people in other age groups. The elderly were more likely to be attacked in or near their homes. Elderly individuals with limited access to transportation may develop life-styles that do not involve traveling great distances; the likelihood of any attacks occurring in or near home is therefore increased. Although attackers were often youths who were unarmed, no indication was found that older persons were more likely to be attacked by gangs.

Cook et al. (1978) argue that it is a popularly held mistaken belief that the elderly are more likely than other people to be victims of crime:

During the early 1970s, it was widely believed that the elderly were more likely to suffer from crime than any other age groups. . . . But since then, studies using data with large national samples . . . have shown that the elderly are the least likely age group to be victimized in many serious crime categories (including burglary, theft, rape, robbery, and assault) and are no more likely than other age groups to be victimized in the crime category of personal thefts (i.e., picked pockets and snatched purses). (p. 338)

While the LEAA studies show that the elderly are not disproportionately victimized, the figures also indicate that the crime rate among the elderly is not negligible. This is especially true of larceny, for which the victimization rate is 317 per 100,000 in the general population and 362 per 100,000 among the population 65 and older. In general, the House Select Committee on Aging has concluded that an elderly person stands a little better than one chance in ten of being the victim of a crime in a 1-year period. The chances of being attacked may be increasing. LEAA reports show that violent crimes against the elderly increased by 46% between 1973 and 1974.

Vulnerability

Do special legal programs need to be developed to protect the elderly against potential victimization? This question can only be answered by examining the effects of crime on people in different age groups. As an official of LEAA testified to the U.S. House of Representatives Select Committee on Aging (1976a):

While there may be some uncertainty about crime victimization among senior citizens, there is, I believe, little question about their vulnerability—physical, psychological and financial. Take, for example, the instance of the theft of a television set. The effect on a younger person does not carry the same impact as it does upon a person who is 65 years and older and of limited means. Take the instance of physical violence. It has a particularly debilitating effect on the older person. The theft of a social security check has a tremendous impact upon a person of lower income. (p. 5)

This testimony points to a number of factors that make the elderly especially vulnerable to crime. A low income makes it difficult for many older persons to recoup from robbery, and it also makes them susceptible to confidence games that hold out the promise of quick wealth. Older individuals faced with the threat of violence may not have the physical strength to fight off a potential attacker and thus may be viewed as easy victims. The elderly also tend to reside in changing areas of the city where unemployment and general social problems abound. Many of these elderly residents receive their checks for social security, SSI, or pensions on fixed dates of each month. These dates are often common knowledge in the neighborhood and become red-letter days for attackers. The development of a system of direct deposit of checks is helping to reduce this problem. The elderly are also easy prey for attackers because they often live alone and go out shopping by themselves rather than in groups.

Effects of Victimization

The LEAA official's comments on the financial and psychological effects of crime on the elderly can be supplemented by the Cook et al. (1978) investigation of the physical effects of victimization. An examination of the 1973 and 1974 LEAA data indicates that individuals 40–49 are the group most likely to be injured in criminal attacks; the second most likely are the elderly. While the elderly suffered fewer broken bones or teeth when attacked, they were more liable to internal injuries and became unconscious more often than other age groups. Few of the elderly who reported these injuries required medical treatment, and the authors hypothesize that this may be due to a lesser amount of force being used against the elderly by their assailants. An amount of force equivalent to that used against younger adults might be extremely harmful to the older person, whose susceptibility to complications from broken hips and falls is greater.

Confidence Schemes

While the debate about the degree of violent crime against the elderly continues, there is less controversy about the special susceptibility of the elderly to confidence games. In addition to the physical weakness and living habits that increase the vulnerability of the elderly to violent crime, the American aged have a number of other characteristics that make them "marks" for consumer fraud. Especially important are their fear of growing older and the loss in functioning they assume aging will include. Devices that promise to prevent or repair losses in hearing or vision may be especially attractive to older adults, and those who suffer from chronic illnesses frequently jump at the opportunity to purchase medications that promise to relieve their pain. All of these factors are most at play among less educated elderly. Older individuals with more education show less interest in overpriced merchandise and less susceptibility to fraudulent schemes.

The most common of confidence games is the "pigeon drop." In this scheme, an elderly person is approached by someone on the street who informs him or her that a bag of money has been found. The money will be shared if the older person shows good faith by going to the bank and withdrawing some funds, which will be held by an attorney until the bag of money is legally released to them. The con artist, once given the money, disappears. Other con games are variations on this theme, which promise the elderly person some easy reward for providing some of her or his funds as a sign of good faith or as security.

A second form of fraud is engaged in by unscrupulous retailers and salesmen who encourage the elderly to buy items that are unnecessary, inadequate, or overpriced. The most common consumer frauds perpetrated against the aged involve hearing aids, eyeglasses, funeral arrangements, dentures, and health insurance. In many cases, the elderly are encouraged to buy prosthetics, such as hearing aids that will not make up for their auditory losses, or they are encouraged to buy overpriced aids. In 1978 there were reports of individuals selling the elderly overpriced health insurance.

Crime Prevention and Assistance

Robberies, attacks, consumer frauds, and confidence swindles can beset the elderly individual. Because victimization can take so many forms, the programs that have been devised to protect the victims are also extensive. They are run under a variety of auspices, including general or special units of the police department. In many cases, these programs are supported by funds from the LEAA. Some programs are operated by the local Area Agency on Aging or a social service agency.

Educational Programs

A report by the Select Committee on Aging of the U.S. House of Representatives (1977b) emphasizes the need for crime-related educational programs for the elderly. These educational programs focus on informing older residents about how to avoid street crimes and recognize confidence swindles. A second type of program related to crime prevention encourages increased cohesion in the community and the implementation of support services, such as an escort service. Finally, most areas now have some form of "victim assistance" program that provides both financial compensation and counseling to victims of crime.

At the national level, the AARP has worked to develop a training program that is available to senior citizen organizations. In four 2-hour sessions, this program informs the elderly about methods of avoiding street crime and burglary, about the most common types of confidence schemes, and how to work with the police to reduce crime. In Evansville, Indiana, the police department holds a 2-day symposium every year for the elderly which is geared to common crime problems (International Association of Chiefs of Police, n.d.). In Cottage Grove, Oregon, the police department has developed a program that trains senior citizens to be crime prevention specialists. Having completed training, they contact other elderly residents in the community, informing them about building security and how to mark their valuables for identification. In Jamaica, New York, the Jamaica Service Program for Older Adults has formed a safety committee. This committee has established a liaison with the local police precinct and sponsors a variety of programs directed at senior citizens, including a safety fair, monthly programs on safety, and a project designed to encourage older persons to report crime. In Baltimore, Maryland, the mayor's office has utilized LEAA funds to develop videotapes dealing with assault, robbery, and burglaries. These tapes concentrate on techniques that can be used when the individual is confronted with these crimes. In Kansas City, Missouri, the Mid-America Regional Council began a national demonstration program, including educational components designed to "decrease unrealistic perceptions and fears of crime of the elderly in specific areas" (U.S. House of Representatives, Select Committee on Aging, 1977b, p. 51).

In Los Angeles, the Interagency Task Force on Crime against the Elderly has been formed from the law enforcement agencies, the area agencies on aging, social service agencies, libraries, and educational institutions in the area to design educational programs dealing with victimization of the elderly. The task force's efforts have included the use of television and radio announcements. California has also attempted, through its Consumer Information and Protection Program for Seniors, to provide education for the elderly on prevalent types of consumer frauds.

Security Programs

In many areas with a high concentration of elderly, educational efforts have been combined with increased security measures. LEAA has funded a project in Syracuse, New York, to establish security units in eight low-income elderly housing projects. In Plainfield, New Jersey, a $6,000 program has been developed to control access into senior housing units through the use of closed-circuit TV systems. In South Bend, Indiana, LEAA provided $3,000 for the installation of door locks for elderly residents who could not afford them. This project was operated by the South Bend police. Aside from these efforts, LEAA allotted $300,000 during FY 1976/1977 to provide training for police in the special problems and needs of the elderly.

The federally funded Blow the Whistle on Crime program has made efforts to provide whistles to individuals in over 300 cities. In the Crown Heights section of Brooklyn and in high-crime areas of Milwaukee, Wisconsin, and Wilmington, Delaware, "security aides" provide escort services for the elderly. The Wilmington program utilizes both older individuals and teenagers as escorts.

Victim Assistance

A final group of programs is aimed at providing assistance to individuals who have been the victims of crime. The previously mentioned Jamaica, New York, effort provides sessions for elderly crime victims and attempts to help them cope with their "reactions." In March 1976, the New York City Department of the Aging began a program to assist elderly people in obtaining the social and financial services they would need to overcome the strains of crime. In both New York and Kansas City, crime victims are contacted by social workers and informed of the services available to them. By taking the initiative, these programs attempt to prevent the elderly from feeling isolated and ineffective in dealing with the problems created by a crime.

LEAA has also funded "victim centers" in 20 cities. These centers serve all age groups and are often located within police departments. As LEAA officials describe them,

> specially trained officers concentrate on the allied offenses and try to relate to the victims and provide the type of direct assistance the victim often needs. In certain instances, the victim centers attempt to restore to the victim any property or resources which have been lost. In other cases the centers are geared to meet the needs of special classes of victims such as rape victims or elderly persons who have been victimized. (U.S. House of Representatives, Select Committee on Aging, 1977a, p. 11)

Many of the elderly who become crime victims are reluctant to serve as witnesses. LEAA has also funded "witness centers" in conjunction with the local courts. The witness is informed about court procedures as well as provided with necessary services, such as transportation. The centers will provide protection for witnesses if necessary.

Unfortunately, many elderly people find that they are not reimbursed by insurance for what they lose as a result of victimization. A study by Marquette University (U.S. House of Representatives, Select Committee on Aging, 1977a) found that the average nonreimbursed costs for medical injury to the elderly were $200. The noninsured property damage and loss was $432. Loss of income averaged $373. Many states have now instituted victim compensation laws which provide reimbursement for the costs sustained by all individuals.

The state-by-state variation in these victim compensation laws is great. The maximum amount of compensation for medical expenses or loss of earnings and the maximum time within which a victim may file a claim vary. A sample case in Wilmington, Delaware, illustrates the principle of victim compensation. The victim, a 72-year-old woman, was assaulted. She paid $102 for medical expenses. Since she cooperated with the police, was a victim of a violent crime, and a resident of Delaware, the compensation board also reimbursed her for other out-of-pocket expenses related to the crime for a total of $350 (U.S. House of Representatives, Select Committee on Aging, 1976b). In Baltimore, the Commission on Aging has established a victim's assistance unit composed of a director, attorney, and counselor. The unit works with elderly individuals who have been victimized. The majority of these elderly victims are referred to the unit by the police.

As people have become aware of the existence of the compensation programs, the time lag between claim filings and awards has often increased. In 1977, New York state officials testified that the volume of cases needing action had resulted in a 10-month interval between submission of claims and reimbursement (U.S. House of Representatives, Select Committee on Aging, 1977a).

Despite all of this activity, the effectiveness of these programs is not yet clear. The loss of a feeling of community and the general fear that pervades many American cities is still strong. In the 1970s, an old fashioned eye-for-an-eye philosophy began to replace the 1960's emphasis on rehabilitation of the criminal offender. Whether a punitive approach toward offenders will reduce crime rates or the fear of crime remains to be seen.

Legal Representation

As services have increased, the elderly have become more involved with a variety of public and private bureaucracies which determine their eligibility for these programs. Disputes about eligibility may necessitate legal representation. For older people, legal issues which most often arise are questions about social security and SSI benefits, landlord-tenant disputes, Medicare claims, food stamp certification, and wills and probates.

There is little doubt that the elderly have not received adequate legal assistance, partially because lawyers are not likely to earn high fees working with the elderly. Many older persons also remain unaware of their legal rights or are afraid of dealing with lawyers, just as they do not report crimes out of fear of dealing with the police. Elderly individuals who do possess higher educational backgrounds and are more confident about legal transactions may lack the transportation necessary to reach a lawyer's office.

Legal Services Corporation Programs

Legal representation for the elderly has begun to improve in recent years, mainly through the efforts of the Legal Services Corporation (LSC) authorized under federal legislation in 1975. This corporation is an independent successor to the poverty law program that existed within the now-defunct Office of Economic Opportunity. The LSC has lawyers in offices throughout the country and services all individuals who fall below the federal poverty level, including the elderly. Specialized programs for the elderly have been supported by funds from Title III of the OAA, revenue sharing funds, and Title XX of the Social Security Act. Title III funds for legal services increased in 1975 as a result of the 1975 amendments to the OAA, which specified four priority areas for state and community programs: transportation, home services, legal and other counseling services, and home repair and renovation programs. In Memphis, Tennessee, $220,000 from revenue sharing funds was allocated by the city for a legal program for the elderly, and $150,000 was set aside in Sacramento, California, for a similar program. In San Diego, California, the Bank of America has supported a program to increase legal representation for the elderly. The LSC and the AoA have provided support to the National Senior Citizens Law Center (NSCLC).

Of the elderly, 15–20% are eligible for legal services through the LSC. As Stephens (1977) notes, a large percentage of the legal problems presented by the elderly fall under the heading of public benefit claims. In some cases obtaining benefits may be merely a matter of obtaining important information. A major case cited by the LSC was the refusal of the Social Security Administration to release the official SSI manual, which contained vital information on emergency benefits. The threat of a lawsuit from LSC resulted in 1,000 of these manuals being distributed around the country (Nathanson, 1977).

The threat of legal action is also helpful in situations where private pension plans contain major loopholes and possibilities of abuse by employers. In one case, a truck driver for a major supermarket chain retired after 34 years of work, expecting a pension of $300 a month. When his first check arrived, he found that it was for only $250. The employer informed him that his pension had been reduced because he retired a month too early, even though this date was advised by an official of the firm. A student at the Protection for Elderly People program of the George Washington University Law School wrote to the supermarket chain informing them of the problem. After 2 months, the retired driver received a check for $1,200, an apology from the company for the mistaken advice, and credit for the additional month (National Law Center, 1976).

While the efforts of the LSC and the NSCLC are admirable, these two organizations alone are unable to provide sufficient legal representation to serve the multiple needs of the elderly. Some law schools have set up special clinics to serve the elderly, but it is unlikely that in the upcoming years we will see any rush on the part of lawyers toward major private practice with older populations. A number of other approaches to utilizing lawyers are now being tried. In Tennessee a legal aid program sends lawyers on a regular circuit of 3–15 counties in the state. On these trips, the lawyers visit senior centers and run seminars for the elderly on important legal issues. In addition, the NSCLC provides "support and information" for lawyers representing elderly clients. The NSCLC will provide information on previous cases or draft pleadings for legal aid lawyers who request this assistance. NSCLC also provides technical assistance to states on a variety of issues including housing for the elderly and formulations of pension plans.

Pro bono representation is now a policy of the American Bar Association, but attempts to specify the amount of time lawyers should donate to clients have been resisted. While efforts are being made to increase lawyers' gratis representation of the elderly, it is likely that much of the increased legal counseling will be undertaken by paralegal counselors.

Paralegal Assistance

As of 1977, over 100 paralegal programs existed in the United States, with many focusing attention on the legal problems of the elderly. The common definition of a paralegal as "any person who deals with the products of the legal system, that is statutes, regulations, administrative agencies and court" (Buford, 1977, p. 109) has been objected to by Buford. This definition, he contends, is vague and omits the crucial fact that the "paralegal is an employee of an attorney who has been trained to work on tasks formerly done by attorneys" (Buford, 1977, p. 109). Although paralegals are not licensed by bar associations, they are allowed by federal regulations to handle cases of individuals seeking such public benefits as social security, SSI, welfare, public housing, and food stamps. In cases where a lawyer is required, paralegals may prepare the briefs for lawyers.

At George Washington University, the Paralegal Training Institute has developed a program training elderly individuals as paralegals. By training the elderly as paralegals, the institute hopes to alleviate the communication problems that often exist between the older clients and attorneys, as well as to provide important new roles for a group of older adults. The paralegal training takes 1 academic year and covers both classroom and clinical experiences. The syllabi cover social security, SSI, medical benefits, food stamps, administrative law, private pension plans, insurance, probate problems, and age discrimination in housing and taxes (National Law Center, 1976).

A second group of individuals who can provide assistance to the elderly are what the Paralegal Institute has termed community services advocates (CSA). CSAs may be individuals with backgrounds in many other fields. The common denominator is that they come into frequent contact with the elderly. Caseworkers or home health workers may thus play an important role as CSAs, and the National Paralegal Institute has made efforts to train social service workers as CSAs. Not employed by an attorney, CSAs are limited in the legal representation they can provide the elderly in actual hearings. However, they can be strong advocates for the elderly and provide important information and referral resources for the elderly who are having legal problems, particularly in relation to public benefits.

The funding of legal services for the elderly should continue to increase. In the 1978 OAA Amendments, legal services were classified as one of the three priorities. The act provides for legal services and representation by an attorney (including, to the extent feasible, counseling or other appropriate assistance by a paralegal or law student under the supervision of an attorney) and includes counseling or representation by a lawyer where permitted by law, to older individuals with economic or social need. [Section 302a (4)]

As part of its aging plan, each state must show that the Area Agencies on Aging are contracting for legal services while making efforts to involve private bar organizations in legal services at reduced rates or for free.

Despite the seeming specificity of the legal services provisions of the OAA's 1978 amendments (Appendix A), the failure of the Congress to specify dollar amounts that area agencies must spend on legal services may create problems. As can be seen in Section 306b (2), the act also permits an Area Agency on Aging to waive the requirement for legal access and in-home services if it can be demonstrated that these services are already being adequately provided.

Legal services that are to be provided with Title III funds are aimed at the elderly "in the greatest economic or social need." Many of the elderly who fall into this category may be ineligible for assistance from the LSC; yet

> in carrying out its responsibility to concentrate on the elderly with the greatest need, no project shall, in any way, give a means test or asset test to any applicant; no applicant shall be questioned about his or her means or assets; and no applicant should be directed to seek services through a Legal Services Corporation project. (U.S. House of Representatives, 1978, p. 65)

The net result of this policy is that individuals who come into legal service offices not operated by the LSC may *not* be queried about their income and then referred to an LSC branch. Given the large group of elderly individuals now having economic or social need of legal assistance and the restriction on referrals, it is doubtful that many of the Area Agencies on Aging will be able to utilize any waiver clauses of the OAA.

Protective Services

While in many cases legal representation of an elderly person can increase the person's self-sufficiency, protective service measures remove many of the rights an individual has to make his or her own decisions:

> Elderly persons who are thought to be unable to manage their personal or financial affairs in their own best interests are subject to the imposition of protective services designed to protect them from themselves and from unscrupulous third parties. (Horstman, 1977, p. 227)

Elements of Protective Services

Protective services have two major components: (1) intensive services provided with the individuals' consent to those who appear to need major supportive assistance, and (2) services provided for individuals without their consent after a hearing, which involve "legally enforced supervision or guardianship which, temporarily depriving the client of certain rights, enables an agency to assist the person" (Regan & Springer, 1977, p. 4). These services and guardianship may be imposed on individuals of any age, but the concept of protective services has been most widely applied to individuals over 60.

Recipients

We can define the type of person for whom protective services might be appropriate by examining an individual case.

> Mr. E., seventy-three, a tall powerfully built man with no surviving family, formerly a skilled iron worker, had become settled, but not rooted in one area of town after an early adulthood of country-wide transiency. He had never married but was proud of earlier feminine conquests. Inarticulate, having had a large investment in his body image, he now lacked the kind of strengths which formerly had helped him achieve his goals. With a foreign childhood rearing and little formal education, Mr. E. was now frustrated by the ravages of illness and old age. He reacted behaviorally with extreme intolerance of others, suspicion, and severe verbal abusiveness. At the point of referral, Mr. E. was in grave danger of dying and was thwarting efforts of interested agencies to induce him to accept proper medical attention through hospitalization. Despite his cleanliness of person, his disabilities had affected the maintenance of his small apartment which was cluttered and dirty. A friendship of twenty years with a male friend indicated some underlying capacity for human attachment. The grave medical problems were compounded by the limitations of an income of $105 monthly from social security. (Wasser, 1974, p. 103–114)

Mr. E. can obviously benefit from many forms of assistance, including a variety of personal services. He may also be one of the 25% of the elderly often estimated to have major mental health problems.

During the famous social experiment in protective services at the Benjamin Rose Institute in Cleveland, individuals such as Mr. E. were provided with intensive casework assistance from experienced social workers with master's degrees in social work. These social workers functioned under one overriding directive: do, or get others to do, whatever is necessary to meet the needs of the situation (Blenkner et al., 1974, p. 68). In order to be effective, the social workers had to utilize a variety of concomitant services needed by clients of the protective services program. These included financial assistance, medical evaluations, home aides, and psychiatric consultation. In 20% of the cases, legal consultation was utilized; and in 12%, guardianship proceedings were instituted and completed. The Benjamin Rose program provides a model for the types of assistance that protective services might supply, its basic assumption being that clients of the program require more intensive assistance than is normally provided by most agencies.

Guidelines for Guardianship

Contemporary legal guidelines for guardianship and commitment are inadequate. The complex questions raised by protective services have been outlined by Blenkner et al. (1974):

1. If the services provided to an individual such as Mr. E. are inadequate and are resisted by Mr. E., who should have the right to define Mr. E. as a problem and deprive him of his ability to make decisions?

2. If older persons resist services, do their provision against their will provide them with assistance or merely satisfy the "psychological discomfort" of the social worker?

3. Is providing protective services the answer to the problems of Mr. E., or is the real issue for the elderly the conditions they have imposed on them, and under which they are forced to live?

4. If the proposed solution to Mr. E.'s problems is placement in a long-term care setting, will this solve the problems for the family and neighbors upset by his behavior but be destructive to his own personal functioning?

5. Can any services, whether voluntary or imposed, help many of the individuals who come under the wing of protective services improve to a "normal" functioning level?

Even if answers to these questions affirm the need for protective services, there remains the necessity of careful criteria for legal intervention models.

Consequences of Guardianship

An individual placed under "guardianship" suffers a variety of losses. These include the right to sue, charge purchases, engage in contracts, deed property, marry, divorce, open a bank account, or vote. In some states, the individual's eligibility for program benefits including Medicare and pensions will come under scrutiny when a guardian is appointed.

> An incompetent is defined traditionally as one who, by reason of mental illness, drunkeness, drug addiction, or old age is incapable of self care, of managing business or of exercising family responsibilities or as one who is liable to dissipate an estate or become the victim of designing persons. (Regan & Springer, 1977, p. 36)

In most states the individual must be declared incompetent for a guardian to be appointed. Vague bases for declarations of incompetency such as "old age" have contributed to the abuses now associated with the protective services approach.

In many states, the major basis for a commitment or guardianship decision is evidence presented by physicians. The ability to define an individual as mentally impaired and suffering from organic brain syndrome is usually based on limited evidence because of the problems in accurately diagnosing this condition. The same is true of overused diagnostic labels such as "undifferentiated schizophrenia." Even if more precision were available in diagnosis, these labels do not deal with the level of functioning of the individual, who may be able to cope with most of the major social requirements for individuals living in the community.

While the procedures differ, any individual may file to have an elderly person declared incompetent. A notice is then sent to the subject of the hearing, informing him or her of its date and time. Although he or she is not usually informed of the fact, the subject does have the right to be represented by counsel. The subject is required to be physically present, although as California law states, the person can be excused if

> he is not able to attend by reason of physical inability or by reason that the presence of such person in court would retard or impair the recov-

ery of such person or would increase his mental debility. (California Probate Code, Section 1461, cited in Horstman, 1977, p. 253)

A doctor's letter satisfies this requirement and can often easily be obtained by the parties instituting the proceedings.

Once incompetence is declared, a guardian deemed appropriate by the court is appointed. A conservator, if appointed, takes control of the property and handles the financial needs of the ward. The conservator is accountable to the court and must obtain court permission for transfers of property.

The powers of the guardian and conservator are clearly extensive and give them almost complete control over the ward's life, including where she or he lives. Unfortunately, the elderly person may not have a family member or relative able to take on the complex tasks of guardianship. Although many states previously limited guardians or conservators to family members, attitudes on this matter are changing. As Regan and Springer (1977) observe, the ward may not be able to depend on an individual who,

> when needed, might be absent, ill, or distracted by other affairs. In contrast a social agency appointed as guardian could do more to treat the ward, create opportunities for recreation and friendship and evaluate the client's physical and psychological needs and changes. (p. 41)

Under some state laws, particular agencies have been authorized as public guardians. In Maryland, for individuals over 60, this task falls to the state Office on Aging. In Georgia, the Commissioner of Human Resources is the public guardian for welfare recipients. A public guardian may also be a court official or a specific local official. The court may appoint a public guardian even if the petition for guardianship was filed by a private individual. The public guardian may be paid from public funds but may file a claim on the estate when the ward dies to pay for the services rendered.

The guardianship-conservator model is long term in nature. There is, however, a rationale for an emergency intervention model for individuals whose needs are immediate or expected to be temporary. In most states individuals believed to be dangerous to themselves and others may be confined for a period which averages 72 hours. After that time, a formal hearing must be held to determine whether an individual should be committed for a longer period. In Maryland, three criteria must be evident before individuals can be committed to a state mental facility: the individuals must (1) be dangerous to themselves or the community, (2) require inpatient treatment, and (3) be mentally ill.

Alternatives to long-term commitment have not existed until recently and have not always been explored by protective service workers. Alternative settings were a major point in the landmark *Lake* v. *Cameron* (1966) decision, in which the D.C. Court of Appeals ruled that Mrs. Lake could not be held in St. Elizabeth's Hospital unless all other possible less restrictive alternatives were explored. Unfortunately for Mrs. Lake no alternatives available at that time (1966) were deemed appropriate, and she was remanded to St. Elizabeth's.

Changes in Protective Services

The potential for abuses in protective services is obvious, and a number of major changes are being promoted throughout the country to prevent undue restriction of the elderly's civil rights. These include: (1) changes in the law to redefine competency according to the level at which an individual is capable of functioning, rather than by a vague medical diagnosis; (2) requirements that the individual be informed of the importance of guardianship hearings, the right to counsel, and the right to cross-examine witnesses; (It is interesting to note that one study in Los Angeles found that in only 2% of the guardianship hearings was counsel present for the subject. In Ohio, a negative correlation of .94 was found between representation by counsel and decisions to commit an individual to a long-term care institution.) (3) legislation to authorize a full range of protective social services throughout the country; and (4) establishment of a system of public guardianship for people without private guardian resources.

Horstman (1977) has argued for a "bill of rights" for all aged people which would define their constitutional rights in relation to confinement. Under his plan, confinement would be utilized only when the following five conditions were present:

1. The individual had been declared mentally incompetent to determine the viability of seeking or refusing treatment, and
2. Less restrictive alternatives to total institutionalization have been fully explored and found to be inadequate to protect and maintain the individual, and
3. The individual is unable to live safely in freedom either by himself or with the assistance of willing and responsible family members or friends, and
4. The individual is untreatable, and
5. Institutionalization is in the individual's best interest. (p. 288)

One of the most important methods for ascertaining the existence of these five conditions has been the development of geriatric evaluation services (GES) in some states. These services provide a mandatory evaluation by an interdisciplinary team (usually nurse, psychiatrist, and social worker) to determine whether long-term care is needed. The GES evaluates clients being considered for commitment to a mental hospital, appointment of a conservator, emergency protective services, or protective placements. With these changes, the stress in protective services shifts to delineating the ability of the individual to function in the community with or without supportive assistance.

It could be argued that a nationwide development of protective services might cut down the need for guardianship or commitment hearings. The Benjamin Rose Institute study stressed caution in aggressively expanding protective services. The research did not show significant differences on a number of measures between individuals in the experimental and control groups. As summed up by Blenkner et al. (1971):

> For the participant, himself, however, there was no significant impact with respect to increased competence or slowed deterioration and greater contentment or lessened disturbance. Furthermore, although he was more "protected," the participant was no less likely to die when given protective services than when left to the usual and limited services of the community. In fact, the findings on functional competence together with those on death and institutionalization force consideration of the hypothesis that intensive service with a heavy reliance on institutional care may actually accelerate decline. (p. 494)

This negative evaluation placed a brake on the development of protective services and raised important questions in many social workers' minds about the degree to which the development of extensive services promoted dependency of the aged on the worker. A reanalysis by a new group of researchers at the Benjamin Rose Institute (Bigot et al., 1978) indicates, however, that the original staff may have underestimated the positive effects of the intensive social work services.

The positive and negative effects of protective social casework services offered by agencies remains unclear. The effects of legal procedures for the elderly that remove their rights are much clearer in their negative implications. Legislative enactments as outlined by Regan and Springer (1977) will afford due process for the elderly and restrict the power to unduly remove the civil liberties of the elderly.

These legislative revisions should be a prime concern for advocates of aging programs and practitioners in aging.

References

Antunes, G., Cook, F., Cook, T., & Skogan, W. Patterns of personal crime against the elderly: Findings from a national survey. *Gerontologist*, 1977, *17*(4), 321–327.

Bigot, A., Demling, G., Shuman, S., & Schur, D. *Protective services for older people: A reanalysis of a controversial demonstration project.* Paper presented at the annual meeting of the Gerontological Society, Dallas, Texas, 1978.

Blenkner, M., Bloom, M., Nielsen, M., & Weber, R. *Final report: Protective services for older people.* Cleveland: Benjamin Ross Institute, 1974.

Blenkner, M., Bloom, M., Wasser, E., & Nielsen, M. Protective services for older people: Findings from the B.R.I. study. *Social Casework*, 1971, *82*(8), 483–522.

Buford, A. D., III. Non-lawyer delivery of legal services. In M. Rafa (Ed.), *Justice and older Americans.* Lexington, Mass.: Lexington Books, 1977.

Cook, F., Skogan, W., Cook, T., & Antunes, G. Criminal victimization of the elderly: The economic and physical consequences. *Gerontologist*, 1978, *18*(4), 338–349.

Horstman, P. Protective services for the elderly: The limits of parens patriae. In J. Weiss (Ed.), *Law of the elderly.* New York: Practicing Law Institute, 1977.

International Association of Chiefs of Police, Technical Research Services Division. *Crime prevention programs for senior citizens.* Gaithersburg, Md., n.d.

Lake v. Cameron, 364 F.2d 657 (N.C. Cir. 1966).

Nathanson, P. Legal services. In M. Rafa (Ed.), *Justice and older Americans.* Lexington, Mass.: Lexington Books, 1977.

National Law Center, George Washington University. Paralegal training for seniors. *Institute of Law and Aging Newsletter*, 1976, *1*(1), 2–3.

Regan, J., & Springer, G. *Protective service for the elderly: A working paper prepared for the U.S. Senate Select Committee on Aging.* Washington, D.C.: U.S. Government Printing Office, 1977.

Stephens, W. Legal aid programs in Tennessee. *Aging*, November–December 1977, pp. 16–17.

U.S. House of Representatives. *Report No. 95–1618 Comprehensive Older Americans Act of 1978.* Washington, D.C.: U.S. Government Printing Office, 1978.

U.S. House of Representatives, Select Committee on Aging. *Elderly crime victimization* (Federal Law Enforcement Agencies—LEAA and FBI). Washington, D.C.: U.S. Government Printing Office, 1976. (a)

U.S. House of Representatives, Select Committee on Aging. *Elderly crime victimization* (Wilmington, Delaware, Crime Resistance Task Force). Washington, D.C.: U.S. Government Printing Office, 1976. (b)

U.S. House of Representatives, Select Committee on Aging. *Elderly victims crime compensation.* Washington, D.C.: U.S. Government Printing Office, 1977. (a)

U.S. House of Representatives, Select Committee on Aging. *In search of security: A national perspective on elderly crime victimization.* Washington, D.C.: U.S. Government Printing Office, 1977. (b)

Wasser, E. Protective service: Casework with older people. *Social Casework,* 1974, *97,* 103–114.

9
Employment and Volunteer Programs

For many elderly, retirement is a long-awaited event that promises to allow them to engage in long-postponed activities. Retirement may also mean relief from the drudgery of a job that has been endured but never enjoyed. For other older workers, retirement is a dreaded moment, a termination of a career with its attendant status, a loss of important collegial relationships, and a future that promises to consist of hours of unfilled time. Activities for the elderly must therefore include both paid jobs and volunteer opportunities. Jack Ossofsky, Executive Director of the National Council on the Aging, has attempted to place the issue of employment and volunteer activities in a framework that transcends purely economic issues:

> Maintaining options for the older American is the heart of the issue. . . .
> The greatest loss among the elderly is not of economic status, income
> or health, serious as these may be. It's the loss of options, the opportu-
> nity to stay employed, volunteer for social work, start a second career.
> (Cattani, 1977, p. 13)

In this chapter we will examine both paid employment programs and volunteer opportunities available to the elderly.

Employment Legislation

Age and Retirement

In 1900, two-thirds of the men over 65 were still in the labor force. In fact, until 1950, over one-half of the men over 65 were still working (National Council on the Aging, 1978). As Figure 9.1 indicates,

Figure 9.1. Percentage of 65 and Older Work Force, Male and Female, 1950–1990

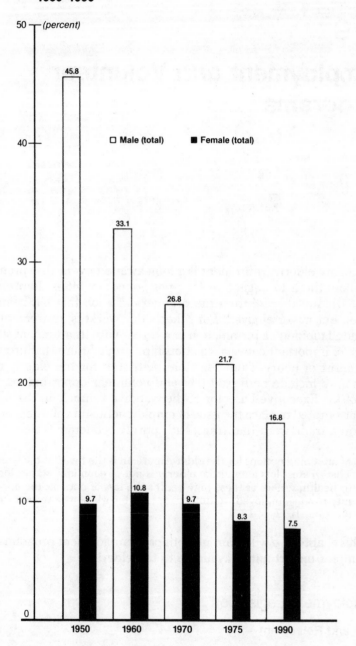

Source: Reprinted from *Fact Book on Aging,* by Charles S. Harris, for The National Council on the Aging, Inc., Washington, D.C., © 1978, by permission.

the drop in the proportion of older individuals working has been most evident in the last 20 years. The average retirement age for all workers is now below 60 (U. S. Senate, 1979). While some workers elect early retirement, others feel forced out of jobs without any considerations being given to their experience and competency. As Ahrens has summed up the situation:

> The economic effects of early retirement can be devastating. . . . It is true that many workers look forward to retirement and appreciate company policies that allow early retirement at minimally reduced pension benefit levels. But, it is not true that all older workers enjoy being "put out to pasture" nor should they. Consider the fact that, on the average, a man reaching his 65th birthday could expect to live 13.4 years longer; a woman 17.5 years.
>
> Over the years, those who retired on seemingly adequate pension and social security benefits will see their purchasing power diminish as the cost of living climbs. (U.S. Senate, 1979, p. 16)

Social security regulations have restricted the work options of the elderly since benefits have been reduced in proportion to earned income. Formerly, when an individual obtained $3,200 in earnings, social security payments have been terminated. The removal of any social security limitations on earned income may encourage more older individuals to seek employment. The problem of employment for the elderly has thus been twofold: (1) finding employers who did not discriminate against them and (2) finding sufficient numbers of part-time jobs which provide additional money without exceeding the limit allowed by social security regulations. In 1971, the National Commission on Employment and Unemployment reported that over 1 million individuals were discouraged from seeking employment because of poor prospects, and 27% of these were over 55.

Age Discrimination Legislation

The major ally of the elderly in their effort to obtain employment has been the Age Discrimination Employment Act of 1967 (ADEA), which outlawed discrimination based on age (unless age was a bona fide requirement of the job), and the Age Discrimination Act described in Chapter 2. Originally the provisions of the ADEA covered employees in private firms, public agencies, and labor organizations who were between 40 and 65. In 1977, 86 suits were filed under this act; but in 1976 and 1977, over 5,000 complaints were registered with the Department of Labor, the agency formerly responsible for enforcing the act's provisions (U.S. Department of Labor, 1977a).

For the elderly, the most important changes in the ADEA took place in 1978. The 1978 amendments increased coverage of the act to individuals up to 70 years of age in private and nonfederal employment. Mandatory retirement for most federal employees was abolished. The exceptions to the new provisions were tenured faculty at universities, who would be included beginning in 1982, and high-level executives eligible for retirement benefits of at least $27,000. Since 20.9 million workers have been employed under compulsory retirement provisions, the effects of these changes will need to be carefully observed. Individuals covered under collective bargaining agreements in effect on September 1, 1977, could still be forced to retire at 65 until January 1, 1980, or the end of the agreement, whichever came first (U.S. Senate, 1979). Regulations accompanying the passage of the 1978 amendments to the ADEA transferred the enforcement of the act from the Department of Labor to the Equal Employment Opportunities Commission. This shift brought the ADEA enforcement under the wing of the agency charged with overseeing all other antidiscrimination activities.

Employment Programs

Attaining part-time and full-time jobs requires well-coordinated placement services that match skills of the worker to possible positions. Efforts in this direction are underway. Much less common are efforts to retrain older workers for new positions which require the attainment of extensive new skills.

Counseling

The first stage of the employment efforts in many areas entails helping older workers gain a better understanding of their skills. This type of counseling has been part of the programs of voluntary agencies in Cleveland and Baltimore dating from the middle 1960s (Health and Welfare Council, 1965; Occupational Planning Commission of the Welfare Federation of Cleveland, 1958). The counseling clinics attempt to provide the worker with supportive help, foster the development of self-assurance, and help with occupational adjustment. Meeting these goals involves attempting to overcome some of the common problems found among older individuals interested in working. These may include poor motivation or poor work histories, a long lag period since their last job, and a lack of appropriate skills for a changing labor market. Added to these deficits may be physical or emotional problems. Once counseling has helped to overcome these problems and enabled workers to achieve a realistic understanding of their own work potential, adequate placement becomes critical.

Using a variety of federal and local funds, placement programs are operating in a number of states and localities. This number could easily be expanded. In 1978, 100 nonprofit placement centers were estimated to be in operation, but the number of centers that could be utilized nationally has been estimated at 268 (Cattani, 1978). Many of these programs are funded through provisions of the OAA, but a number of the most well-developed programs predate AoA's funding for employment programs. In 1959, the Atlanta Branch of the National Council of Jewish Women (Cattani, 1978) started a program that now places 500 older workers per year. In Evanston, Illinois, Senior Action Services operates a storefront and places 120 seniors each year. This placement record represents one out of every three applicants. These workers hold jobs as typists, house sitters, companions, and chauffeurs. Locally funded, Senior Action Services' efforts are coordinated through Operation Able, a coordinating group for all Chicago-area senior programs (Cattani, 1978).

Older Americans Act Employment

On a national scale, the largest provision of funds for the older worker stems from Title V (formerly Title IX) of the OAA. Prior to the emphasis on employment in the OAA, Title X of the Public Works and Economic Development Act of 1965 provided some job opportunities for the elderly. This program, targeted for high unemployment areas, made some funds available for older workers. By 1975, approximately 4,800 seniors had obtained employment under this funding mechanism (Braver & Bowers, 1977).

The original Title IX of the OAA authorization of 1975 was aimed at helping needy older persons obtain a higher income level. It was also hoped that employment would provide these workers with a renewed sense of involvement with the community while they acquired new skills or upgraded existing ones. The 1978 OAA defined low income as 125% of the federal poverty level.

The OAA also saw older persons as resources able to provide communities with needed additional human service workers, especially to fill major gaps in providing services to the elderly. The Senior Community Service Employment Program (SCSEP) of Title V has been contracted by the Department of Labor to a number of major organizations including the National Council on the Aging (NCOA), the National Farmers Union, the National Retired Teachers Association/American Association of Retired Persons, the U.S. Forest Service, the National Council of Senior Citizens, three minority organizations, and individual states. In 1975, 22,400 slots were authorized under the program (U.S. Department of Labor, 1977a), but this figure had risen to 52,500 by 1980; and the total budget, to approximately $267 million. A formula has allocated 45% of the available SCSEP funds to the national contractors and 55% to the states. Individual states receive funds in accordance with the percentage of state residents over 55 and the per capita income of the state. A major concern of the program is to avoid political problems that would result if SCSEP workers filled job classifications normally held by full-time employees and were seen as competitive with these workers (National Council of Senior Citizens, 1978).

The program administered by the NCOA had enrolled over 3,000 individuals over 55 by 1977. Of these workers, 58% were providing services to the elderly; the remaining 42% were employed in jobs serving persons of all age groups. The breakdown of the types of jobs undertaken is shown in Table 9.1. This breakdown parallels the types of jobs being emphasized in other elderly employment programs. A concrete example of these efforts is the assistance seniors in Los Angeles have provided elderly Filipinos in obtaining citizenship. In Hoboken, New Jersey, elderly workers have been spending 4 hours a day with the children of recent Italian immigrant families, teaching them math and phonetics (Taylor, 1978). The SCSEP administered through the AARP provides similar opportunities for 8,000 individuals in public or private nonprofit organizations and is now in operation in 47 urban and rural areas (American Association of Retired Persons, 1979). The National Council on Senior Citizens Senior Aide program provides limited employment in 53 areas for older persons working in community service organizations for the elderly. This includes activities such as delivering meals to the homebound or providing shopping services (National Council of Senior Citizens, 1978). In all SCSEP efforts, the older adult has been limited to a maximum of 1,300 hours of work per year and payment of either the federal or state minimum wages, whichever is higher.

While these programs are administered through agencies oriented to the elderly, additional efforts are being undertaken by the

Table 9.1. Types of Agencies, Organizations, or Programs Employing SCSP Participants

Elderly Community	Number	Percentage	General Community	Number	Percentage
Outreach/referral	476	26	Social services	365	28.0
Nutrition programs	361	20	Education	356	27.2
Recreation/senior centers	315	17	Health and hospitals	155	11.9
Health and home care	148	8	Housing/home rehabilitation	80	6.1
Transportation	120	7	Transportation	75	5.7
Housing/home rehabilitation	96	5	Recreation, parks, forests	72	5.5
Project administration	96	5	Employment assistance	31	2.4
Employment administration	53	3	Environmental quality	17	1.3
Other	171	9	Other	156	11.9
Total	1,836	100	Total	1,307	100

Source: Adapted from p. 23 of *The Senior Community Service Project—Activities and Accomplishments: The 1973–1977 SCSP Report*, compiled by Walter Taylor, for The National Council on the Aging, Inc., Washington, D.C., © 1978, by permission.

Department of Labor and the Department of Agriculture. The Green Thumb program operated by the National Farmers Union with funds from the Department of Labor employs individuals with rural or farm backgrounds in a variety of part-time conservation or beautification efforts, or in outreach services for the aged. On-the-job training is provided for individuals over 45. The Green Thumb program is operational in over 45 states. In 1979, 65% of its 16,000 employees were over the age of 65 (National Farmers Union, 1979). The Conservation Employment Program of the U.S. Forest Service utilizes low-income individuals over 55 in a variety of projects in National Forest lands.

CETA and CSA

Funds made available to localities through the Comprehensive Employment Training Act of 1973 (CETA) could also be used to hire unemployed elderly. Unfortunately, only a small proportion of CETA funds has been utilized to subsidize employment of older individuals, but the Senior Opportunities and Services Program of the Community Services Administration does give preference to employing low-income elderly. These employees act as service providers for older community residents not receiving adequate assistance through other federal programs.

Meeting Employment Needs

While all of these efforts are valuable, they still fail to adequately meet the needs and desires of many older individuals seeking meaningful employment. Officials at the NCOA estimate that they receive eight applications for each job opening, and the statistics they have compiled indicate that there are still major groups of elderly whose needs are not being met. Over half of the workers in the NCOA program are between 55 and 65, and half have completed high school. Similar results were obtained by the U.S. Department of Labor (1977b) in an analysis which indicated that 52% of the elderly workers were women, 73% were between 55 and 69, and 74% were white. Special efforts need to be made to attract more substantial numbers of older, low-income, minority elderly to these programs. Among those older individuals fortunate to obtain employment, the evaluation of these programs is overwhelmingly positive. Of those in the NCOA program, 97% indicated that they felt the job made them feel more useful in the community. These feelings of usefulness were shared by supervisors and employers, 64% rating their older employees as outstanding or above average (Taylor, 1978).

Volunteer Programs

Many of the volunteer opportunities for the elderly are administered through ACTION—the federal agency that encompasses the Peace Corps and VISTA.

VISTA workers are employed in impoverished rural and urban areas and are paid monthly food and living allowances and minimal salaries. In 1975, over 500 VISTA volunteers were over 55. The Peace Corps performs similar tasks abroad, and in 1975, it had 346 volunteers over 50 and 36 who were between the ages of 71 and 80 (U.S. Administration on Aging, 1975).

ACTION also administers three programs more directly oriented toward the older person: the Retired Senior Volunteers Program (RSVP), the Foster Grandparents Program, the Senior Companions program, and the Service Corps of Retired Executives (SCORE). These programs are administered through ACTION's Division of Older Americans Volunteer Programs. RSVP was authorized under the 1969 amendments to the OAA. When ACTION was formed in 1971 as the federal volunteer agency, the program was transferred to this new organization.

RSVP

RSVP roots can be traced to a pilot program developed by the Community Service Society of New York in 1965. This project attempted to enlist older adults in volunteer work in the community and make use of their neglected talents and experience. The planners of project SERVE (Serve and Enrich Retirement by Volunteer Experience) hoped that the involvement of the elderly in the program would provide them with a renewed sense of self-esteem and satisfaction as well as filling important gaps in community resources.

The present RSVP program continues this tradition. Programs are locally planned and sponsored. Local communities must also provide 10% of the costs of the projects for the first year, 20% the second, and 80% for each subsequent year. Individuals enrolled in RSVP work in "volunteer stations" which include courts, schools, libraries, nursing homes, children's daycare centers, and hospitals. Volunteers in the program include a retired minister who operates a commissary cart at a local nursing home and a retired lawyer who works 1 day per week at an Indian community center providing legal advice. Many volunteers are reimbursed for transportation to and from their assignments and for out-of-pocket expenses. The programs also provide the volunteers with accident and liability insurance. In FY 1978, nearly 700 projects were utilizing 250,000 volunteers (ACTION, 1978).

Foster Grandparents

The Foster Grandparents Program is designed to provide low-income elderly with important social experiences while they assist children who have special physical or psychosocial needs. As ACTION notes, "Foster Grandparents do not displace salaried staff, but complement staff care to special children with the love and personal concern essential to their well being" (ACTION, 1979). Foster Grandparents work 4 hours a day in a variety of settings including correctional facilities, pediatric wards of general hospitals, homes for the mentally retarded or emotionally disturbed, schools, and daycare centers. In 1979, Foster Grandparents received a nontaxable stipend of $2 per hour in compensation for their efforts, reimbursement for transportation and meals, and accident insurance. The recruitment and training of Foster Grandparents is the responsibility of the individual program. The local programs also provide the older individual with counseling and referrals on personal matters. In FY 1978, the Foster Grandparents Program budget of $35 million enabled 16,640 volunteers to be recruited to work with 41,600 children around the country. Because of its emphasis on assisting poverty-level elderly, ACTION has concentrated on working with local agencies to develop Foster Grandparents programs in low-income areas. In 1978, over one-third of enrolled Foster Grandparents were minority elderly.

Senior Companions

The Senior Companion Program, which was authorized in 1973, is modeled after the Foster Grandparents Program except that its stress is on low-income elderly working with other elderly, assisting them in nursing homes, hospitals, or their own homes. Other places are possible as long as the local projects emphasize elderly providing assistance to elderly with "physical, emotional, or mental disabilities" (ACTION, 1979). Longview, Washington, had 53 older adults enrolled in its Senior Companion Program in 1978. Of these volunteers, 34 were providing assistance to homebound elderly and 20 others were working in nursing homes helping residents participate in activities. The remaining volunteers were placed with an adult daycare program (State programs, 1978).

SCORE

The fourth program for older Americans is the Service Corps of Retired Executives (SCORE). Sponsored by the Small Business Administration, SCORE places retired executives in small businesses such as groceries, restaurants, bakeries, pharmacies, and other organizations which can benefit from their managerial experience. In Wharton, Texas, a SCORE volunteer is helping a bottling company revise its accounting system. In Chicago, a SCORE volunteer helped a small supermarket qualify for a Small Business Admininstration loan. As in the other ACTION programs, SCORE volunteers are reimbursed for out-of-pocket expenses (ACTION, n.d.).

References

ACTION. *Retired Senior Volunteers Program (RSVP)*. Washington, D.C., 1978.
ACTION. *Senior Companions Program history*. Washington, D.C., 1979.
ACTION. *Service Corps of Retired Executives*. Washington, D.C., n.d.
American Association of Retired Persons. Personal discussion with staff, 1979.

Braver, R., & Bowers, L. *The impact of employment programs on the older worker and the service delivery system: Benefits derived and provided.* Washington, D.C.: Foundation for Applied Research, 1977.

Cattani, R. The elderly: Fight for job rights. *Christian Science Monitor,* January 9, 1977, pp. 12–13.

Cattani, R. Government job programs provide limited help to elderly. *Christian Science Monitor,* January 11, 1978, p. 15.

Health and Welfare Council. *Older workers project: A demonstration on the job training program for workers over 50.* Baltimore, Md., 1965.

National Council of Senior Citizens. *Senior aides: A unique federal program.* Washington, D.C., 1978.

National Council on the Aging. *Fact book on aging.* Washington, D.C., 1978.

National Farmers Union. Personal discussion with staff, 1979.

Occupational Planning Commission of the Welfare Federation of Cleveland. *Measuring up: A career clinic for older women workers,* 1958.

State programs vs. senior companion models. *Prime Times,* 1978, *1*(2), 9.

Taylor, W. *The senior community services project: Activities and accomplishments: The 1973–1977 SCSP report.* Washington, D.C.: National Council on the Aging, 1978.

U.S. Administration on Aging. *AoA fact sheet.* Washington, D.C., 1975.

U.S. Department of Labor. *Age Discrimination in Employment Act of 1967.* Washington, D.C.: U.S. Government Printing Office, 1977. (a)

U.S. Department of Labor. *News,* March 9, 1977. (b)

U.S. Senate. *Developments in aging, 1978: Part I.* Washington, D.C.: U.S. Government Printing Office, 1979.

10
Nutrition Programs

The nutrition program, formally authorized under the 1973 amendments to the OAA provides at least one hot meal a day primarily in a congregate setting for those age 60 and over. Originally criticized by some as a new version of the depression soup lines, this program has ultimately become the most popular and universally well-received program of the 1970s. Its success can be attributed, at least in part, to the fact that it provides a measurable service (namely, the preparation and serving of a meal) in a setting that brings people together informally while integrating its efforts with other available services in the community.

The goals of the program identified in 1973 by the AoA illustrate the dual emphasis of the program:

1. Improve the health of the elderly with the provision of regularly available, low-cost, nutritious meals, served largely in congregate settings and, when feasible, to the homebound.

2. Increase the incentive of elderly persons to maintain social well-being by providing opportunities for social interaction and the satisfying use of leisure time.

These first two goals also provide a summary of the success of the program. Nutrition is essential to good health but is greatly affected by the social situation. Eating is a social activity, and regardless of other resources, the older person is less likely to prepare adequate meals when eating alone. The other goals of the program are:

3. Improve the capability of the elderly to prepare meals at home by providing auxiliary nutrition services, including nutrition

and homemaker education, shopping assistance, and transportation to markets.

4. Increase the incentive of the elderly to maintain good health and independent living by providing counseling and information and referral to other social and rehabilitative services.

5. Assure that those elderly most in need, primarily the low-income, minorities, and the isolated, can and do participate in nutrition services by providing an extensive and personalized outreach program and transportation service.

6. Stimulate minority elderly interest in nutrition services by assuring that operation of the projects reflect cultural pluralism in both the meal and supportive service components.

7. Assure that Title VII (changed to Part C under Title III in 1978) program participants have access to a comprehensive and coordinated system of services by encouraging administration coordination between nutrition projects and Area Agencies on Aging (AAAs).

This latter goal was strengthened in the 1978 OAA, which brought the administration of the nutrition program under the direction of the AAAs for the first time. Before 1978, the formal links with the AAAs were optional.

The Congregate Nutrition Program

History

Although there have been conflicting data on the nutritional deficiencies of older Americans based largely on the differences among urban, rural, ethnic, and economic variables, some general patterns of deficiency have emerged (Rawson et al., 1978):

> Calcium appears as the most common denominator, noted as deficient in most of the studies cited. Iron and Vitamins A and C are the next most commonly identified deficiencies . . . within the elderly, the problems of nutrition intake increase as the individuals grow older and are based as much in quantitative dietary shortcomings as in qualitative deficiencies. (p. 27)

Although the elderly malnourished have been a part of our society for a long time, formal, sustained programs to provide for those who do not have personal or financial resources are relatively new.

The most significant research prior to the planning and development of a national nutritional program was the 1965 National Study on Food Consumption and Dietary Level sponsored by the Department of Agriculture. This study showed that 95 million Americans did not consume an adequate diet; 35 million of these had incomes at or below the poverty level. Subsequent analyses indicated that 6–8 million of those age 60 and over had deficient diets. This data laid the foundation for a federal nutrition program for the aged (Cain, 1977).

A task force set up to develop recommendations based on the results of the national study recommended demonstration projects for a 3-year period to determine the best mechanisms for delivering nutritional services. Demonstration projects were needed because of the lack of information on how such programs should be designed and, more important, the extent of their effectiveness (Bechill & Wolgamot, 1972). The purpose of the demonstration projects was to "design appropriate ways for the delivery of food services which enable older persons to enjoy adequate palatable meals that supply essential nutrients needed to maintain good health . . . in settings conducive to eating and social interaction with peers" (Cain, 1977, p. 142).

While this overall goal seems straightforward, the demonstrations were expected to examine multiple issues. Besides the major effort to improve the diet of older adults, the meals were to be served in social settings which would allow for the testing of the effects of different types of sites. These sites would be evaluated in terms of their ability to promote increased interaction among the older clients. The effects of a nutrition education program on the eating habits of the elderly would be evaluated as well as the general ability of the congregate meals approach to reduce the isolation of older persons. Of course, the AoA was also concerned about the comparative costs of different methods of preparing and delivering meals and the problems that were entailed in any effort to increase the nutritional quality of the older person's diet (Cain, 1977).

The AoA funded 32 demonstration and research projects under Title IV. An intensive evaluation of the demonstrations produced the support for the national nutrition program first authorized in the 1973 OAA Amendments. The 32 demonstration projects were designed to control for variations in income, living conditions, ethnic background, environmental setting, sponsoring agency, method of food preparation and delivery, staffing, and record keeping. This intricate design allowed national guidelines to be developed that would incorporate the successful components of each project. More important, the Title IV projects indicated to the AoA and to the U.S. Congress that the proper provision of congregate meals for groups of elderly people fostered social interaction, facilitated the delivery of supportive services, and met emotional needs while improving nutrition.

Since the beginning, the congregate nutrition program has grown from 32 demonstration sites to 1,047 nutrition programs with approximately 9,000 sites. In 1977, 383,000 meals were served daily, 67% of which went to low-income elderly (U.S. Administration on Aging, 1978).

Program Operation

Under the provisions of the OAA, the AoA is mandated to develop a nutrition program for older adults

> 1. which, five or more days a week, provides at least one hot or other appropriate meal per day and any additional meals which the recipient of a grant or contract may elect to provide, each of which assures a minimum of one-third of the daily recommended dietary allowances as established by the Food and Nutrition Board of the National Academy of Sciences . . .
> 2. which shall be provided in congregate settings; and
> 3. which may include nutrition education services and other appropriate nutrition services for older individuals. (Title III, Part C).

Because the nutrition program was developed at the federal level under the authorization of the AoA and was, thus, ultimately administered through a single agency, the guidelines for operation have been clearer than in other programs (such as home-delivered meals) which have developed out of different local and national program units.

Each state is allotted funds in proportion equal to the number of older persons in the state as compared with the older population nationally. However, each state is guaranteed a minimum of .5% of the national appropriation. The nutrition program is administered by the state agency on aging, unless another agency is designated by the governor and approved by the Secretary of HEW. Based on a previously approved state nutrition plan, the moneys are allocated to AAAs or public and nonprofit agencies, institutions, and organizations for the actual provision and delivery of meals. Before the 1978 amendments, one-half of the local nutrition programs were under the sponsorship of the AAAs, the other half under the local sponsorship. Within 2 years of the 1978 amendments, all nutrition programs were to be administered through the local AAAs to ensure service delivery coordination. However, AAAs are authorized to contract the nutrition programs to other local groups as appropriate.

The state units on aging and local nutrition administrative units must provide for advisory assistance that includes consumers of the service at the state level, members of minority groups, and persons knowledgeable in the provision of nutrition services. Nutrition advisory groups can advise on all aspects of the program as well as play an advocacy role for the continuation and growth of the program. Programming, allocations, recruitment of participants, meal sites, and service linkage are common areas of concern for nutrition advisory committees.

All persons age 60 and over and their spouses are eligible for services under the nutrition program. Special emphasis is placed on serving the low-income and disadvantaged elderly. This is achieved by locating nutrition centers, when possible, in areas that have a high proportion of low-income elderly. Through this system, any variation of a means test is avoided, thus increasing the general acceptability of the program to the elderly, who often avoid programs that appear to be "charity."

Actual centers or sites are located in any space appropriate for the serving of congregate meals. The centers can serve as few as 5 or as many as 250 participants on a given day; however the average center serves between 20 and 60 participants each day. Church basements, schools, high-rise apartments, senior centers, and multipurpose centers are the more common locations for nutrition sites. Because transportation is so important to the success of the program, centers are usually located in high-density areas, where walking is possible, or on bus or subway lines. In suburban and rural areas, the centers are located in areas where some form of transportation to and from the center can be provided by the site. Unless the nutrition program is incorporated into senior centers that offer all-day programming, nutrition sites or centers are open up to 4 hours a day. The location of the center, transportation available, and additional resources affect the length of time of the daily operation of the program. For example, those programs in school cafeterias are often sandwiched between student lunch programs.

Location also affects the type of programming developed by the site. Sites that are not used for other purposes allow greater freedom for alterations, decorating, and storage space than locations that have other activities scheduled in the same space. Shared space has posed a hardship for many nutrition programs in meeting the national guidelines for program development.

The meals themselves are either prepared on site, delivered to the site in bulk, or delivered to the site in individual trays or containers. Because of cost and health code regulations, the on-site preparation is the least popular form of meal preparation. Catering services contracting with many nutrition sites in a given area can provide 6- to 8-week-cycle menus that both meet the nutritional requirements of the program and are interesting to the participants. Costs per meal range from $1.50 to $4.50. Private firms, hospitals, and long-term care institutions are the most likely sources for meals because they can incorporate special diet meals into the program and already have an understanding of the nutritional needs of older persons. School cafeterias and restaurants are less successful meal sources. Catered meals arriving in individual trays provide the most flexibility for nutrition center locations, as health code requirements are minimal.

Eating and Socializing

Because the purpose of the nutrition program is to provide both meals and socialization, programming is an important part of the services offered. When the nutrition site is incorporated into a high-rise for the elderly, a senior center, or a recreation center, programming is usually part of the additional available resources. When the nutrition site is its own center, programming responsibility rests with the nutrition site managers under the direction of the nutrition project director for the region. Programming is diverse and related to the interests and backgrounds of the participants. The programming available is similar to that found in senior centers but with special emphasis on nutrition education, meal preparation, buying practices, health maintenance, and physical fitness. Not all participants become involved in the programming. An example of what appears to be most popular (based on a personal survey) is programming which requires self-selective active participation, menu swapping, food demonstrations, exercise programs, and handcrafts. Lectures, movies, and other passive activities are less successful at nutrition sites.

Eating and Needs

People who attend the nutrition centers very often have other service needs. The nutrition program guidelines have stated from the beginning that only up to 20% of the nutrition funds can be spent on other services including transportation. Because of this, the nutrition program has had to reach out and develop linkage with other community services in order to respond to the needs of the participants.

This limitation placed on expenditures for supportive services has contributed to the success of the nutrition program. The nutrition programs have not built a duplicate service system but have, instead, integrated other agency services into their programs. Visits by social security representatives, health department officials, and recreation leaders are part of nutrition programming. The limit on service funds has also been a factor in the location of nutrition sites. Many times priority is given to sites located in existing community programs. For example, the nutrition program has led to the expansion of the multipurpose senior center system and has made possible many geriatric daycare programs. County departments of recreation have been able to expand their programming because of the available lunch program. Housing developments for the elderly have also been able to build around the lunches being served.

The same limit imposed on funds for services was imposed on funds for personnel staffing with the same result. Project directors have reached to other programs to supplement nutrition center staffing needs and have, in some cases, used senior aides, CETA employees, and RSVP volunteers to provide support staff. Guidelines indicate that staffing preference should be given to older persons. In locations where the nutrition center or site is separate from other services, the staff usually consists of one part-time site manager assisted by volunteers. In this manner, the participants themselves become involved in the actual operation of the program and see it as "their program" for which they feel responsible.

Funding

Funding for the basics of this program came from the federal government, with an initial outlay fund of $98 million. In 1975 and 1976, the amount was raised to $125 million, although the actual money expended was higher owing to the delay in the appropriation of the initial moneys. For FY 1977 and 1978, $203,525,000 and $250 million, respectively, were expended. Expenditures for FY 1980 were expected to reach $300 million. Because of inflation, the increases have not allowed for a substantial growth in the number of elderly served per day. To help compensate for the funding limitations, sites are requiring reservations, advance notice of cancellations, and in some cases, a 3- or 4-day rotating system of attendance, all of which create hardships for older persons who have become dependent on these programs for an adequate diet.

Participants are encouraged to contribute something for the meal. The guidelines provide that individuals, from their own consciences, shall determine how much they should and can afford to pay (Cain, 1977). Nutrition centers furnish envelopes or have similar systems in which participants pay what they feel is appropriate. Despite the original intent that donations should be anonymous and of whatever amount appropriate to the given individual, suggested contributions of $.25 or $.50 have become common at nutrition centers. Even though the compensation mechanism has become more formalized since the beginning of the program and contributions more uniform, the opportunities for self-identified compensation have been maintained. This is the only national aging-related program with such a compensation system. With the limited funding in some local areas in relation to the participant demand, participants have decided among themselves to contribute higher amounts in order that more people can be served. This, then, provides an opportunity for the participants to see the direct result of their contributions.

As funding becomes more restricted, the question of eligibility will become more important. With limited resources, can everyone continue to be eligible? Should outreach be eliminated? Should it be available on a first-come, first-served basis or restricted to the low-income, minority, isolated, and handicapped?

The OAA nutrition program serves basic physiological and social needs, is measurable, and is relatively inexpensive. For these reasons, it has become one of the most successful programs of the last 10 years.

Home-delivered Meals

Home-delivered meals are provided to homebound persons, and enable those persons who cannot buy food or prepare their own meals to have good nutritional meals on a regular basis. Approximately 90% of all those receiving homebound meals are 60 and over. The purpose of the program is to provide either one or two meals per day, 5 days a week. Being able to obtain these delivered meals may enable many of these aged to remain living in the community.

History

Programs of home-delivered meals began in England immediately
following World War II. The first program in the United States began
in Philadelphia in 1955. The longest continuously operating program
is "Meals on Wheels" of Central Maryland, Inc., which began in 1960
in Baltimore and was modeled after the English programs.

The early models of home-delivered meal programs were operated locally and largely by volunteer organizations. Originating in a
church kitchen, these programs would serve from 15 to 100 clients,
generating payment from clients either through a fixed fee or on a
sliding scale. From 30 to 300 volunteers would be involved in any
given local program. Referrals would come from friends, families,
professionals in the field, or the elderly themselves. Whether one or
two daily meals were delivered and the costs of the meals both
depended on the facilities available for meal preparation. Menus,
number of meals served, amount, and cost were determined by the
local organization sponsoring the program. Volunteers were primarily retirees and nonworking women, each of whom volunteered approximately 2 hours a week. The hot meal was delivered at
noontime, and if a second meal was provided, it was a cold evening
meal delivered at the same time as the hot meal.

The early programs were sponsored by local churches, community groups, or nonprofit organizations and were largely self-sufficient based on the fees charged the participating clients. This early
model has continued to the present time and grown to where there
are approximately 1,000 such programs nationally (Buchholtz, 1971).
The number is difficult to determine because of the relative auton-
omy of the various programs.

In the early 1970s, as more government funds became available,
either new programs under government sponsorship or links between nonprofit local programs and government agencies began to
emerge. With the introduction of these new support mechanisms,
uniform standards, quality control, and uniformity began.

In the early 1970s, moneys for social services under Title XX of
the Social Security Act community action funds were the prime
support for home-delivered meals efforts. In 1973, under Title III of
the new amendments to the OAA, the congregate nutrition program
had formally begun. In the guidelines, up to 10% of the meals served
could be home delivered. Later, the 10% ceiling was dropped. The
figure has risen to 15–20%, depending on the congregate program
and the needs of the participants. The 1978 amendments to the

OAA for the first time designated a separate authorization for home-delivered meals. This program was to be administered through the nutrition program; and now federally sponsored, locally run home-delivered meal programs are added to the preexisting community-based programs. In some situations, there were no preexisting home-delivered meal programs; in other communities the two existed. AoA funded home-delivered meal services served primarily clients who were congregate-site participants while locally funded programs served other eligible clients. Because congregate nutrition participants pay only what they feel they can (usually $.25–$.50) while those being served by a locally self-supporting home-delivered meal program pay a fixed fee, the meals-on-wheels cost to a client is often as much as five times higher. This can cause confusion when a client moves from one program to the other.

The 1978 legislation with separate authorization for home-delivered meals—funded for the first time in 1979—brought the issue of privately operated, largely volunteer groups vis-à-vis federally sponsored programs to a head. The authorizing legislation stated that home-delivered meal programs under the separate authorization were to be administered through the federal nutrition program with preference for funding given to local preexisting voluntary home-delivered meal programs.

Program Operation

Basically, in a home-delivered meal program, two volunteers—one acting as a driver and one as a visitor—visit 8–10 different clients each day, spending 5 minutes with each while delivering the meal. The home-delivered meal program's primary function is to prepare and deliver the meals, but it also provides a few minutes of friendly visiting. If additional services are needed, the client is referred to other support systems.

The meals are prepared by volunteers in church kitchens or are catered by private services, hospitals, long-term care institutions, schools, or colleges. When catered, the meals are either packaged by volunteers (delivered in bulk) or packaged by the meal producing agency. The extent to which special diet meals are available is determined by the amount of funds available and the source of the meal preparation. Low-salt and diabetic diets are the more common special diets available. The development of better serving boxes for keeping food warm and of better individualized food-storage containers have improved the system of food delivery. Because of the importance of keeping food above 120° or below 45° until reaching the point of individual delivery, appropriate delivery equipment is essential to an effective program. Either a 6- or 8-week-cycle menu ensures the variety necessary in such a program while guaranteeing that the one-third required daily allowance is met in each meal.

For many of the home-delivered meal programs, the volunteer aspects of the program are themselves a service to older persons. In a study of the volunteers in "Meals on Wheels" of Central Maryland (Olsen, 1979), one-half were over 60 years of age themselves and indicated that being able to serve in this program gave meaning to their lives; 29% of the volunteers were widows and living alone. Although primarily for the homebound, the program obviously also provides a service to those preparing and delivering the meals.

There has been some experimentation with dehydrated, dried, and frozen food, but such alternatives have not yet been readily accepted by the programs or the elderly. These alternatives have been under experimentation for the purpose of providing meals to those clients for whom daily visits are impractical, especially the rural elderly (Rhodes, 1977). Some of these alternate methods of food preparation have been evaluated; and preliminary results indicate that the food itself, preparation, and cost are competitive with current situations.

When the home-delivered program is attached directly to the nutrition congregate site, the nutrition participants themselves often package and deliver the meals. In this way, those that are attending can keep in touch with participants who are unable to attend. As was pointed out in Congressional testimony (Cain, 1977), the longer the congregate nutrition program is available, the greater potential for home-delivered meals as part of the program. One project found that after 3 years, up to 30% of the participants were now receiving the home-delivered meals because of changes in their physical condition. The interrelation of the two programs is important in order that those who are eligible for the nutrition program can have an opportunity to continue, even when physical limitations temporarily make visiting the center impossible. The home program can speed recovery and perhaps, in many situations, make a return to the congregate site possible.

Under the 1978 amendments, for the first time those under 60 years of age will be eligible for a service under the OAA. Because home-delivered meal programs have served anyone homebound, the new legislation allows the younger, homebound to continue to be eligible for those programs shifting to the Title III funds.

Funding

Funding for home-delivered meals has always been diverse. Either a fixed fee based on the cost of the meal or a sliding scale that averages the cost of the meal has been the common method until recently. Fees per meal range between $.75 and $2.00 in most locations. Eligible clients have been able to use food stamps in most locations to supplement the cost of the meals. Currently, funds from Title XX of the Social Security Act, and Title III of the OAA are the key sources for revenue. These funds can be used not only for the cost of the meals themselves but to pay those that prepare, package, and deliver the meals. Because of the availability of federal funds, there is a shift from volunteer to paid help for meal preparation and delivery. Local United Ways, church, community service, and neighborhood groups also contribute money, equipment, or transportation to the program. With the inclusion for the first time of home-delivered meals into the OAA and the separate authorization for funding, the home-delivered meal program will continue to expand its important role in the community service delivery system.

Nutrition and the Older Person

Providing nutritional meals with opportunities for socialization is a basic service to the elderly. Meal programs are measurable, cost effective, and meet a basic human need. It is partly for these reasons that the nutrition programs have been so successful in the United States. Unfortunately, after 6 years of expansion, the programs are now limited to a modest annual growth rate because of funding limitations. More reliance will need to be placed on local support, in-kind matches, and volunteerism to enable the programs to meet the demand for service. Fortunately these programs are well-integrated into the community and have just such a capacity for local support they can call upon if their funding becomes constricted.

References

Bechill, W. B., & Wolgamot, I. *Nutrition for the elderly: The program highlights of research and development nutrition projects funded under Title IV of the Older Americans Act of 1965, June 1968, and June 1971.* Washington, D.C.: U.S. Government Printing Office, 1972.

Buchholtz, F. *Home delivered meals for older Americans.* Washington, D.C.: U.S. Government Printing Office, 1971.

Cain, L. Evaluative research and nutrition programs for the elderly. In *Evaluative research on social programs for the elderly.* Washington, D.C.: U.S. Government Printing Office, 1977.

Olsen, J. *The effect of change in activity in voluntary associations on life satisfaction among people 60 and over who have been active through time.* Unpublished doctoral dissertation, University of Maryland, 1979.

Rawson, I., Weinberg, J., Herold, J., & Holtz, J. Nutrition of rural elderly in southwestern Pennsylvania. *Gerontologist,* 1978, *18,* 24–29.

Rhodes, L. NASA food technology, a method for meeting the nutritional needs of the elderly. *Gerontologist,* 1977, *17,* 333–340.

U.S. Administration on Aging. *Fact Sheet.* Washington, D.C.: U.S. Government Printing Office, 1978.

Part IV
Services for the Aged

In contrast to programs, the existing services in aging offer a large number of components and always seem to be under pressure to expand. Since these services are community based, these expansionist pressures often come from seniors in the community and their families. Pressures for expansion are increasingly being generated by a federal government that is demanding more accessibility to services for seniors and more accountability on the part of service providers.

In this part we will examine some complicated and vital service delivery systems including multipurpose senior centers, housing services, in-home services, adult daycare centers, and nursing homes. As is evident, these services are being presented in an ordering that relates to their orientation to elderly with differing levels of need. Multipurpose senior centers serve ambulatory elderly, while housing services may be oriented to ambulatory elderly with some housekeeping and personal needs for which they require assistance. In-home services and adult daycare centers serve seniors with more extensive physical or emotional problems. Finally, nursing homes are oriented toward a population which cannot survive in the community even with the provision of extensive services.

It should be noted that although these services are discussed individually they are not mutually exclusive. Seniors may be taking advantage of more than one service. Ambulatory elderly who attend a senior center may also be living in elderly housing and receiving some homemaker assistance. Clients of adult daycare centers may also be the recipients of extensive in-home services.

11
Multipurpose Senior Centers

The multipurpose senior center is probably the most diverse service now available to the elderly. This diversity is emphasized in NCOA's definition of a senior center:

> a community focal point on aging where older persons as individuals or in groups come together for services and activities which enhance their dignity, support their independence and encourage their involvement in and with the community. (National Council on the Aging, 1978, p. 15)

This definition emphasizes the senior center as a community focal point, the key ingredient of present senior center philosophy. Senior center programs operate from a separate facility, serve as a resource for information and training, and promote the development of new approaches to servicing the older adult.

Title V of the OAA emphasized the multipurpose senior center's role as a community facility for the organization and provision of a broad spectrum of services for the older person. The success of senior centers, however, lies not only in the breadth of services they provide but in the voluntary participation of the users in center activities. Seniors can choose not only whether they want to participate in a center program but in what way they want to become involved. Individuals thus maintain their independence while reaching out to others and to the community in a variety of activities.

History and Legislation

Associations of peers have always been sources of support for individuals. Clubs organized for older people only can be traced as far back as 1870. However, centers for older people began with a program in New York City in 1943. The idea came from workers in the New York City Welfare Department who felt that the older people with whom they were working needed more than a club.

> The organizers of the project, besides securing a meeting place, had contributed games, had suggested the serving of refreshments to foster sociability, and having gathered the old people together, expected that they could manage by themselves. They had in this way provided them with a more sociable means of passing time, which then seemed adequate provision. No one had thought beyond this point. (Maxwell, 1962, p. 5)

The idea of this form of association quickly spread, as private groups began setting up centers throughout the country. The San Francisco Senior Center, begun in 1947, was created through efforts of the United Community Fund, the American Woman's Volunteer Services, the Recreation Department, and individual local citizens (Kent, 1978). In 1949 the new "Little House" in suburban Menlo Park, California was able to attract a clientele of white-collar and professional clients (Maxwell, 1962). The centers in New York and Menlo Park became the prototypes for the two conceptual models of the senior center that are now dominant. One conceptual approach embodied in the social agency model views senior centers as "programs designed to meet the needs of the elderly and postulates that the poor and the disengaged are the more likely candidates for participation in senior centers." The alternative "voluntary organization model hypothesizes that the elderly who are more active in voluntary organizations and who manifest strong attachments to the community are also the ones who make use of senior centers" (Taietz, 1976, p. 219).

Senior centers grew primarily as locally supported and directed institutions. Established either by local nonprofit groups or by local units of government (departments of social service or departments of recreation), centers were designed to be primarily responsive to local needs. However, most of the growth in senior centers has occurred since 1965. Before that time small clubs were the most common form of social organization. Even in 1970, there were only 1,200 centers as opposed to 6,000 in 1978 (National Council on the Aging, 1978).

In the 1970s, federal legislation made more funds available for the development of senior centers. The most important piece of authorizing legislation was Title V of the OAA. The 1973 amendments, Section 501, inserted into the act the new "Multipurpose Senior Centers" title. Although not funded until 1975, this title identified senior centers as a unique and separate program. Because Title V provided funds for "acquisition, alteration, or renovation" of centers but not for construction or operation of centers, Title III made it possible to fund senior centers for the development and delivery of a variety of specific services. Title V provided resources for the facilties, while Title III provided operational moneys.

The 1978 amendments to the OAA consolidated the Title V program into Title III, repealing Title V. With this change, Title III can "provide for acquisition, alteration, renovation, or construction of facilities for multiple purpose senior centers as well as provide for the operations of these centers." This consolidation provides for a greater opportunity to organize senior centers under the direction of the AAAs. The new Title III also allows the AAAs to fund senior centers from the beginning to the fully operational stages.

A number of other legislative enactments provide mandates for senior centers:

1. The local Public Works Development and Investment Act of 1965 provided funds which may be used for the development of multipurpose senior center facilities. Under Title I of this act, funds may cover 100% of the cost of construction, renovation, and repair of buildings to be used as centers.

2. Title XX of the Social Security Act, authorized in 1974, provides funds for group services for older persons in senior centers. Many of the programs offered through senior centers are eligible for funds under Title XX, because Title XX's purpose is the provision of social services for low-income persons. Only individuals who meet the eligibility requirements can receive services. Because of this requirement, it is often difficult to coordinate Title XX programs with those funded through the OAA, which has no eligibility requirements other than the age of the recipient.

3. The Housing and Community Development Act of 1974 provides funds for the expansion of community services, principally for persons of low and moderate income. Construction funds are available through this act (U.S. Administration on Aging, 1977).

Characteristics

Senior Center Users

Since 1943, the senior center concept has grown to the point where
more than 5 million older Americans from 60 to 95 years are members and participants in over 5,000 senior centers (Kent, 1978). In
any 2-week period, about 6% of all older Americans attend a senior
center and about 18% have attended a senior center recently (Kent,
1978). A 1974 study sponsored by the National Institute of Senior
Centers found further that the majority of senior center clients were
between 65 and 74. Approximately one-fourth of the clients were
between 75 and 84 years of age. Of the participants, 85% were white,
and women comprised 75% of center clients. Participants from blue-
collar backgrounds made up 47% of the membership; white-collar
clerical workers an additional 16%; and professional and managerial
groups accounted for another 16%. One-third of the center users
reported they would have had difficulty paying fees if required.
There were 59% of the membership who lived alone.

The study also compared center users and nonusers to see what
differences, if any, existed between the two groups. Basically, users
saw themselves as more healthy than nonusers. Otherwise, the differences between the two groups varied by age. In the under-65 group,
nonusers were better educated and had a higher income. For those
over 65, users had a higher income. Users were also more likely to
be widowed but less likely to be single, separated, or divorced.
Whereas users and nonusers of the centers were similar in their
previous patterns of organizational membership, users currently be-
longed to more groups than nonusers. Although people who use the
centers are somewhat more active than people who don't, a sizable
minority of users could not be characterized as joiners or doers. This
does not vary by age. Finally, users had a significantly higher life
satisfaction score than nonusers (Leanse and Wagner, 1975).

Two more recent studies (Hanssen et al., 1978; Toseland &
Sykes, 1977) have shown some variance from the earlier description
of senior center participants. Toseland and Sykes found that there
was no significant difference between the life satisfaction of users and
nonusers and that senior centers did not always serve a self-selected
group of highly satisfied, healthy, elderly people. Hanssen et al.
found that users were more socially oriented, enjoying more out-of-
home and structured activities. They also found that those with life-
long patterns of affiliation were more likely to participate in senior
centers. However, Hanssen et al. did concur with the earlier study's

finding that nonparticipants were more likely to have activities focused in the home and in passive endeavors that were the least consistent with the structured, social programs offered at the senior centers.

Models

There are several alternative models for senior centers. As indicated earlier, Taietz (1976) clarified the basic conceptual difference between the social agency model and the voluntary organizational model. These two models evolve out of the support system on which they are based. Early research identified the social agency models as the most commonly developed. As Taietz notes, the social clubs for the elderly have been most meaningful to individuals who are isolated from social relationships, the clubs helping to relieve the older person's loneliness. For the older person who is active in a number of informal and organizational roles, the existence of age-graded social clubs may not seem an exciting opportunity.

The voluntary organizations are usually groups that have many social activities but also possess regular memberships, have organizational bylaws, and conduct scheduled meetings of the members on a variety of topics (Taietz, 1976). In a study of senior centers in 34 communities, Taietz noted the similarities between senior centers and other voluntary organizations which include both service components and professional staff. One major difference, however, was that, while veterans and fraternal groups tend to be sex exclusive, senior centers provide men and women with equal access to programs. However, because the centers under this model are similar to formal voluntary organizations, their major clientele will tend to be active elderly rather than the more isolated senior.

In *Alternatives to the Single Site Center* (Fowler, 1974), three different mechanisms for categorizing senior centers were developed. The first defines centers in terms of activities generated. The center can be identified by whether it provides primarily services, activities, individual services and casework, or a combination of the three. The second mechanism for categorizing centers is by administration. The center administrative core may be either centralized (everything in a central facility), decentralized (located in several neighborhood facilities), combined (central location, with satellites), or a multiplicity of operations with some linkage. Finally, centers can be classified by the origin of their services. The services can be offered exclusively by center staff, by center staff and community agencies, or by community agencies with the center staff providing coordination. The description of the models themselves show how complex and diversified the structure can be and still come under the rubric of senior centers.

As part of the NCOA study of centers, another model emerged, one based on size and complexity of operation and including four levels:

1. Multipurpose senior center
2. Senior center
3. Club for older persons
4. Program for all persons, with special activities available for elderly

The differences between centers and clubs do not rest solely in their activities or membership but rather in the breadth of services available to clients, the permanent nature of the physical facility, and the numbers of unpaid staff. Many senior centers are also incorporated entities. In the NCOA survey, 51% of the responding organizations were centers, 46% clubs, and 3% could not be placed in any existing category (Leanse and Wagner, 1975).

Cohen (1972) attempted to further delineate the center from the club. The center he viewed as having the following five characteristics:

1. Community visibility based on a good facility and easy identification
2. A central location for services, either through central site or satellites
3. An ability to serve as a focal point for concerns and interests
4. An ability to serve as a bridge to the community
5. A program purpose that focuses on the individual, family, and community.

The diversity of structure, size, and functioning capabilities are a result of the origins of senior centers. The centers have emerged from the community; are sponsored primarily by voluntary, non-profit, or public community-based organizations; and still receive a substantial percentage of funding from locally determined sources.

Programming

Although center programming is diverse, it falls into two basic types: recreation-education and service. The programming provided is most likely to be successful when it is built as part of the larger community structure and under the direction, or at least with the support, of the older people who will be served by the center.

Recreation and Education

Recreation-education is the type of programming most commonly conceived as the central component of a senior center. It is this that sets it apart from other service delivery agencies in the community and builds the center as a neighborhood focal point for seniors. The development of activity and the selection of the activities to be offered are related to the target group identified by the center. If the center plans to serve everyone within a given geographic area, the programming should reflect the diversity of the population served. Whether clients are men or women, people of high or low income, people of various ethnic backgrounds, or from urban or rural settings should be reflected in the activities designed for the center. If not, unrepresented components of the population potentially served will not utilize the center because their activity needs are not being met. Taietz (1976) warned program directors of the danger of neglecting the special efforts required to attract isolated and alienated elderly to the centers. Hanssen et al. (1978) add another cautionary note with the identification of another subgroup for whom activity programming is not always available:

> The senior center does not consistently accommodate those seniors with perceived physical limitations and those who are mildly depressed. This finding highlights a critical problem for senior centers. If they are to provide services beyond recreation, they must help those persons with greater perceived health problems and that have other limitations. (p. 198)

Many senior centers are beginning to make special efforts to serve elderly with special needs. These elderly may have serious chronic illnesses and physical impairments. In Detroit, senior centers are cooperating with the Metropolitan Society for the Blind to co-sponsor a program which brings blind elderly into senior center activities. In Springfield, Illinois, a senior center is conducting a lip-reading program for older persons with hearing problems (National Institute of Senior Centers, 1979). With increased emphasis in federal programs on the "frail elderly," we can expect these programs to expand.

A center can choose as a target population a particular subgroup of the seniors eligible within a certain geographic area. In making this decision, however, the center staff needs to work with the larger community to be assured that there are similar resources available for the other components of the population group.

The recreation-education component of center programming can be as varied as the community resources allow and as the participants' interests indicate. Common activities include arts and crafts, nature, science and outdoor life, drama, physical activity, music, dance, table games, special social activities, literary activities, excursions, hobby or special interest groupings, speakers, lectures, movies, forums, round tables, and community service projects. When center participants themselves identify their interests and plan the activities with expert assistance from staff, there is a greater chance of adequate participation and success.

Services

The service component of programming is the other essential ingredient for a successful senior center. What identifies the senior center as the community focal point for older people is the combination of both activity and service in one location. The availability of a lecture on horticulture, dental screening, or square dance lessons along with social security advice at the same site and with the same friends makes the senior center a unique community resource.

The services available through a senior center depend on the facilities, the resources, and the community supports available. These services can be provided directly by center staff, by agency staff assigned to the center, through satellite centers close to the agency, or by the agencies themselves rotating through the center.

Services likely to be available through senior centers fall into a number of categories (Cohen, 1972):

1. Information, counseling, and referral, including general information, intake and registration, personal counseling, referral resource files, and special group education around special problems.

2. Housing and living arrangements and employment, including helping the older person locate appropriate housing situations, job referral and counseling programs, and job retraining.

3. Health programs, including screening clinics for a variety of health problems; pharmaceutical services; specialty services, such as dentistry, podiatry, hearing, and speech; and health education programs. These programs are most likely to be developed in conjunction with county health departments, doctors, nurses, extended-care facilities, hospitals, and outpatient clinics in the area.

4. Protective services, including preventive services such as

planning for the appropriate use of funds, securing safe living arrangements, supportive services to help enable the older person to be as self-sufficient as possible, and intervention services including assistance in gaining access to such legal resources as commitment or guardianship.

5. Meals, such as those provided through the OAA nutrition program. The development of the nutrition program since 1973 has been the single biggest contributor to the development of senior centers. Since the nutrition program needed sites for the congregate meals, and senior centers needed a meal program in order to continue adequate daily programming, the nutrition program has given the centers a much needed resource.

6. Legal and income counseling, including helping determine eligibility for Supplemental Security Income (SSI) and the preparation of wills.

7. Friendly visiting as an outreach program, with the participants of the center providing the visiting and outreach services.

8. Homemaker assistance.

9. Telephone reassurance and buddy programs.

10. Handyman and fix-it programs.

11. Daycare services.

12. Transportation programs.

13. Nursing home resident activities within the senior center facility.

In the NCOA study, the majority of self-identified multipurpose centers were found to be at least offering educational, recreational, and either information and referral or counseling services. Many multipurpose centers were also providing health services and opportunities for volunteers. Specifically, the most frequently offered services were transportation to the center, arts and crafts, lectures, employment counseling, health screening, friendly visiting, and health counseling.

The programs garnering the greatest participation of elderly were meals, information and referral, and sedentary recreation. However, the activities that generated the most enthusiasm were tours and trips, particularly among women and blacks. Some members joined the center in order to be eligible for the outings that were planned. Overall, participants indicated that their reasons for attending the centers were to meet others and for opportunities to use leisure time. Thus participants are able to select activities and programs based on individual preference and to participate in evaluations on how well the expectations are met. (Leanse and Wagner, 1975).

It is clear that effective programming is essential for a senior center to fulfill its role as community focal point. Because senior center participants are more likely to attend by choice or at least see themselves as first coming to the center by choice rather than need, the importance of relevant programming determines the continued

Programming Examples

Perhaps the best way to gain an overview of the multipurpose senior center is to examine some examples of centers that illustrate the wide range of programs that can be offered in these facilities. The senior center in Franklin County, New York, is run under the auspices of the county's office on aging. Because the office serves a rural population, the primary service of the eight senior centers is transportation; 12- and 20-passenger vehicles provide 9,000 rides a year to the center, stores, and health facilities. In addition, the centers provide full-time nutrition, education, physical fitness, and craft programs. Assistance is also provided to seniors who are applying for special government programs. In the smaller communities in the county, senior citizen clubs meet monthly for social purposes. The clubs' membership links up with the senior centers for trips and other cooperative events.

The Waxter Center in Baltimore provides one of the most comprehensive services in the country. Built as a result of a $4 million bond issue, the center now has over 11,000 members. Housed in a large, especially designed three-story building, Waxter offers a range of activities including swimming, language classes, crafts, a library, lectures, and trips. Because a large number of separate rooms are available, 15 to 20 different activities can be carried out at the same time, giving each member a wide choice of individual or group settings. The center also operates an extensive health screening clinic, an adult daycare program, and a special program to integrate nursing home patients with center members. Representatives from social security, SSI, Legal Aid, home care agencies, and other public agencies are at the center on a daily basis. The center, including the nutrition program, is open 7 days a week.

The Hudson Guild–Fulton Senior Center in New York City has a membership of 1,300, with 300 members present on any given day. An advisory committee helps to make decisions affecting the staffing operations of the center and to initiate programs that respond to their own interests and talents. The center views itself as a supermarket, with members selecting what they need from the center's offerings. The center's classes include crafts, exercise, drama, music, discussions, and languages. Tickets are available through the center to the wide range of concerts, theater, and opera offerings that are available in New York throughout the year.

The Hudson Guild–Fulton center provides assistance to its members for Medicaid, Medicare, social security, and other public-assistance problems. Personal and housing problems as well as legal concerns also receive attention from the center staff and volunteers. Clients are assisted in finding jobs and volunteer placements. Health screening programs and a telephone reassurance program help to maintain the health of the elderly and keep them in contact with the center. A minibus is utilized to transport members to health care appointments. The center also provides breakfast to about 30 seniors and lunch to an average of 200 older adults at the center and to 75 in their homes.

Facilities

Because senior centers can present an image that encourages older persons' participation in center programming, the choice of a facility has always been a very important part of senior center development. The fact that under the old Title V of the OAA moneys were available only for the development of the center's physical plant underscores the importance of appropriate facilities:

> A senior center should be a place in the community which is attractive and makes older people feel that it is a place where they want to come. In addition, an attractive facility represents a message to the community that older people are valued by both the community and themselves. (U.S. Administration on Aging, 1977, p. VI-1)

In order to maximize opportunities for securing a wide range of clients, attempts are always made to locate a senior center in an area convenient to transportation. This location should also be in a neighborhood that is accessible to the target population of the center. Adequate parking facilities, outside activity spaces, and easy accessibility for the handicapped are also vital elements of the center's physical plan. The interior of the center should provide a variety of room sizes including private areas for counseling, a kitchen-dining area, and adequate space for staff and supplies.

The most commonly utilized facilities for senior centers are separate buildings that are designed or converted solely for center use. Alternatively, churches or synagogues, recreation centers, government facilities, community centers of voluntary organizations, housing authority sites, civic organization facilities, and privately owned commercial facilities have been used to house senior centers. Public housing has not been more frequently used because it is not available in suburban and rural areas. According to the findings of the NCOA study, only 20% of the surveyed centers were in new buildings; 42% of the centers were utilizing renovated facilities; and an additional 37% were still located in old buildings that had not been renovated to meet the needs of the program. Inadequate room sizes and arrangements were hampering many of the centers. Programs often had to be curtailed or altered because of the limiting room situations (Leanse and Wagner, 1975).

With the rising costs of building, rehabilitating, and renovating facilities, it is anticipated that development of adequate facilities could continue to be a barrier to expanding the senior center programs. Fortunately, in many communities, unused schools have been changed to senior centers. The recycling of buildings that had related purposes can help keep down costs.

Funding

Funding mechanisms for senior centers reflect the importance of integrating the center into the community. There is rarely a single source of support for all the activities that a center may wish to inaugurate. Instead, funding from a variety of sources is utilized to cover different components of the center's activities. The auspices under which the center is operated may thus be a crucial determinant of the sources of funds a center is able to tap, since the perspective various resource groups have of the center's sponsor will affect their willingness to make funds available for a senior center program.

A number of federal funding sources are available to centers including:

1. Title III of the OAA, which authorizes funds for multipurpose senior center construction, operation, nutrition services, and special programming. Title IV authorizes training and research funds as well as model projects. Title V of the OAA can fund senior community service employment programs through senior centers.

2. CETA can help to provide staff for the center, and the Public Works and Economic Development Administration Act of 1965 can be drawn upon for construction funds.

3. Block grants from the Department of Housing and Community Development can be utilized for developing, improving, and coordinating senior center activities and facilities.

4. As determined by the locality, General Revenue Sharing funds can be allocated to senior centers.

5. The volunteer programs of ACTION can provide additional personnel resources for the senior center.

6. Title XX funds of the Social Security Amendments can be used to offer social services in the centers.

7. Title I funds of the Higher Education Act can assist centers in developing funding for educational activities and for the training of center staff to implement a variety of learning projects.

In addition to federal funds, state and local funds are also available. Centers have been funded through legislative appropriation in many states, and several centers have been financed through a bond issue, either city or state supported. Civic and religious organizations often make contributions to senior centers. Because the center is visible, contributions made by these groups not only provide needed resources to the centers but bring some visibility to the contributing organization. These groups can most easily donate labor, space, materials, and equipment for the center. Private philanthropists and nonprofit groups also are likely to make contributions; and United Way, as well as local private foundations, can be a source of annual support. Finally, the center itself can generate some income from either membership dues, fund raising projects, or the sale of center-generated products.

Most centers attempt to combine moneys from a variety of sources, with the primary source being Title III of the OAA. However, significant support has been made available by ACTION, the Department of Labor, state and county funds, state and local revenue sharing, in-kind contributions, United Fund, religious organizations, foundations, membership fees, civic groups, and project income. Because in-kind contributions account for a substantial amount of support, center budgets are difficult to estimate. Free space, volunteers, and service agency personnel are all important but hard to evaluate in dollar-and-cents terms.

A center's success can be related to the types of funding supports that are built. With each source of funding, new advocates and supporters are generated. Even though donations might be small, local groups who contribute reinforce the community connection to and support for the senior center.

References

Cohen, M. *Senior centers: A focal point for delivery of services to older people.* Washington, D.C.: National Council on the Aging, 1972.

Fowler, T. *Alternatives to the single site center.* Washington, D.C.: National Council on the Aging, 1974.

Hanssen, A., Meima, N., Buckspan, L., Henderson, B., Helbig, T., & Zarit, S. Correlates of senior center participation. *Gerontologist,* 1978, *18,* 193–199.

Kent, D. The how and why of senior centers. *Aging,* May–June 1978, pp. 2–6.

Leanse, J., & Wagner. *Senior centers: A report of senior group programs in America.* Washington, D.C.: National Council on the Aging, 1975.

Maxwell, J. *Centers for older people.* Washington, D.C.: National Council on the Aging, 1962.

National Council on the Aging. *Senior center standards: Guidelines for practice.* Washington, D.C., 1978.

National Institute of Senior Centers. Senior centers and the "at risk" older person. *Senior Center Report,* 1979, *2*(5), 1, 2, 7–8.

Taietz, P. Two conceptual models of the senior center. *Journal of Gerontology,* 1976, *31,* 219–222.

Toseland, R., & Sykes, J. Senior citizens center participation and other correlates of life satisfaction. *Gerontologist,* 1977, *17,* 235–241.

U.S. Administration on Aging. *Program development handbook for state and area agencies on multipurpose senior centers.* Washington, D.C.: U.S. Government Printing Office, 1977.

12
Housing

Housing Conditions of the Elderly

Of the U.S. population age 65 and over, 95% live outside institutional settings. Even though problems of reduced income and physical impairment can become more acute as people move through the retirement years, their desire to live independently, to remain in familiar surroundings, and not to be isolated is well documented (Tucker et al., 1975). Housing is a major factor for maintaining independence, as older persons spend a greater portion of time in their living units than any other group over 5 years of age (Tucker et al., 1975).

Because housing is the life setting for the physical and social entirety, supportive services and the atmosphere of activity and interchange become as important as the physical characteristics of the housing space. The goals of housing have changed from the provision of physical shelter to improving the quality of life (Carp, 1976a).

There are basically two kinds of housing for the elderly: relatively affluent retirement communities and low-cost publicly supported facilities. However, only 3% of the elderly are housed in the Housing and Urban Development (HUD) program housing. About 90% of the elderly live neither in institutions nor in special housing in their communities. Very little is known about the housing of this group or their needs in regard to the living environment. Their needs are difficult to determine because of the complicated factors involved in making a decision to alter a current housing situation (Carp, 1976a).

Households headed by elders live in somewhat more modest dwellings, both in terms of size and quality, than American households at large. Geographically, 55% of the elderly-headed households live in boundaries of metropolitan areas; 40%, in smaller communities; and 5% live on farms. Elderly couples have the highest income households, followed by older individuals living alone. The poorest is the multiperson household headed by a person 65 and over.

One-fifth of the elderly live in substandard housing, and one-half live in housing built before 1939. Examining the total housing picture for the elderly, Carp (1976a) found that 70% of the older population owned their own homes, a figure higher than the national average. An additional 25% were living in apartments and boarding homes, with the remainder in institutions. As a result of their limited resources, older individuals are often not able to move even if they know what housing options are available to them. Among persons expressing a desire to move in 1970, 61% of young adults, but only 37% of elderly, actually relocated.

Economically, the elderly tend to pay more for housing than younger age groups; 29% of all elderly-headed households spend more than 30% of their income on housing. However, within this group, 43% of single individuals and 50% of renters pay over 30% of their income for housing. Rural elderly households spend substantially less on housing, and husband-wife households have the lowest economic burdens for shelter. Unfortunately, low-income older adults comprise the largest proportion of elderly spending more than they should on housing: over 60% of the 1.1 million households with annual incomes under $2,000 spend over 30% of their income on housing, and an additional 20% spend at least 50% of their income on this basic necessity (Struyk, 1976).

Because of their high housing expenses, public housing programs must first assist the low-income renter household. Although the results are as yet inadequate to meet their needs, existing federal housing programs have focused on this group. In this chapter, some of the specific housing services available to the elderly—both those which are publicly and privately sponsored—will be discussed.

Federal and State Housing Programs

The primary focus of federal housing programs is to provide housing for moderate- and low-income renters. Since the inception of federally assisted programs for the elderly in 1956, there has been an impressive amount of construction. Under its various programs, HUD has rehoused approximately 750,000 older people (Carp, 1976a; U.S. House of Representatives, 1976). In the period between 1970 and 1973, local housing authorities owned 108,000 housing units, of which 49% were for elderly. However, the House Select Committee (1976) projects that over 3 million elderly are in need of publicly assisted housing.

History

The concept of federally supported housing began in the 1930s with the National Housing Act of 1934 and the United States Housing Act of 1937. The 1934 act inaugurated the first home mortgage program—a restructuring of the private home financing system—under the Federal Housing Administration (FHA). Under the 1937 act, the government offered subsidized housing to low-income families. Although the primary purpose of this latter legislation was to clear slums and increase employment, new housing resulted.

  - Under the Housing Act of 1949, the national goal of "a decent home and suitable living environment for every American Family" (Housing Act of 1949) was first stated. The act also included programs for urban renewal, increased funds for subsidized housing, and new programs for rural housing. During the 1950s, housing programs were more directed toward rehabilitation, relocation, and renewal.

Section 202 began under the Housing Act of 1959. The program provided low-cost loans to developers of private housing. It was the forerunner of later mortgage subsidy programs. In the Housing Act of 1961, below-market interest rate mortgages were begun to assist rental housing for moderate-income families. This section, 221(d)(3), is still operating today. In 1965, two rent subsidy programs were begun. In one program, residents would pay 25% of their income in privately owned housing units built with FHA financing. Under the Section 23 leasing program, the government would lease regular units for low-income families.

In 1968, Congress found that "the supply of the nation's housing was not increasing rapidly enough to meet the national housing goal of 1949" (U.S. Department of Housing and Urban Development, 1973). Congress then established a production schedule of 26 million housing units—6 million of these to be for low- and moderate-income families over the next 10 years. One of the programs of this act was Section 236—a program that provides a subsidy formula for rental housing. In 1969, the Brooke Amendment was passed, which limited the amount of rent that could be charged by local housing authorities to 25% of adjusted tenant income. This amendment is currently in effect.

In September 1973, President Nixon halted all housing programs, except the low-rent public-leasing program, in order that a thorough review could be accomplished of what was then viewed as a spendthrift and inadequate program (U.S. Department of Housing and Urban Development, 1973). Following a study, during which no new federally subsidized housing starts were approved, the Housing and Community Development Act was signed into law in August 1974. The act removed the suspension that had been placed on construction and required contracts annually of at least $150 million to help finance development or acquisition costs of low-income housing projects. Because most of the money was to be channeled through the new Section 8 program, which was authorized under this act, funding was slow to begin. Administratively, at least 2 years elapsed before the Section 8 program was fully operational (U.S. Senate Special Committee on Aging, 1975).

The Section 8 Program

Authorized under the Housing and Community Development Act of 1974, this program 'filled the void of the 1973 moratorium. It provides no direct funding to the developer but instead pays monthly rent so that housing can be developed on the private market. As of 1975, of the 207,057 units applied for, 86,539 units were for the elderly (U.S. House of Representatives, 1976).

Section 8, or subsidized rent, is the rent for a unit in a development which is receiving federally subsidized Section 8 housing assistance payments. The Section 8 rent differs from the market rent in that it depends strictly on the amount of income of the tenant. Tenants pay 25% of their adjusted income for rent, with the Section 8 housing assistance payment making up the difference between tenant-paid rent and the full market rent. The tenant could pay as little as $40 or $50 per month or nearly as high as the market rents, depending on the monthly adjusted income. Rents under Section 8 cannot exceed the fair market rent for the area as established by HUD. Rents are reviewed annually, and the tenants must move if 25% of their adjusted income meets the fair market rent for that particular housing project.

In Washington, D.C., in 1978, fair market rents ranged from $274 for a walk-up efficiency to $633 for a detached four-bedroom house. Fair market rents are reviewed annually and take into account construction costs and maintenance fees for individual locations. In 1978, 80% of median income, the eligibility factor for a family of two for Section 8 housing, was $11,700 in Baltimore, $14,400 in Washington, D.C., and $11,600 in Wilmington, Delaware. A family would have to leave Section 8 housing if its income exceeded the amounts given above.

Projects with Section 8 rental units are owned by private parties, profit and nonprofit, and by public housing agencies. Under Section 8, HUD will make 20-year contracts with private parties for the rental units unless the project is owned by or financed with a loan or loan guarantee from a state or local housing agency, in which case HUD will guarantee the rental units for 40 years. Efforts have been made to increase the private guarantee time of 20 years because, in some situations, it is a disincentive for private parties to become involved in the program. Any type of financing may be used for the purchase or rehabilitation of a project which houses Section 8 rental units, including HUD-FHA mortgage insurance programs, conventional financing, or tax-exempt bonds.

Under Section 8, the owner handles the whole program and is responsible for leasing at least 30% of the subsidized units to very low-income families (families whose income is 50% of or below the local median income). Under the Section 8 legislation, priority is given to projects with 20% of their units in Section 8 only to guarantee an income mix in the housing project. However, if the rental units are to be used for the elderly, there is no restriction on the number of Section 8 rental units per project.

The purpose of the Section 8 program is to develop rental housing for medium- and low-income families within the structure of the private housing market. Section 8 units can exist in houses, small apartment buildings, or any other location that has units to rent. Suburban, rural, and urban areas are equally eligible. However HUD determines how many Section 8 rental units can be awarded to a given area in each state. Usually, applications far exceed the units available for the specific areas in question.

The Section 8 housing program had a slow beginning after it was authorized in 1974. In 1975, there were 200,00 applications, but only 30 new units actually materialized (U.S. House of Representatives, 1976). The cumbersome application and administrative procedures were blamed for the delays. In addition, because it was an entirely new program involving low-income families, the private financial community—the group that had to generate the construction moneys—did not appear ready to fund the building of units which would house Section 8 families until the program had grown to become one of the key housing programs for the elderly. Section 8 covers only the actual rental units but is most successful when combined with other housing construction and service programs.

The Section 202 Program

Authorized under the Housing Act of 1959, Section 202 provides federal loans at 3% interest directly to nonprofit sponsors to provide rental housing for the elderly through new construction or rehabilitation of existing structures. The property should include needed support services and can have such rooms as dining halls, community rooms, infirmaries, and other essential services. Many of the nonprofit homes for the aged, such as Cathedral Residences in Jacksonville, Florida—a large housing complex which serves over 700 elderly—were partially constructed with money under Section 202.

The Section 202 program was very successful throughout the 1960s but was phased out after that time in preference to Section 236, another federal loan program. However Section 236 was frozen in 1973 when all federal housing programs were halted to allow for review. Section 202 was reinstated as part of the Housing and Community Development Act of 1974, but it did not return to full activity until the summer of 1975. Under the 1974 act, a $215 million borrowing level was approved for FY 1975, but it was not used until the following year. Regulations in 1976 reaffirmed the importance of the program in providing both construction and long-term financing for housing projects.

Private nonprofit corporations and consumer cooperatives are eligible for Section 202 financing. Loans can carry the average market yield plus 1% during construction and .5% thereafter for administration and program losses. Housing developments under Section 202 cannot exceed 300 units. Section 8 participation is required, and approval of Section 202 loans is based on the feasibility of getting Section 8 financing. In other words, if the number of Section 8 units for a section of the state have already been obligated, Section 202 construction financing cannot be granted.

Section 202/8 allocations are made in accordance with Section 213, a fair share needs formula. The formula, which determines the number of eligible units for a given geographic area, is based on the following criteria:

1. The number of households with the head or spouse age 62 or older

2. The number of such households which lack one or more plumbing facilities

3. The number of such households with incomes less than the regionally adjusted poverty level

4. The prototype production costs for public housing units as adjusted by average cost factors within the loan region

The application process for Section 202/8 housing is extensive and consists of five stages. It usually takes 3–5 years from the time of idea to actual implementation, and approval is given only to those developers with a proven track record.

Other Federal Housing Incentives

Section 236 authorizes interest-reduction payments on behalf of owners of rental housing projects designed for occupancy by lower income families for the purpose of reducing rentals for such tenants. Section 235 provides the same interest-reduction payments for home ownership. Abuses in the use of moneys under Sections 236 and particularly 235 was a key motivation for the halt in all federal housing programs in the summer of 1973. Since that time, Section 236 has not played as significant a role in housing for the elderly.

Under Section 231 HUD is authorized to insure mortgages on structures for housing for the elderly. The construction funds are obtained on the private market, and the rents charged must meet expenses. The federal government provides only the mortgage insurance. Residents with incomes up to $19,000 (in 1978) a year are eligible under this program. Finally, Section 224 authorizes coinsurance to minimize risk. State housing agencies and the private sector, as well as HUD-FHA, bear the risk on defaulted insured loans.

State Housing Programs

State housing agencies have become an important source of financing for the actual building or rehabilitation of housing units. These agencies provide mortgage money directly to developers, who generate the funds through sale of notes and bonds. Construction financing may be provided through the sale of notes having a term of 1–3 years, with permanent loan funds being provided through the sale of 40-year bonds. The bonds sell at an interest rate of 1–2% below that of conventional sources of real estate financing. Because of this interest rate, private developers can get lower mortgage rates from the state units than from private banks. The state housing agencies pass on the savings on the notes and bonds to developers in the form of lower interest rates, which, in turn, should result in lower rents and mortgage carrying charges for market-rate tenants and home buyers. The differences can amount to as much as $40 a month in rent reduction. In 1978, tax-exempt financing could generate rents marketable to families with net annual incomes of between $9,000 and $19,000. Families with incomes even above this range can sometimes be admitted to the program.

The purpose of the state housing agency programs is to attract private developers to the low- and moderate-income housing field with the aim of providing housing for a broad range of income levels. The usual return on equity limit is 8%.

Services

The various HUD programs and state housing agencies support housing that ranges from public ownership and complete public financing to private financing, building, and renting, with federal insurance on the mortgage only. The upper-income limits allowed vary by program, with the most stringent limits being placed on the direct public housing (up to $9,000) and the least stringent limits on the mortgage insurance only program (up to $19,000).

As indicated earlier, nonprofit developers are free to design as much additional space as they wish and are encouraged to add supportive services to the housing units financed under Section 202. However, because of the income limitations placed on those living in federally financed housing, the developer has to keep the rents within the fair market rates and within the rates that the limited-income residents can pay. This, in turn, places limits on the amount of additional support services which can be provided. For example, a high-rise for the elderly in Baltimore, financed under Section 202/8, has the entire top floor overlooking the city as a carpeted and draped multipurpose room. The cost of building as well as maintaining this large, well-equipped, and well-used room must be absorbed in the rental fees allowed for each individual apartment. With the rental ceilings being determined by the government, the room can only be marginally maintained.

Amenities built into the housing programs depend on finances available and on the cost of these amenities in relation to the cost of the overall building. The support from the community in maintaining additional housing facilities and regional preferences will also be determinants of a final design package. The potential resources that can be included in elderly housing are extensive, ranging from transportation, nutrition, and health-screening programs to craft rooms, groceries, and even small restaurants.

Elderly housing projects can thus be part of the larger service delivery system of the community. Because federal housing funds only cover actual housing costs, services run under outside auspices may need to be incorporated into the housing units. Two excellent examples of a housing complex with integrated services are Worly Terrace, Columbus, and Glendale Terrace, Toledo, Ohio. Geared to the elderly who are returning from mental hospitals and to low-income community residents—many of whom were losing their homes through urban renewal—these housing developments operate a unique series of integrated financing and service systems. While HUD paid for the basic construction of the units, the state of Ohio paid for the rooms not eligible under federal regulations (in this case, dining room, community building, clinic, and craft room); and the local housing authorities manage the completed housing units. Worley Terrace is located near public transportation, shops, and several churches. The complex has a six-story high-rise building with 106 living units, four one-story buildings with 120 units; and a centrally located community building. There are furnished and unfurnished quarters for as many as 270 residents, with apartments for single persons, couples, or two unrelated single persons to share an apartment. Available services include hot meals; beauty and barber services; preventive health services including health screening, services of a full-time registered nurse and licensed practical nurse, part-time physician, and podiatry; social activities; and recreation (U.S. House of Representatives, 1976).

The services available in publicly financed or insured housing depend on the developer, the sponsor, the interest of the residents, and the community resources available. Early planning and community support for the project enhances the chances for adequate support services.

Elderly Satisfaction with Housing

Several research studies by Carp (1975, 1976b) have shown long-term satisfaction of residents with subsidized housing for the elderly.

The cornerstone of this satisfaction seemed to be physical conditions of adequate and convenient housing, which were a dramatic improvement over their earlier situations. Even after eight years, the tenants continued to be aware of and to value the good qualities of the physical environment. (1976b, p. iii)

There have been studies which considered whether the elderly really preferred age-segregated housing over types of age-integrated housing. Sherman (1975) concludes that either age-segregated or age-integrated situations are appropriate for the elderly if the individual has had the opportunity of choosing between these alternatives.

Elderly residents in subsidized housing have indicated a preference for modern buildings with commercial facilities, a safe entryway, and lobbies that provide space for interacting with other tenants (Hartman et al., 1976). No preferences were indicated among high-rise, low-rise, furnished, or unfurnished apartments. Elderly residents did, however, attach some weight to balconies in the apartments. Past experience has also shown that, with active and structured meetings, the elderly can play a major part in the design and development of housing for their community.

Older persons who are eligible for senior citizen apartment buildings often choose not to go into such housing even though the subsidized housing offers features not found in their present living situations. Blonsky (1975) found that negative feelings toward elderly housing among seniors were significantly related to the older person's comparisons between their own apartments and homes and the apartments offered by the new buildings and to whether they had an opportunity to see the apartments that were available. The amount of living space and its arrangement were key contributors to the rejection of the housing, since many seniors turned down apartments that did not have separate bedrooms.

Despite the importance of having supplemental programming within housing complexes, the long-term success of these developments is tied to the design and arrangement of the housing units themselves. Improved functioning of the person is enhanced through supplemental services. However, at least from the perspective of the residents, it is the physical housing unit, its design and special features, that determines the success of the projects.

Home Repair and Renovation

Many older homeowners find it necessary to seek alternative housing because of their inability to carry out the maintenance necessary to keep their home in good condition. They also may lack the funds to hire contractors to perform necessary repairs. As homeowners quickly learn, minor repairs that are delayed for a substantial period of time can easily become major costly repairs. In 1975, a report prepared by the state of Michigan commented:

Many seniors reside in structures which are in desperate need of repair. Often a senior will relocate to a new structure when repair to his former living unit would have been more cost-efficient to the government. (Charter Township of Meridian, n.d., p. 4)

The Michigan investigators found that 40% of the single-family homes owned by the elderly in the state needed minor or major repairs.

Home repair programs aimed primarily at low-income elderly have now been organized around the country. Many of these programs have dual purposes: (1) bringing substandard homes up to local code levels and (2) providing supplemental income by hiring older persons to work on these projects. In Meridian Township, Michigan, $42,000 was spent repairing 26 homes between 1975 and 1977. Much of the work on these homes was done by workers over 55 who were paid $4–$5 per hour for part-time labor. In the Virgin Islands homemakers refer clients to the home repair program. Repairs are carried out by a variety of individuals including CETA workers (King, 1976). On Navajo reservations, efforts to upgrade the housing of the elderly have been cooperatively undertaken, with younger workers contributing their time.

In Evansville, Indiana, a major repair program for elderly residents was carried out in a number of neighborhoods. As in other geographic areas, the repair efforts were concentrated on functional aspects of the home including wiring, vermin control, replacement of broken window panes, and new plastering. The hope of the project coordinators was that instituting the repair program would produce a ripple effect which would encourage the elderly to continue making their own repairs and also encourage other neighborhood residents to undertake long-needed repairs. One of the reasons this ripple did not occur was because a majority of the elderly did not even tell their neighbors about the program. This silence was attributable to their ambivalent feelings about accepting aid. In order for the program to be more visible within the community, the evaluators argued that the repairs would have to be undertaken on a continuous basis rather than bringing repairmen into the individual home for an intensive but brief period of time (Abshier et al., 1977).

Home repairs that are to be anything more than cosmetic are also costly. In Michigan, the Meridian Township program spent $6,500 per house to bring these homes up to code standards. As labor costs continue to increase, we can expect that this figure will be appropriate to similar efforts around the country, although volunteer labor can reduce costs significantly. Funding for these home repair programs can be developed from a variety of possible sources including Title III of the OAA, Title XX of the Social Security Act, Community Development Block Grants, or local appropriations.

Specialized Housing Services for the Elderly

Congregate and Sheltered Housing

Housing for the elderly should respond to the wide variation in the needs of older persons. The growth in the interest and availability of sheltered or congregate housing is a response to the need for housing among those elderly who cannot continue to maintain full independent living and yet are not in need of some form of full-service institutional setting. The increase in need for this type of housing is related, at least in part, to increased average longevity, a phenomenon in which a greater proportion of the total population is over 75 years of age and have conditions that require some form of care in addition to basic housing needs.

In addition, there is a commonly occurring pattern in housing for the elderly, federally assisted as well as private. That is, service needs increase as the tenant ages. Tenants who entered the housing program as healthy, independent persons find they need additional service supports with advancing age. New, unanticipated services are then required. Congregate housing is a housing environment which provides enough services to enable many impaired elderly to remain in a community-based residential situation. Lawton (1976) focuses more precisely on the services that might be available in such a congregate housing situation:

> Congregate refers to housing that offers a minimum service package that includes some on-site meals served in a common dining room, plus one or more of such services as on-site medical/nursing services, personal care, or housekeeping. (p. 239)

In contrast, "sheltered" housing as operated in many states offers a more extensive package of services with an emphasis on meals and personal care.

The growth in congregate housing has come long after the availability of both independent-living housing situations and institutional settings. Congregate housing was authorized in 1970 in the congregate housing provision of the Housing and Urban Development Act. Lawton attributes the lag in this important service to the federal desire to avoid developing housing that had the aura of an institution. Space for professional services was also often omitted from construction plans.

In the case of Section 202, any additional services were either to be provided by the sponsor or to come from other federal or local resources. Money to operate additional programs within the housing complex is still not available from HUD. Economic and social considerations impede the relaxing of regulations concerning the use of funds. As Lawton (1976) points out,

> Maintenance of independent function is facilitated by an environment that demands active behavior from its inhabitants, and conversely, the presence of too easily accessible services will erode independence among those who are still relatively competent. (p. 240)

Whatever the validity of this belief, providing additional services does require additional money which cannot be fully recouped from fees charged the residents. Instead, housing programs can maximize the units available by directing funds totally toward housing. Further, the provision of additional services could possibly duplicate other community resources available.

As this discussion indicates, two basic issues emerge in the identification and development of congregate housing for the elderly. The first is whether congregate housing, as a separate entity, should exist. The alternative is to bring community-based programs into the housing situations and to continue to offer assistance through the auspices of community agencies. For example, a home health agency could support those who need it within the housing units, as opposed to having some type of personal care service built into a congregate housing situation. Congregate housing competes with in-home services, community-based programs, and informal assistance offered through family, friends, and informal networks. From this perspective, congregate housing is not readily distinguishable from other housing and supportive service markets that attempt to help elderly people maintain semi-independent life-styles (Heumann, 1976).

The second issue is whether resources can be effectively rearranged so that programs can be provided in a congregate housing situation. The difficulty in developing a congregate housing situation is in identifying the resources for the specific services and making them available within a congregate setting. For example, federal housing does not have the physical space to support office space for services or congregate space for other services (kitchens and dining rooms, for example) or funds to pay for the ongoing services. Funding for services, such as Title III of the OAA and Title XX of the Social Security Act, are contracted primarily to agencies that provide given services to all those eligible. Subcontracting some of these funds into congregate settings is difficult because of state and local guidelines. There is no particular source of funds earmarked for congregate housing programs for the elderly; and the more funding sources required, the more difficult it is administratively to develop and sustain the program.

The need for congregate housing is also difficult to define. Because sheltered housing has not been readily available in the past and because the services are delivered in a housing setting, the demand may not be as high as anticipated, even if the need exists. Data on relative disability, services available, and family support are difficult to identify accurately. Because of these data problems, there has been little effort to assess the over-all demand or need for congregate housing in a local area.

Currently, where congregate housing exists in the community, it is developed with facilities from sections of federally financed housing units, boarding homes, private apartment units, or new construction specifically for this purpose. In addition to shelter, congregate housing can provide housekeeping services, dining and congregate eating services, emergency health services, and recreational services. Sheltered housing helps with personal needs but is not a care facility. The individual residents remain responsible for their own care with the support services available as needed. Sheltered housing does not have ongoing health services.

Currently, congregate housing is emerging as its own system, serving a group that requires some personal care assistance in addition to housing. It is an extension of housing for the elderly, retirement housing, and boarding homes, which serve a heterogenous group of elderly based on their individual needs. As Brody et al. (1975) found, seniors who chose to move into intermediate housing (remodeled row houses with services available as needed) exhibited "improved overall satisfaction with living arrangements and apartments; increased enjoyment of life and social contacts" (p. 355).

Foster Care

For many years, the concept of foster care has been familiar to those who work with children, but the service has only been made available to the elderly since the early 1970s. However, even 10 years later, the foster care program is not as readily available a resource as it should be.

Foster care focuses on a population that cannot sustain full independence. It thus attempts to prolong independence and delay institutionalization. Foster care is a specialized form of sheltered housing whereby the client is placed in a new setting which has family supports. Foster care "is for persons in need of care and protection in a substitute family setting for a planned period of time" (Newman & Sherman, 1977, p. 436). Its uniqueness lies in its family setting and its size. In most foster care programs, the number of older persons per family unit is no more than four.

Foster care programs are generally administered by local departments of social services and rely heavily on Title XX funds for operation. There are strict income limitations attached to the Title XX funding, which makes moderate- or high-income elderly ineligible for foster care through Title XX funding. Although more limited, moneys are also available through state departments of health or mental health and through the Veterans' Administration. More liberal income policies are in effect when funds from these sources are being used. In some programs, the foster family is paid a percentage of the SSI check directly by the recipient of the foster care. In these cases, the foster family does not always break even on the costs.

Eligible homes are usually solicited through appeals to the general public. After eligibility is determined, the family is paid a fee, plus certain expenses, for the care of the older person in foster care. According to a study of the New York Foster Homes program, 93% of the caretakers—those providing the foster home care—were female, and only 58% of them were married (Newman & Sherman, 1977). Less than a third of the home situations provided the participants with involvement in family that included a husband, wife, and at least one child. In Baltimore, the majority of caretakers were women age 55 and over, black, on pensions, living alone, who had held service-oriented positions (Personal data, 1978).

One of the limitations to expanding the foster care program is in the recruitment of families. In some cases, the demand is double the number of homes available. Most recruitment comes from friends and families who have had experience as caretakers (Newman & Sherman, 1977).

One-fourth of the New York State participants in foster care programs were between 60 and 65 years old; 75% were women. Of the foster care residents, 33% had never been married, but 50% were widowed and 5% were divorced. Most of the foster home residents who had worked had held unskilled or semiskilled positions (Newman & Sherman, 1977).

Three-fourths of the caretakers said they included the resident in their family activities and felt they were a member of the family. Three-fourths of the residents took walks or in other ways interacted in the neighborhoods where they lived, while two-thirds participated in community activities. As noted in the report, the sense of family is created even when the caretaker is the only member other than the residents. Being a caretaker can provide meaningful roles to older people as well as provide family situations for those who need some type of sheltered care.

Foster care has been found to be especially effective for older discharged mental patients. The largest foster care program in the United States is run by the Veterans' Administration. In a study of foster residences operated by five VA hospitals (Linn & Caffey, 1977), both younger and older patients were found to have improved after placement in foster care residences. Despite evidence that well-operated foster care is effective for older mental patients, it remains an "appropriate and underutilized resource" (p. 345).

Single-room Occupancy Hotels

Housing situations that are often neglected in discussions of this topic are single-room occupancies (SROs). However, about 600,000 elderly persons live as roomers, either as nonrelatives in households or as occupants of rooming houses and other group quarters (Carp, 1976a). SRO housing is primarily cheap hotels and rooming houses located in commercial areas adjacent to the downtown business district and operated through the private market. There is no licensing of SRO housing beyond the local fire and safety codes imposed by individual local jurisdictions.

Many of those living in SRO hotels do so by choice:

> The avoidance of intimacy and the routinization of suspicion that are endemic features of the SRO can be seen to be compatible with the voluntary self-isolation of these elderly residents. They are life-long isolates and for them, the SRO is a familiar environment. (Stephens, 1975, p. 231)

Residents of SROs are likely to show long histories of being independent, self-reliant, and socially isolated. They are more likely to have histories of time spent in mental hospitals, jails, and prisons and in unskilled work situations (Erikson & Eckert, 1977; Stephens, 1975).

Importantly, residents have usually avoided any dependency on government income programs but instead show a work history, even though it is likely to be unstable.

Most residents of SROs remain isolated from each other, only talking in the public spaces and conducting conversations that are primarily superficial in nature. Deep friendships almost never emerge. However, as pointed out by Stephens, this pattern is a continuation of a lifetime pattern, rather than a change with age. The SRO provides an opportunity to continue the isolated pattern within a framework of affordability, and for many who live in such situations, it is a conscious choice. The most effective supports to these people are from the hotel staffs and nearby shopkeepers (Erikson & Eckert, 1977). It is important to formalize and strengthen these already existing informal support systems as well as to bring in nonprofessional outreach workers to help the residents connect with more formal service systems. However, the choice of isolation that this living style affords can preclude successful response to available programs and services.

Retirement Communities

One of the more recent phenomena developing as a result of the large number of people who are retiring, particularly with good retirement incomes, is the retirement community. Retirement communities can range from small mobile home subdivisions to sizable communities like Youngtown and Sun City, Arizona. The latter had, in 1969, an estimated population of 37,000 (Anderson & Anderson, 1978). The communities can include apartments, semidetached houses, and units that can be purchased or rented. Beyond the living units themselves, varying forms of recreation and supportive services can be offered. The country's first development for senior citizens—Youngtown, Arizona—was founded in 1954 and incorporated as a retirement community in 1960. Currently, it has $2 million in recreation facilities alone; nearby Sun City has $12 million in recreation facilities.

Most retirement communities have age requirements as the key entrance requirement. In Sun Lakes, Arizona, only people over age 40 can purchase property, and no one under age 19 can be a permanent resident. The age limit for buying a home in Sun City is 50, and children or residents must be at least 18 years of age. Residents of any of the Rossmoor Leisure Worlds must be at least 52 years old, and the same age requirement holds for five retirement communities in New Jersey (Heintz, 1976).

"Retirement communities are planned, low-density, age restricted, developments constructed by private funds and offering extensive recreational services and relatively low cost housing for purchase" (Heintz, 1976). The general characteristics of retirement communities include entrance requirements, complete community planning, and relatively low-cost housing coupled with high levels of amenity. The concept of low-cost housing, however, is not universal in retirement communities. Some homes in the Leisure World developments sold for over $70,000 in 1978.

In a study of five retirement communities in New Jersey, Heintz identified characteristics of people who elected to join such communities. She found that residents were primarily Caucasian, retired, and semiaffluent, between 65 and 74 years old. Families in retirement communities had the same household size as the national average, but there were more male-headed households (82.3%). The retirement community population was better educated and more likely to have worked in a high-status or highly skilled occupation. Even though the average age for entrance was only 52, 86% of the residents were actually retired. In 1975, the mean income of residents in these retirement communities was $11,999. The satisfaction of residents with the retirement communities was expressed in the fact that there was an annual turnover rate of only 2–5%. Only 6% of the residents expressed a desire to move from the community.

The communities themselves devoted 80–95% of the acreage to housing, with the remaining land being used for recreation. The usual construction pattern is of single-family attached and detached houses in cul-de-sac arrangements, with the community focal point being the clubhouse. The housing costs in the five communities studied ranged from $16,407 to $30,996, with monthly maintenance charges ranging from $51.69 to $77.80.

An example of a successful retirement community is Leisure World in Laguna Hills, California. Begun in 1963, by spring 1977 it had nearly 12,000 residences and a population of 19,000. "Leisure World was designed to provide security, quick accessibility to good health care, good nearby shopping, good transportation, excellent facilities for recreation and adult education and additional activities to ensure freedom from boredom" (*Leisure World Brochure*, 1977).

The importance of security in a retirement community is illustrated in the efforts Leisure World has made:

> Hundreds of Leisure World residents say one of the principle reasons they came to live in Leisure World is security. . . . The entire residential

area is surrounded by about 8.5 miles of six-foot wall or fence. In some places the wall is topped by barbed wire. Entrance to the residential areas is only through one of eleven guarded gates. Cars of residents have a special symbol attached to the front bumper; all others are stopped for identification and for permission by a resident to pass through ... a security force of 255 officers is backed up by full-time, armed officers who have specific police training. (*Leisure World Brochure*, 1977)

The facilities in Leisure World are extensive. Minibuses circulate over 11 routes, fare free, carrying 88,000 passengers a month. There are five clubhouses, concerts, movies, stage presentations, and 167 clubs and organizations. The enormous sports and recreational opportunities range from swimming pools and horseback riding to a variety of crafts facilities. All of the activities offered by Leisure World are free to residents except golf and horseback riding. Health facilities are available but on a fee-for-service basis.

The success of Leisure World in Laguna Beach is evidenced by the fact that the houses are sold by lottery drawn from the extensive waiting list.

Despite potentially large purchase costs and monthly maintenance fees, retirement communities appear to be growing in popularity, particularly because they offer security, recreation, good housing, and social opportunities with neighbors of a similar age. As a resident of Youngtown put it, "We adults love our children and our grandchildren. ... However, we wish the freedom to live in a community of our choosing, where children are only visitors. At Sun Lakes, we have chosen our lifestyle and are enjoying it" (Anderson & Anderson, 1978). Retirement communities are at the opposite end of the spectrum from congregate housing. It may be hoped that, despite the fits and starts that have characterized housing programs in the United States, we are beginning to see developed a range of housing alternatives that will meet the diverse desires and needs of the elderly.

References

Abshier, G., Davis, Q., Jans, S., & Petranek, C. *Evaluation of the Cape-Smile home repair program.* Evansville: Indiana State University, 1977.

Anderson, W., & Anderson, N. The politics of age exclusion: The adults only movement in Arizona. *Gerontologist,* 1978, *18,* 6–12.

Blonsky, L. The desire of elderly nonresidents to live in a senior citizen apartment building. *Gerontologist,* 1975, *15,* 88–91.

Brody, E., Kleban, M., & Liebowitz, B. Intermediate housing for the elderly. *Gerontologist,* 1975, *15,* 350–356.

Carp, F. Impact of improved housing on morale and life satisfaction. *Gerontologist*, 1975, *15*, 511–515.

Carp, F. Housing and living environments of older people. In R. Binstock & E. Shanas (Eds.), *Handbook of aging and the social sciences*. New York: Van Nostrand Reinhold, 1976. (a)

Carp, F. User evaluation of housing for the elderly. *Gerontologist*, 1976, *16*, 102–111. (b)

Charter Township of Meridian. *Home repair assistance for low income senior citizens*. Okemos, Mich.: Department of Development Control, 1975.

Erikson, R., & Eckert, K. The elderly poor in downtown San Diego hotels. *Gerontologist*, 1977, *17*, 440–446.

Hartman, C., Horovitz, J., & Herman, R. Designing with the elderly. *Gerontologist*, 1976, *16*, 303–311.

Heintz, K. *Retirement communities, for adults only*. New Brunswick, N.J.: Center for Urban Policy Research, Rutgers, 1976.

Heumann, L. Estimating the local need for elderly congregate housing. *Gerontologist*, 1976, *16*, 397–403.

King, G. Bugs, barrels and bush: Home repair in the Virgin Islands. *Aging*, November–December 1976, pp. 8–11.

Lawton, M. P. The relative impact of congregate and traditional housing on elderly tenants. *Gerontologist*, 1976, *16*, 237–242.

Leisure World Brochure. Laguna Hills, Calif. 1977.

Linn, M., & Caffey, E. Foster placement for the older psychiatric patient. *Journal of Gerontology*, 1977, *32*, 340–345.

Newman, E., & Sherman, S. A survey of caretakers in adult foster homes. *Gerontologist*, 1977, *17*, 436–437.

Sherman, S. Patterns of contacts for residents of age-segregated and age-integrated housing. *Journal of Gerontology*, 1975, *30*, 103–107.

Stephens, J. Society of the alone: Freedom, privacy, and utilitarianism as dominant norms in the SRO. *Journal of Gerontology*, 1975, *30*, 230–235.

Struyk, R. *Housing for the elderly: Research needs for informed public policies*. Washington, D.C.: Urban Institute, 1976.

Tucker, S., Combs, M., & Woolrich, A. Independent housing for the elderly: The human element in design. *Gerontologist*, 1975, *15*, 73–76.

U.S. Department of Housing and Urban Development. *Housing in the seventies*. Washington, D.C.: U.S. Government Printing Office, 1973.

U.S. House of Representatives, Select Committee on Aging. *Elderly Housing Overview: HUD's Inaction*. Washington, D.C.: U.S. Government Printing Office, 1976.

U.S. Senate, Special Committee on Aging. *HUD's response to the housing needs of senior citizens*. Washington, D.C.: U.S. Government Printing Office, 1975.

13
In-home Services

The Growth of In-home Services

Unprecedented numbers of individuals are surviving to an advanced age at a time when financial resources that are available in the United States for health and social care are becoming increasingly more limited. The 7.6 million people now 75 or over represent 38% of the total older population (aged 65 and over)—a significant jump from the 33% figure of 1950. The over-75 senior is also six times more likely to use hospital facilities or special residential accommodations than a person aged 65–74 (Brody, 1974).

Health figures indicate that approximately 16% of the elderly are hampered in some major activity (Brody, 1974), while 6% are actually housebound (U.S. Senate, 1972). According to the General Accounting Office report (Comptroller General of the United States, 1977), about 17% of those 65 and over are either greatly or extremely impaired, and about one-third of this group are in long-term care institutions. Almost a third of the impaired elderly live alone, and nearly three-quarters of these individuals will eventually enter long-term care institutions. Impaired elderly who live with families are more likely to remain in the community.

Unfortunately, admission to nursing homes, chronic care hospitals, and other long-term facilities is often utilized as a solution to problems of impairment when all that the older person may need is limited periods of care during the day. Although institutionalization is costly, the existing funding systems encourage this approach rather than any possible alternatives (Robertson et al., 1977).

In-home services are provided to individuals who live in their own home or apartment. The hope is that these services can "through coordinated planning, evaluation and follow-up procedures, provide for medical, nursing, social, and related services to selected persons . . . with a view toward shortening the length of hospital stay, speeding recovery, or preventing inappropriate institutionalization" (U.S. Senate, 1972, p. 25). These services have received a relatively low priority in the United States until the present time. Support for the development of viable home services has been minimal. The funding that has been available has been enmeshed in regulations that define in-home services so narrowly as to make their actual provision negligible in terms of meeting real need (U.S. Senate, 1972).

In-home services to the elderly are fairly evenly divided between health and welfare agencies, a phenomenon that has resulted from the parallel but relatively independent growth of social and health services to the homebound. Welfare agencies were the first to offer in-home services. In the early 1900s, private charitable family agencies provided homemakers to care for children whose mother was sick. During the 1930s, poor and unemployed women were hired as housekeepers for other poor persons who were in need of the service. By 1958, 145 agencies offered homemaker or home health aid services, of which one-half served adults (U.S. Administration on Aging, 1977).

After 1958, the number of agencies providing in-home services grew rapidly, with the percentage of public agencies comprising a larger portion each year until 1967. With the introduction of Medicare and Medicaid in the mid-1960s the emphasis of service shifted from family and child care to serving the elderly. With this shift in recipient population came a shift in the type of care given, from home maintenance to personal care. The care of the sick, elderly person required an emphasis on personal care, and Medicare and Medicaid reimbursed only for the personal care aspects of the in-home work.

By 1973, 1,716 agencies offered in-home homemaker services. Of these, 28% were voluntary agencies; 56% were public agencies (a drop from 1967); and 9% were proprietary agencies. The number of proprietary agencies providing in-home homemaker services rose following the introduction of Medicare and Medicaid.

Health agencies—long established to provide health services in community and institutional settings—started to add home health aid service to their in-home services when reimbursements through Medicaid and Medicare became available. Skilled nursing care had been available through health agencies for some time before the new funding became available. With the availability of new funding, welfare agencies offering homemaker services and health agencies offering home health aid services began offering the same or similar basic services. Both personal and homemaking services are required to enable persons to remain in their own homes. Because of the overlapping of the services—personal and homemaking, by both social and health agencies—HEW developed in 1965 standards which established that a single person, a homemaker–home health aide, could provide both homemaking and personal care services. Unfortunately, some confusion still exists because some funds which pay for the services still retain the separate titles; that is, Medicaid and Medicare reimburse home health aides while Title XX reimburses homemaker services (U.S. Administration on Aging, 1977).

Today, the general shift toward providing services to the elderly has continued, as most in-home services are now given to adults, particularly the elderly. Only 5% of in-home service agencies serve only children, while 14% serve only the elderly. Of the agencies nationally that provide in-home services, 36% are primarily rural; 37% are primarily urban; and 27% cover both urban and rural areas. One-fourth of the agencies have only homemaker–home health aide services, while three-fourths are multiservice. Maintenance organizations, visiting nurse associations, mental health agencies, neighborhood centers, prepaid health plans, and religious organizations are the more common types of agencies providing in-home services (U.S. Administration on Aging, 1977).

Service Patterns

In-home services encompass several levels or types of services. However, the services and levels of services being given should be flexible and readily changed as the client's needs change. Because they are administered in the home of the client, in-home services are an extension of the individual's functioning ability—the ability that allows that person to continue to live in and be a part of the community. Because they are personalized to individual situations, there is a potential need to change the service components as persons respond to the services being given. Thus, coordination of services is an integral element of successful in-home services. A smoothly functioning network of services must be available to ensure that the individual receives exactly what is needed at the time it is needed. Strong links and easy accessibility among the services are essential to ensure cooperation for the benefit of the client. For example, Baltimore recently began a coordination program involving 10 in-home service agencies, whereby, through a central intake system, the client could be matched with the most appropriate services. As service needs change, the central intake system can continue to reassign the appropriate services.

Available in-home services can be grouped into three general categories, based on the level of intensity of service (U.S. Senate, 1972).

1. *Intensive or skilled services.* These services are ordered by a physician and provided under the supervision of a nurse. Skilled care would be given to clients with such problems as cardiac difficulties, bone fractures, open wounds, diabetes, and terminal illnesses involving catheters and tube feedings. The services could require physician visits, regular visits by a nurse and frequent physical and occupational therapy treatments in addition to less technical services such as nutritional services, delivered drugs and medical supplies, home health equipment, transportation, and other diagnostic and therapeutic services which can be safely delivered in the client's home.

The intensive or skilled service level usually involves a complex grouping of services which themselves might not be needed for a long period of time but modified amounts of which would probably be part of client planning for an extended period of time. Coordination is particularly important for this level of in-home services because of the potential for change and probable number of different service components that could be needed.

2. *Personal care or intermediate services.* Those eligible for personal care services are clients who are medically stable but who need assistance with certain activities of daily living, such as bathing, ambulation, prescribed exercises, and medications. These services can be given to persons who are convalescing from acute illnesses or to persons with temporary disabilities related to a chronic illness, or as part of a chronic illness. Personal or intermediate care services can be given independently or in conjunction with skilled care.

3. *Homemaker-chore or basic services.* These services involve light housekeeping, preparation of food, laundry services, and other maintenance activities that help sustain the client at home. In those circumstances where the clients can care for themselves but do not have the capacity to care for their personal environment, these basic services help sustain the home situation for them. Basic or chore services can be given in conjunction with both intermediate and skilled services and usually are given on an ongoing basis.

The key in-home service worker, particularly for both personal and homemaker-chore areas of service, is the homemaker–home health aide. Homemaker–home health aide services comprise the personal and homemaking services needed to enable persons who cannot perform basic tasks for themselves to remain in their own homes. The basic duties performed include cleaning, planning meals, shopping for food, preparing meals, doing the laundry, changing bed linens, bathing, giving bed baths, shampooing hair, helping the persons move from the bed to a chair, checking the pulse rate, helping perform simple exercises, assisting with medications, teaching new skills, and providing emotional support. The homemaker–home health aide can perform primarily personal care services, homemaking services, or both, as the training usually involves skill development in both areas. The combining of these positions in recent years has allowed greater flexibility to respond to the specific personal and homemaking needs of the client through a single person (U.S. Administration on Aging, 1977).

Heavy house cleaning and simple home maintenance, such as painting and simple carpentry repairs, are usually performed by a person specifically employed for that purpose and are not included in the homemaker–home health aide functions. Special programs which match high school or college students with the chore needs of older persons have enabled this type of work to be done. Usually, the older person pays a minimum wage for the services, as such services are not covered under most funding programs.

Service Agencies

In-home services are provided by a variety of agencies which are usually based in the community and defined by the source of the funding and the service specialty:

> "An agency eligible to receive Medicare and Medicaid funds is a home health agency, a public or private agency which in addition to requirements for sound administration, adequate records, professional supervision, assessment and review, has as its primary function the provision of skilled nursing service and at least one additional therapeutic service" (U.S. Senate, 1972, p. 21).

Thus the agency is defined by the type of service that it provides.

Home health agencies can be both hospital and community based, public, private nonprofit, or proprietary:

• *Home care units of community hospitals.* These units have emerged as a part of the hospital program, primarily as a method of discharging patients as soon as appropriate. As a hospital affiliate, the patient can retain the same doctor and can move in and out of the hospital as needed for ongoing care. Hospital-based programs are particularly effective for terminally ill patients who can spend some time at home but who need a close affiliation with emergency health services. These home care units are staffed primarily with public health nurses and have on call the medical units from the hospital itself. These units provide primarily skilled-care services.

• *Departments of social services.* Local departments of social services usually provide intermediate- and basic-level in-home services under their adult services units. Because their background is a welfare agency, these homemakers are more likely to be involved with household activities and to a lesser extent with personal care services.

• *Private nonprofit community agencies.* Included in this group are such agencies as Associated Catholic Charities, Jewish Family and Children's Services, Family and Children's Services, and Visiting Nurse Associations. These types of agencies provide homemaker–home health aides, nurses, and other in-home service workers as part of larger community-related programs. Each agency usually selects which specific service area it will provide, such as personal care services only or nursing services, and incorporates them into the other agency services being given.

• *Community health centers.* Community health centers can provide some in-home services as part of their community health services program. The in-home services are usually tied to those clients who are participating in the health center as an extension of the services given.

• *Proprietary agencies.* Proprietary agencies, such as Upjohn, provide in-home services to the homebound on a fee-for-service basis. The services are usually at the skilled level of care and provided for short periods of time.

Funding

The most difficult problem in the delivery of in-home services is that of funding. Because of current funding restrictions, the demand for services far exceeds the supply. Further, the demand is primarily for those types of services that are not readily reimbursable through the available funding sources. The community and institutional agencies which provide the services are available and prepared to deliver the services, if the repayment mechanism were available for reimbursement. The greatest unmet need for in-home services is for those with long-term disabilities and for the chronically ill whose conditions are not likely to improve quickly. There are approximately 1.5 million adults that require service intervention beyond that which is now available (U.S. Senate, 1972).

It is ironic that, in most situations, the cost of home health services is less than the potential alternatives for the eligible clients. A Senate Special Committee on Aging report (1972) showed that almost one-half of the patients admitted to home health services would have required hospitalization if the services had not been available. Early discharge programs to home care services in Denver and Philadelphia showed a reduction of 19.2 and 12.9 days, respectively, in average hospital days per patient.

There are five basic ways for payment of in-home services. The first—client fees—is used by most agencies that provide in-home services. In 1977, 27% of all agencies had one fixed fee for all clients; 41% had a sliding fee scale; and 32% charged no fee at all. Of the no-fee agencies, 92% were public, most likely receiving their support from Title XX funds. Voluntary agencies were the most likely to have a sliding-scale fee, while 85% of all proprietary agencies charged a fixed fee (U.S. Administration on Aging, 1977). The voluntary agencies are able to offer sliding-scale fee schedules because they are usually supported in part through contributions from individuals, religious groups, community groups, disease-related groups, or United Way fund-raising organizations.

The second payment method—Medicare—is used by agencies which provide health-related services in situations when the client and the service meet Medicare eligibility requirements. In order to be eligible for Medicare reimbursement, the service must be given by a home health agency which has, as its primary function, the provision of skilled nursing service and at least one additional therapeutic service. The services that are reimbursable focus upon acute or short-term illnesses, not on chronic or custodial ones. In addition, there are varying interpretations as to what is appropriate for reimbursement, interpretations that might be applied after the service has been given. Because of the potential unpredictability of Medicare reimbursements, agencies are often reluctant to give Medicare-reimbursed services other than those specifically defined as eligible services. This makes it difficult for clients to receive appropriate services for their situations.

Actual services provided under Medicare are skill oriented and do not include activities of daily living, which are mostly personal and home maintenance services. Appropriate services include part-time or intermittent nursing care (under the supervision of a registered nurse); physical, occupational, and speech therapy; medical social services (under the supervision of a physician); medical supplies; and the part-time services of a home health aide. All these services are provided on a visiting basis to those confined to their residences and under the care of a physician (Comptroller General of the United States, 1977).

In order to be eligible under Part A of Medicare, individuals must have been in the hospital for at least 3 consecutive days prior to entry into home care. The care to be provided must be for an illness for which the person received treatment while in the hospital and must be provided within the year following hospitalization. Coverage is limited to 100 home care visits per year after the beginning of one illness and before the beginning of another. Under Part B, a person may qualify for 100 home care visits in 1 year without prior hospitalization.

Medicare home health care outlays grew from $199 million in 1975 to $563 million in 1978, or $100 million more than the Medicare outlays for skilled nursing facilities (Comptroller General of the United States, 1977). Despite the spiraling growth in the outlay of Medicare services, there is increasing pressure to expand the type of eligible services under this program. For example, the General Accounting Office report to the Congress in December 1977 stated that —by limiting the requirement that beneficiaries be confined to their homes and be in need of skilled care—expanding the number of eligible home visits, eliminating the prior hospitalization requirement under Part A, and adding homemaker-chore services would not be as costly as expected. The expansion of in-home services would decrease the percentage of those entering institutions. Most people do not exhaust their 100 visit-limit, and by dropping the prior hospital requirement, people would be discouraged from entering the hospital needlessly. Even in the face of the pressure to expand the services covered by the Medicare program, fiscal constraints have forced Congress to continue the narrow definitions of in-home services that are eligible for reimbursements.

Medicaid is the third payment method and is used by agencies which provide health-related services in situations when the client and the service meet Medicaid eligibility requirements. Unlike Medicare, in which every person age 65 and over is potentially eligible for the benefits, Medicaid is available only to those who meet strict income requirements. Although the actual income limit is determined within each state because Medicaid is partially financed by the states, the usual income limit is set to coincide with the SSI limit, plus whatever state aid for income is being given (a total of about $200 a month for a single person).

Home health care became a required service under Medicaid in 1970 and could be given by the same agencies that are eligible for Medicare. Although the services provided under Medicaid vary among the states, basically Medicaid covers nursing services, home health aide services, and medical supplies and equipment. Medicaid benefits do not require that skilled nursing care or therapy be given. The potentially eligible persons do not need prior hospitalization nor is there a limit on the number of visits.

During FY 1977, total state home health care Medicaid expenditures were $154 million; the federal share was $87 million for the same period. In contrast, federal and state expenditures for institutionalized care in skilled and intermediate care facilities were $5.8 billion (Comptroller General of the United States, 1977). It is clear that Medicare is more likely to pay for in-home services, while Medicaid is being used primarily to pay for institutional care. This is discussed in more detail in Chapter 15.

A fourth payment source for in-home services is Title XX of the Social Security Act, a program which provides funds for in-home services by both public and private agencies. Local departments of social services are the major recipients of these moneys. Federal Title XX moneys, matched 25% by state or local sources, are given individual agencies for the purpose of providing eligible services to eligible clients. Unlike Medicaid and Medicare, the services given are not reviewed on a service-by-service basis for reimbursement. This and the emphasis on personal care and home services rather than on health services are the basic differences between Title XX programs and those of Medicare and Medicaid. As with Medicaid, however, a person must have a limited income in order to be eligible for the Title XX services. The income limit, although varying from state to state, is usually about the same as for Medicaid.

Home-based services, such as homemaker, home health aide, home management, personal care, consumer education, and financial counseling, can be provided under a Title XX program. These can be ongoing and are not restricted to a limited amount per year.

The services can go to the chronically ill and disabled for an extended period of time. However, the program is limited by the income eligibility of the client and the amount of money available to the public and private agencies for personnel to provide the services. In FY 1976, the federal government provided $284 million for home-based services through Title XX.

The fifth payment source is Title III of the OAA, which provides moneys for in-home services through the local Area Agencies on Aging. These funds are made available to provide

> services designed to assist older individuals in avoiding institutionaliza-
> tion, including preinstitution-evaluation and screening and home
> health services, homemaker services, shopping services, escort services,
> reader services, letter writing services, and other similar services de-
> signed to assist such individuals to continue living independently in a
> home environment. (Older Americans Act as amended in 1978).

The funds can provide for a variety of services by both public and private agencies for both the chronically and acutely ill. The only eligibility requirement is that the recipient be 60 or over. Although there is no income restriction on the services, efforts are made to make most of the services available to low-income elderly. The service limitation under Title III programs is in the financial limits of the allocations themselves. Because eligible services are broadly defined under this act, efforts are made to use these funds and services for those people who are ineligible for services under the other funding programs—primarily those who are just over the scale for Title XX and those with chronic illnesses.

Variations in Services

Because of the variety of funding sources and varying eligibility standards, programs around the country have attempted to combine various sources of money with other local resources in order to be able to provide as broad a base of service as possible.

As mentioned earlier, because of the growth of in-home service agencies, the Baltimore City Commission on Aging decided to develop a coordinated system for the 10 major in-home service programs in order to expeditiously link clients to in-home service providers. The central coordinating unit serves as the single point of entry for clients and as a clearinghouse to minimize duplication of services. Before the services begin, an in-home assessment is made to assure that the services being provided are appropriate to the situation. Periodically, the client situation is reviewed to make sure that changing needs are being translated into appropriate services. The central intake program is funded through Title III, while the actual services are funded through Medicare, Medicaid, Title XX, and Title XXI—depending on the agency giving the service.

In New York City, a home maintenance program for the chronically hard-to-reach elderly was developed through a local hospital (Brickner et al., 1976). Physicians, nurses, and social workers voluntarily participated on hospital-paid time. The hospital, therefore, actually supported the professional component of the work at a level of $50,000 a year. Funds for the salaries of nonprofessional staff members came through grants from private philanthropic agencies. The program estimated that it saved $150,000 in hospital costs and $340,000 in nursing home costs during the first year of operation. Again, this program was geared to those hard-to-reach clients who had no other mechanism for in-home service eligibility.

In Cleveland, the Home Aide Extension Program involved the consolidation of professional and paraprofessional staff from three agencies in order to make home aide services immediately available to the elderly within the individual agencies who could not receive services because of funding problems (Noelker & Harel, 1978). The people most like to be excluded from other pay situations were the posthospitalized elderly whose home aide care needs did not fit the Medicare eligibility standards or who had exhausted their benefits, and those who were qualified for services from the county welfare department but did not receive them because of shortages of service providers and resources under Title XX.

In order to provide the needed services, the third agency, the Benjamin Rose Institute, using additional operating funds allocated for this purpose, supplied 175 hours per week of home aide service time to the other two agencies that could not provide services to this target group. The other two agencies, however, maintained case management responsibilities and supervised the services being given. The resources from the third agency were used to augment the services already in place through the two other agencies. The system maximized available resources by not setting up a third administrative structure.

A review of the cases after 1 year of operation showed that 53% continued to receive services; 13% entered institutions; 15% had died; and 19% were terminated for other reasons. All of the elderly in this special program had been excluded from existing programs and could not have afforded to purchase the services. A high percentage of these elderly would have been considered as candidates for institutionalization.

Related Services

There has been a growth in the number and types of formal support systems for the homebound that complement in-home services or even substitute for these services when regular contact and visiting are all that are needed. Two such programs, reassurance and friendly visiting, are most frequently available, primarily as adjunct programs within senior centers or agencies providing other programs and services to the elderly.

Reassurance Services

As the number of elderly maintaining independent residence in the community continues to increase, a method for ensuring their daily well-being becomes vital. In housing specifically designed for seniors, systems that require turning off a hall light outside the apartment each morning can be used to indicate that the resident has not suffered any mishap during the previous day.

For individuals living in other types of residences, telephone reassurance has been stressed as a means of maintaining daily contact with older individuals. The telephone reassurance systems can be traced to the efforts of Grace McClure during the 1960s. After attempting to contact an elderly friend for 8 successive days, Mrs. McClure made a personal check of the friend's apartment and found her on the floor after having suffered a stroke. Mrs. McClure's subsequent efforts in Michigan resulted in a telephone reassurance service and a replication of this type of service in many parts of the country.

In the typical telephone reassurance service, the individual is called twice a day. If there is no answer, a policeman with a house key is dispatched to make a personal check. The individual must also inform the police when they are leaving their home in order to ensure that calls are not made when the house is vacant. In New York City, a private service provides two calls a day and includes information about television listings, news, and weather (Conait, 1969).

Among publicly funded services a variety of volunteers have been used to do the telephoning, including residents of a nursing home in Nassau County, New York, and multiple sclerosis patients in other programs in New York State. In rural areas, mail carriers are asked to alert a special office if they notice mail accumulating in an older person's mailbox (National Institute of Senior Centers, 1978).

One possible side effect of these services is the friendships that can form between volunteer callers and clients. This potential for friendships is being built into some services that utilize a buddy system. This approach depends on a team of approximately 10 people who utilize a daily round robin of calling. If the chain is broken on any day, the individual unable to make contact with the next person reports the problem to a central office, and a personal visit is made to the home (Match, 1972).

If well-run, these reassurance services are important links for the aging. More affluent elderly will soon be able to enroll in a service that enables them to hook their home into a central office. Failure to punch a code on a specially designed machine will result in a checkup visit to the home. The key link in the machine-based or telephone-based reassurance service is the reliability of the staff responsible for checking on the elderly client who fails to utilize the designated code or answer the phone. Because of this problem, few services are relying on relatives because of their possible unavailability at crucial times.

Visiting Services

Although they are now available in greater numbers, many cities have operated friendly visiting services for a long period of time. The visitors service in Chicago was begun in 1947. The friendly visitors services utilize volunteers to visit elderly individuals who are homebound. Visitors may chat with the older persons, read to them, help them with correspondence, or play chess and board games.

While they are most often oriented to community-based elderly, a friendly visitor service was begun in Maryland in 1977 to provide companionship for nursing home residents who did not receive regular visits by family and friends. One friendly visiting service utilized members of a senior citizens club as visitors, and programs around the country rely on volunteers of all ages to reach elderly who might otherwise be isolated from social contacts.

The Future

The greatest shortcoming of many in-home services for the elderly is that of eligibility. Narrow definitions of eligibility exclude many seniors whose need for these services is great. Without a service system that bypasses the normal reimbursement sources, these elderly will remain ineligible for any in-home services. It is apparent that both eligibility requirements and funds allocated for in-home services need to be changed and expanded to include more of the high-risk elderly, particularly those with chronic disabilities or health problems. Otherwise these seniors will be pushed in the direction of institutionalization, in many areas still the only alternative to in-home services. Unfortunately the issues of expanding the services are directly tied to the available funding at both federal and state levels. Significant changes will not be made in eligibility requirements until legislatures can be shown that more extensive in-home services can result in lower overall health care costs. In the meantime, agencies that provide in-home services will need to look to the informal support system—family, neighborhood, and churches—for assistance in providing in-home care.

References

Brickner, P., Janeski, J., Rich, G., Duque, T., Starita, L., LaRocco, R., Flannery, T., & Werlin, S. Home maintenance for the homebound aged. *Gerontologist,* 1976, *16,* 25–29.

Brody, S. Long-term care in the community. In E. Brody (Ed.), *A social work guide for long-term care facilities.* Rockville, Md.: National Institute of Mental Health, 1974.

Comptroller General of the United States. *Home health: The need for a national policy to better provide for the elderly.* Washington, D.C.: U.S. Government Printing Office, 1977.

Conait, M. *Guidelines for telephone reassurance services.* Ann Arbor, Mich.: University of Michigan Institute of Gerontology, 1969.

Match, S. *Establishing telephone reassurance services.* Washington, D.C.: National Council on the Aging, 1972.

National Institute of Senior Centers. Senior center programming: Expanding services to the vulnerable elderly. *Senior Center Report,* 1978, *1*(3), 4–5.

Noelker, L., & Harel, Z. Aged excluded from home health care. *Gerontologist,* 1978, *18,* 37–41.

Robertson, D., Griffiths, R., & Cosin, L. A community based continuing care program for the elderly disabled: An evaluation of planned intermittent hospital readmission. *Journal of Gerontology,* 1977, *32*, 334–339.

U.S. Administration on Aging. *Human resources issues in the field of aging: Homemaker–home health aide services.* Washington, D.C.: U.S. Government Printing Office, 1977.

U.S. Senate, Special Committee on Aging. *Home health services in the United States.* Washington, D.C.: U.S. Government Printing Office, 1972.

14
Adult Daycare

The Roots of Daycare

Dependency and Aging

It is unfortunate that daycare services for the elderly often seem to resemble similar programs for children. While the programs may be similar in some aspects, services for the aged should not be based on viewing the elderly as childlike. As one advocate for adult daycare urges:

> We object to the comparison to child care because it is inaccurate. We are not a place where people are left in safety as children are left, until someone is ready to "pick them up" again. Our services have an objective, and those who are consumers are not children. They are adults who may be limited for shorter or longer periods of time in their capacities for total self-care—but they are participants in their own care programs with everything that the term implies. (Lupu, cited in Trager, 1976, p. 6)

The common thread running through services for children and the elderly is that of dependency. Lupu argues, however, that dependency among the elderly and children stems from different sources. The elderly do not lack knowledge of "right from wrong" and have attained the skills necessary to conduct their everyday life. Dependency in the elderly usually stems from physical and mental impairments that make it difficult for them to continue to successfully accomplish routine tasks. These tasks may include what are labeled the "activities of daily living" such as dressing, bathing, using the bathroom, cooking, and self-feeding. The task of the daycare center is to assist the individual in functioning as independently as possible given his or her physical and mental status.

Family Care for the Elderly

The elderly individual suffering from chronic illnesses may by necessity place much of the burden of financial and social support on children and other relatives. While some elderly may be able to bear the financial costs of such programs as daycare, the vast majority of the present generation of elderly have limited financial resources. These resources need to be supplemented by assistance from their families. Over 6 million older individuals receive some assistance from their families. For many families this assistance imposes a heavy burden, not totally remedied by contributions from Medicare, Medicaid, and other supplemental income programs.

Families shouldering the major costs for services for older relatives may be estimating their resources on the assumption that both spouses are working. Care for an elderly person that requires a family member to give up employment may be viewed as costly not only in terms of reduced income but in terms of career losses. Given the recent emphasis on careers for women, fewer women are likely to accept responsibility for caring for an older family member as a full-time task. Paying family members for the services they contribute to their older relatives would help to alleviate the extra financial problems encountered when the family attempts to provide the assistance needed by the older person.

Financial compensation would not, however, adequately deal with all of the social and psychological issues involved. There are a variety of personal issues that face the relatives of older individuals requiring extensive assistance. This includes being able to schedule their time so as to have opportunities to engage in recreation, take vacations, or take care of their own children. When an elderly parent lives with their children, the appropriate family role for the older person often becomes a bone of contention. The inability to resolve these issues frequently leads to unnecessary institutionalization.

One extreme case of inappropriate institutionalization involved an elderly couple who had been waiting for the husband to retire so that they could travel extensively. Once this long-awaited retirement occurred they found that the obstacle to their travel was not a lack of funds but rather their need to care for the wife's 90-year-old mother, who required a family member to be on hand and available for a variety of basic and social activities. The mother thus fit into the large category of elderly people who could live in the community with some supports. Faced with this problem, the couple saw no alternative to placing the mother in a nursing home. While this move violates the growing emphasis on the "least restrictive alternative," it was the only clear option that the children viewed as meeting their legitimate needs.

History of Daycare

Daycare is one possible response to the need for families to have a respite from caring for an impaired older person on a daily basis as well as providing them with some free time. Kaplan (1976) has summarized the basic assumptions about daycare as a belief in (1) "the instrinsic worth of living within one's community," (2) the merit in keeping the family together, (3) the beneficial nature of allowing a person to continue independent living, and (4) independent living as beneficial in the broader concept of social well-being for older persons and their families.

Daycare for adults originated in Britain during the 1940s, when outpatient hospital centers for psychiatric patients were set up. These centers, located in psychiatric hospitals, were designed to decrease the numbers of individuals who would require admittance to inpatient units. By the late 1950s, the British had extended daycare programs to geriatric patients; by 1969, 90 programs were already in operation.

In 1947, the first geriatric day hospital in the United States opened under the auspices of the Menninger Clinic, and in 1949, a similar operation was begun at Yale (McCuan, 1973). Bolstered by the increased interest and funding for aging programs in the 1970s, daycare programs have now begun in most states. Approximately 300 daycare centers are now in operation in this country.

Daycare Clients

Eligibility

Because of this short history, a variety of programs with varied focuses now fall under the daycare rubric. Federal guidelines have not yet been set up to determine eligibility for federally funded daycare programs. In 1974, Congress authorized demonstration daycare programs. In its guidelines for these demonstration programs, HEW defined daycare as a program "provided under health leadership in an ambulatory care setting for adults who do not require 24-hour institutional care and yet, due to physical and/or mental impairment, are not capable of full-time independent living" (U.S. Health Resources Administration, 1974, p. 1).

An individual with physical and mental impairment is further defined under these guidelines as a "chronically ill or disabled adult whose illness or disability does not require 24 hour inpatient care but which in the absence of day care service may precipitate admission to or prolonged stay in a hospital, nursing home or other long-term facility" (U.S. Health Resources Administration, 1974, p. 1). It is obvious that the major projected daycare population is an at-risk group whose involvement in daycare programs may provide enough support to enable them to remain out of long-term care institutions. Among existing programs, daycare is not often used for individuals discharged from nursing homes.

Present Users

In examining a number of daycare programs, Weissert (1975) commented on the participants: "Most are aged who need continuing support and will probably leave the adult day care program only to go into a nursing home or at death" (p. 14). The participants in Weissert's sample had between two and five diagnosed medical conditions. The same configuration of conditions was noted by Kaplan (1976) examining a daycare program in Ohio. Kaplan found that 75% of the participants had many of the same symptoms usually found among nursing home patients. As Gurian (1976) argues, daycare clients can thus potentially come from three major groups: (1) individuals enrolled in day hospital programs in mental hospitals which provide mental health treatment during the day, (2) nursing home patients, or (3) elderly living in their own homes or with their families. Interestingly, although the vast majority of elderly live independently, Weissert (1975) found that, on average, only 31% of the clients in the 10 programs studied by his researchers lived alone. In 1978, Mahoney found that only 26% of daycare clients in three Connecticut centers lived alone. The need for daycare thus may first be perceived by those who become caretakers as the elderly individual's physical or mental condition deteriorates. Referrals to daycare centers may be coming either from the families of elderly persons or from agencies or service providers who come into contact with the families and are aware of the centers rather than being initiated by the elderly themselves. In contrast, the literature on nursing homes indicates that the majority of long-term residents have previously lived alone. It is therefore possible that daycare clients differ from nursing home residents in the degree to which economic, social, and psychological support is being provided by family members.

As the possibility of federal reimbursements increases, the definition of eligible daycare clients should become clarified. Although a number of models have been proposed (Robins, 1976), daycare programs will probably be increasingly categorized as maintenance rather than rehabilitative services. If individuals come into daycare programs from nursing homes, they will be those elderly whose conditions have improved and who are found not to be in need of the 24-hour nursing services offered by these homes. The daycare centers will be expected to provide a gamut of services necessary to maintain the participants near their present level of functioning.

Evaluating Benefit to Clients

The ambiguities that now exist in definitions of daycare create an initial difficulty in evaluating the effectiveness of these programs. If daycare centers are maintenance oriented, it still may be difficult to evaluate the centers that enroll large numbers of seriously impaired individuals. For these individuals it is possible that there will be deterioration, admission to nursing homes, or death despite the extensive care a center may provide. A broken hip, myocardial infarction, or organic brain syndrome may occur at any point in the impaired elderly person's day, and these occurrences may be unaffected by attendance at a daycare center. While it is possible that the day services may delay the onset of these conditions or deterioration in existing conditions, the evaluation of these effects is complex. Daycare centers that are determined to demonstrate complete effectiveness at "maintaining" the elderly may thus attempt to select clients they know to be emotionally, intellectually, and physically stable.

Eligibility for daycare services as well as evaluation of the center's ability to meet its stated goals will be determined to a great deal by the range of services offered by the individual center. Thus the clients served and the criteria used for evaluation will differ between a center that is rehabilitation oriented and has multiple medical services, a maintenance-oriented center with many different services not all offered on site, and a center that is socially oriented and has a minimum of medical services.

It was in acknowledgement of this wide range of daycare programs that the following definition was accepted in 1979 as a beginning statement of the newly formed National Institute of Adult Daycare, which is a program of the National Council on the Aging (NCOA): Adult daycare is a generic term for a variety of programs, each providing a gamut of services. These services range from social and health related to the provision of active rehabilitation and physical and mental health care. Various terminology is applied: daycare, day treatment, day health services, psychiatric day treatment, therapeutic center, day hospital. It is coordinated with, and relates to, other agencies and services such as senior centers, in-home services, and institutional and hospital care. It is an innovative way to organize and blend the more traditional health and social services for disabled older persons (National Institute of Adult Daycare, 1979).

Daycare Center Services

Program Outlines

The range of services that daycare centers currently provide to maintain impaired clients at their optimal level of functioning is clear: screening for physical conditions; medical care (usually by arrangement with an outside physician); nursing care; occupational, physical, and recreational therapy; social work; transportation; meals; personal care (e.g., assistance in going to the toilet); educational programs; crafts; counseling. In contrast to senior centers, daycare services are not available on a drop-in basis. Clients are scheduled, usually on a minimal 2-day per week basis, but often on a full 5-day basis. While many clients are ambulatory, daycare centers endeavor to provide transportation and appropriately designed space to serve individuals confined to wheelchairs.

Most daycare centers are small, typically serving 15–25 clients a day. This size helps to prevent the development of an institutional atmosphere. Centers are located in settings ranging from schools, apartments, and churches to hospitals and nursing homes. Clients usually arrive at the center between 9 and 10 a.m and may have coffee before becoming involved in an individual or group project. A period of exercise matching the client's capability may be held before lunch, which is followed by a rest period and another group or individual project. The projects range from crafts and reading to dances and discussions. At any point in the day, appropriate counseling, nursing care, and medical-social services may be provided. Activities are conducted in accordance with the individual plan of care that the center develops for each client upon his or her acceptance into the program. Clients are transported back to their residences in the late afternoon (3–4 p.m). This schedule would not apply to centers that run an extended-hours program in the morning and afternoon. As would be expected, the staff-client ratio necessary to provide the individualized attention described here is low, averaging around 1:5 or 1:7 at most centers. In order to maintain the client's relationship with the community, many centers make extensive use of volunteers and emphasize frequent outings, including picnics, shopping, and trips.

Program Emphasis

The major disagreement among daycare advocates has revolved around the relative emphasis on particular services. This lack of consensus can be seen in the ambiguous guidelines for the 1974 HEW demonstration programs:

> The essential elements of daycare programs are directed towards meeting the health maintenance and restorative needs of participants. However, there are socialization elements which by overcoming the isolation often associated with illness in the aged and disabled are considered vital for the purpose of fostering and maintaining the maximum possibile state of health and well-being. (U.S. Health Resources Administration, 1974)

The relegation of "socialization" programs to the second sentence of these guidelines reflects uncertainty as to the importance of these elements in the daycare program. Padula (1972) has attempted to distinguish between "day hospital" programs, which are health related and service the disabled or ill elderly, and "daycare," as a social program for "frail, moderately handicapped or slightly confused older persons" (p. 8). A report by the NCOA (National Institute of Senior Centers, 1978) on adult daycare attempts to distinguish between daycare, in-home services, and senior centers: "Daycare differs from in-home services in that the therapeutic care is given in a group setting, which reduces loneliness and social isolation of the impaired older person and facilitates the delivery of multiple services." In 1972, Padula developed a diagrammatic portrayal of the relationships of the social components of daycare to health components (Figure 14.1). As Figure 14.1 indicates, daycare is predominantly a social program. Daycare programs for the elderly, however,

Figure 14.1. Model for Day Care

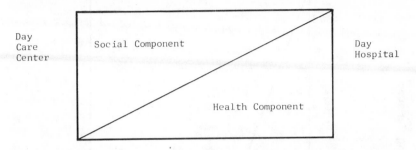

are changing rapidly. Since Padula's first effort in 1972, some major changes have taken place. Daycare centers now more closely approximate the model shown in Figure 14.2, in which the relationship of social to health services for a variety of aging services is indicated. As can be seen from the figure, daycare centers in this model provide almost equivalent amounts of social and health services, in contrast to social clubs, which are 90% social in nature, and hospitals, which are 90% health oriented. The model also indicates the variety among daycare centers, with some giving strong emphasis to social components and others to health services.

Until federal or state guidelines clearly specify the outlines of daycare services, the components emphasized will partially depend on the affiliation or sponsorships of the centers. Daycare centers sponsored by Area Agencies on Aging may have a greater degree of emphasis on social rather than health components, depending for their health services on linkages with medical and nursing schools. Programs such as the Mosholu-Montefiore program in New York place a heavy emphasis on health components because of their strong relationship to major hospital facilities and, in the case of this particular program, because it uses space provided by the hospital. The actual ratio of health to social services depends on the requirements of funding sources. Trager (1976) has succinctly summed up the problems that may result from viewing social and health components as distinct and separate daycare entities:

> The development of centers which set policies and objectives in the context of treatment and physical restoration may tend to exclude those in need of some, but not all of these services. For those who are considered candidates for supervision and socialization, there may be a ten-

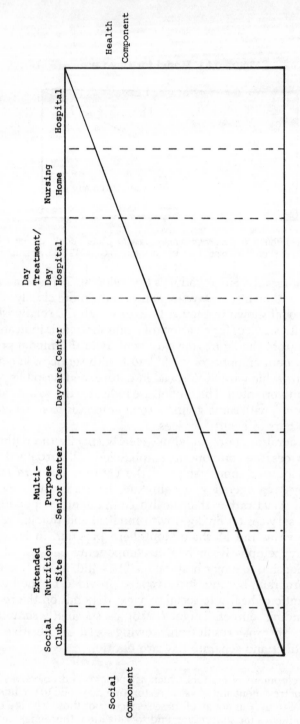

Figure 14.2. Relationship of Social to Health Components in Aging Services

dency to ignore essential health related services. Facilities which are treatment oriented may also tend to take on institutional characteristics and to make a "patient" of the participant—an aspect of institutional care which often is counterproductive in terms of the objectives of treatment. On the other hand, major emphasis on a supervision-socialization policy excludes consideration of restoration and rehabilitation possibilities which may appear to be relatively limited but are of great importance to the participant and such facilities might take on the characteristics of current institutions which are "holding facilities" and ignore essential health needs. (p. 16)

At present the best resolution of this problem may be a variety of community-based centers which offer a mix of services as needed by the potential client population of the area.

Funding

As the discussion of funding sources in Chapter 2 indicates, services for the aging are now being kept afloat through funds obtained from a number of sources. This is exemplified by daycare, where a variety of federal, local, and private funds are used. Because daycare centers do not qualify for Medicare benefits, center directors have had to be creative in their efforts to obtain year-to-year funds. A few centers were funded under demonstration projects in 1972, but most centers now in operation still face a continuous struggle for support. Foundations, churches, and voluntary organizations, as well as local funds of various kinds, provide support for daycare centers. On the federal level, the OAA, plus Model Cities and revenue sharing, have all been called upon for daycare center funds.

In 1976, the Medical Services Administration issued guidelines designed to assist states in preparing regulations for reimbursable daycare centers under Title XIX of the Social Security Act (Medicaid). While the target population of these centers might not differ from the centers already described, the medical service requirement might be more extensive. Programs conducted by a hospital or programs that are recognized as "clinics under state laws" are eligible for Medicaid reimbursements. These reimbursements are authorized under the outpatient hospital provisions of Title XIX.

Under the guidelines, the reimbursable medical services that daycare centers might offer include:

1. Medical services supervised by a physician
2. Nursing services rendered by a professional nursing staff
3. Diagnostic services in addition to initial screening

4. Rehabilitation services including physical therapy, speech therapy, occupational therapy, and inhalation therapy
5. Pharmaceutical services
6. Podiatric services
7. Optometric services
8. Self-care services oriented toward the activities of daily living
9. Dental services
10. Social work services
11. Recreation therapy
12. Dietary services
13. Transportation services

Although existing centers may provide many of these services, provision of all of them is probably beyond the resources of many. The guidelines specify that the packages of services available for any individual must be a combination of some or all of the elements listed. All of the services might be available in a center, but it is expected that the most complex medical services would be found in day hospital settings because of the close hospital-staff linkages. In all centers, the guidelines stress screening of clients by a multidisciplinary team and the development of an individualized treatment plan.

Based on the guidelines, each state has the responsibility to establish and approve a required package of services for reimbursable daycare and day hospital programs. Discussions about the degree of medical supports that will be required by the state to qualify a center for reimbursement are already becoming intense.

Under Title XX, many daycare centers have been funded without the extensive medical services that may be required under Title XIX. Unfortunately, Title XX funds are limited and based on annual population figures for each state. Title XX funds are also allocated on the basis of public hearings and plans developed on a statewide level. Some states have not included day services for the elderly in their plans, while others have viewed Title XX support as only seed money for programs. Programs that have been instituted on the basis of Title XX allocations have now found that these funds are not always available to meet increasing inflationary costs or even that states are cutting back individual program funding in order to distribute small amounts of money to a larger number of centers. In this way the states hope to encourage a larger number of centers, but individual centers have had to scramble to meet the deficits imposed by the cuts in their Title XX funding.

Given these complexities, it is clear at this point that funding for daycare centers remains a continuous headache for their organizers and for families who use their services. Until the debates over the daycare model are ended and the differences about cost and benefits of the services are resolved, it is likely that funding issues will remain a paramount problem.

Cost Effectiveness and Benefits

Even before their social and psychological benefits have been determined, daycare centers have had to face the question of their costliness. Unfortunately, the cost-effectiveness studies fail to provide enough clarity to allow for a final determination of the financial questions. Because of variations in services, costs may differ widely among centers, with health-related services accounting for high expenditures (Weissert et al., 1979). One study cites program costs ranging from $11 to $33 per day for a client. Weiler et al. (1976) calculate $12.99 as the per diem cost per person at a daycare center in Kentucky. Of this $13.00, $4.22 is accounted for by meals, $3.62 by health services, $2.62 by recreation, and $2.53 for transportation. Higher and lower figures have been reported. In some instances, costs borne by programs other than daycare centers are not included in these tallies. Space rental paid by other agencies is a major example.

An additional cost factor that needs to be examined is the ability of daycare programs to provide the totality of services required by an elderly individual. In Connecticut, Mahoney (1978) found that 47% of the clients in three daycare centers also received assistance from other agencies. Clients who were receiving only daycare services were more likely to be living with their families and have fewer functional impairments.

A final problem in cost computations for daycare is that much of the presently available data is based on studies in centers soon after they had opened, when cost may have been higher than, or at least different from, what they would have been at a later point. It thus remains unclear whether a daycare center is more cost effective than a nursing home.

Holmes and Hudson (1975) have argued, however, that cost effectiveness is not the appropriate question to be asked about the daycare approach. Rather, they propose a cost-benefit formula in which the total benefits of participation in the daycare program for the client, family, and community might be explored. These benefits can be related to Kaplan's (1976) basic assumptions about daycare. Acceptance of these assumptions leads to a variety of questions which can be asked about daycare services:

1. Do daycare centers enable impaired elderly to maintain residence in the community?

2. Do daycare services improve or maintain their participants' level of physical or emotional functioning?

3. Do the centers increase the participants' independence on basic activities of daily living?

4. Do daycare services prevent or postpone institutionalization of participants?

5. Do daycare services improve or maintain the participant's interpersonal relationships with family and friends?

6. Do daycare services assist individual participants in reestablishing their desired life-style or increase their life satisfaction?

7. Do daycare services offer supports for family members involved in the care of an elderly individual?

These questions were examined by Weiler et al. (1976) in a controlled study of a daycare center. Positive answers were found to a number of these questions. Most important, the researchers noted that the daycare participants were functioning at a lower level than the community control group when first examined in November but at a higher level than the control group 5 months later. A similar result was obtained by Weissert et al. in a controlled study (1979).

While their studies provide some important evidence, replications with a larger number of centers over a longer time period are needed. As these studies become available, the ability of daycare to meet the psychosocial and physical needs of its client population will become clearer.

References

Gurian, B. Mental health model of day care. In E. Pfeiffer (Ed.), *Day care for older adults.* Durham, N.C.: Duke University Center for the Study of Aging and Human Development, 1976.

Holmes, D., & Hudson, E. *Evaluation report of the Mosholu-Montefiore day care center for the elderly in the northwest Bronx.* New York: Community Research Applications, 1975.

Kaplan, J. Goals of day care. In E. Pfeiffer (Ed.), *Day care for older adults.* Durham, N.C.: Duke University Center for the Study of Aging and Human Development, 1976.

Mahoney, K. *Outside the day care center: Additional support for the frail elderly.* Hartford: Connecticut Department of Aging, 1978.

McCuan, E. R. *An evaluation of a geriatric day care center as a parallel service to institutional care.* Baltimore: Levindale Geriatric Research Center, 1973.

National Institute of Adult Daycare. *Operating procedures.* Washington, D.C.: National Council on the Aging, 1979.

National Institute of Senior Centers. Adult day care: An overview. *Senior center report,* 1978, *1*(7), 3–8.

Padula, H. *Developing day care for older people.* Washington, D.C.: National Council on the Aging, 1972.

Robins, E. Models of day care. In E. Pfeiffer (Ed.), *Day care for older adults.* Durham, N.C.: Duke University Center for the Study of Aging, 1976.

Trager, B. *Adult day facilities for treatment, health care and related services.* Washington, D.C.: U.S. Government Printing Office, 1976.

U.S. Health Resources Administration, Division of Long-Term Care. *Guidelines and definitions for day care centers under P.L. 92-603.* Washington, D.C.: U.S. Printing Office, 1974.

Weiler, P., Kim, P., & Pickard, L. Health care for elderly Americans: Evaluation of an adult day health care model. *Medical Care,* 1976, *14*(8), 700–708.

Weissert, W. *Adult day care in the U.S.: Final report.* Washington, D.C.: Trans Century Corporation, 1975.

Weissert, W., Wan, T., & Livieratos, B. *Effects and costs of day care and homemaker services for the chronically ill.* Hyattsville, Md.: National Center for Health Services Research, 1979.

15
Long-term Care Institutions

Nature and History of Long-term Care

Although adult daycare centers and other services can provide long-term care, the term is usually used to refer to "care provided in an institutional setting over an extended period of time" (Cohen, 1974, p. 18). The forms of care provided can range from assistance in dressing, bathing, and ambulating to sophisticated medical life support systems. The uniqueness of long-term care facilities lies in their constraint on individual choice in everyday situations since the person living in these settings must adjust to being removed from "normal" individual or family living patterns. Existing long-term care institutions include chronic care hospitals, private and public nursing homes, homes for the aged, psychiatric hospitals, and Veterans' Administration facilities. All of these facilities provide varied levels of care ranging from extended, skilled, and intermediate care to personal and boarding care. Long-term care facilities are run under a variety of auspices including public, private-nonprofit, or proprietary organizations.

History of Institutional Settings

The history of long-term care institutions began with the almshouses and the public poor houses of colonial America. When a family or individual could no longer care for the pauper, that person became the responsibility of the government. The disabled, aged, widowed, orphaned, feeble-minded and deranged, and victims of disasters were mixed together in almshouses, hospitals, workhouses, orphanages, and prisons. Officials made little distinction between poverty generated by physical disability and economic distress. Boarding out or foster care programs were not uncommon although often harshly administered (Cohen, 1974). Following the Revolutionary War, almshouses became increasingly popular, and in 1834, the Poor Law of England reaffirmed this approach. This philosophy of isolating the aged and infirm from society continued to be the predominant social policy throughout the 19th century.

Residents of almshouses were usually pressed into working for very low wages as a means of earning at least a meager salary. Any financing for the facilities was the responsibility of the towns and counties in which the facilities were located; all efforts at state or federal support were denied for three-quarters of a century. By the late 19th century, other resources were being located for some indigent populations, but the elderly were still relegated to the almshouses. In 1875, a New York State report noted:

> Care has been taken not to diminish the terrors of this last resort of poverty, the almshouse, because it has been deemed better that a few should test the minimum rate of which existence can be preserved than that many should find the almshouse so comfortable a home that they would brave the shame of pauperism to gain admission to it. (cited in Cohen, 1974, p. 14)

In the beginning of the 20th century, the rise of private foundations and philanthropy began to expand the types of institutional care available. In addition, by 1929, the Old Age Assistance Act began to offer an alternative to institutionalization in most states. In the 1930s, new welfare, loan, housing public works, and rent programs, as well as the Social Security Act (SSA), provided a new concept of income support for the aged.

In the early versions of the SSA, there were prohibitions against federal financial participation in the cost of any relief given in any kind of institutional setting. Later this prohibition continued in relation to public facilities because public institutions were considered a state responsibility (Cohen, 1974). The intent of the legislation was to encourage the elderly to live at home or with foster families. However, the actual effect was the displacement of people from public facilities to private facilities—particularly to boarding homes. As these facilities began to add nurses to their staffs, the name *nursing home* emerged (Moss & Halmandaris, 1977). Some people could not afford to move to the boarding homes—substandard as many were—and so continued in the public homes at state expense (Drake, 1958).

Since the 1930s, institutional long-term care has increased rapidly. In 1939, there were 1,200 facilities in the United States with 25,000 beds. In 1954, there were over 25,000 facilities with about 450,000 beds. In 1976, there were 23,000 facilities with over 1,300,000 beds. It is apparent from these figures that there has been —particularly in the late 1960s and early 1970s—an alteration in the configuration of ownership of beds in long-term care institutions in order to better respond to funding patterns, service delivery patterns, and economic viability (Cohen, 1974; Moss & Halmandaris, 1977).

In 1953, federal participation in the cost of assistance for indigent persons in private institutions was first authorized, but the ban on payment to public institutions continued. However, if states wanted to participate in the federal program, they were required to establish some standards for the institutions. Also, in the 1950s, several federal acts authorized moneys through grants and loans for constructing and equipping long-term care institutions. The Hill Burton Act, the Small Business Administration, and the National Housing Act provisions were the most prominent.

The passage of Title XVIII (Medicare) in 1965 and Title XIX (Medicaid) in 1967 opened new and major funding sources for long-term care institutions. With this legislation, service delivery requirements were reshaped and clarified. Prior to the enactment of Medicare and Medicaid, there was very little consistency among what were institutions of long-term care. Nursing homes, homes for the aged, convalescent hospitals, chronic care facilities were all defined separately by each state. The new funding sources set common definitions and basic national standards for service delivery in this important area of long-term care (Winston & Wilson, 1977).

Extent of Long-term Care Programs

As mentioned, the number of long-term care beds has greatly increased over the past 20 years. Between 1960 and 1976, the number of beds increased from 331,000 to 1,327,358, for a 302% increase. During this period, the number of long-term care patients increased from 290,000 to over 1 million, for a 245% increase, while the population aged 65 and over increased from 17 million to 21 million, for a 23% increase (Moss & Halmandaris, 1977).

Despite the extensive increase in the number of long-term care patients, only 4–5% of people aged 65 and over are residents in nursing homes at any one time (Ingram & Barry, 1977). In metropolitan Detroit, 23% of the aged deaths occurred in nursing homes and other long-term care facilities (Wershow, 1976). As people get older, their chances of being in a nursing home increase. Only 2% of those aged 65–74 are institutionalized, while 16% of those 85 and over are institutionalized (Moss & Halmandaris, 1977).

Not only has the number of beds increased, but the size of the homes, which reflects the change from family businesses to larger corporations. In 1963, the average nursing home had 39.9 beds, and this had increased to 74.8 beds by 1974 (Ingram & Barry, 1977).

Long-term Care Patients

Although the average length of stay is 2 years, there is a fairly significant turnover in nursing home occupancy (Gottesman & Hutchinson, 1974). In 1975 there were over 1 million admissions and discharges from nursing homes. In Alabama, as many as 44% of the deaths in nursing homes occur within a month after admission (Wershow, 1976). Of the 387 million resident days of nursing home care in 1974, 60% was paid by Medicaid at a cost of $7.5 million (Horn & Griesel, 1977).

The average nursing home resident is 82 years old, and 70% of the residents are over 70 years of age. Women outnumber men 3 to 1 in nursing homes. Only 10% of all nursing home residents have a living spouse; 63% of the residents are widowed, but 22% were never married. Importantly, more than 50% have no living close relatives, which may account for the fact that 60% receive no visitors. These figures indicate that one of the contributing factors to nursing home admissions is the lack of family support that might enable the person to continue living in his or her own home.

Almost a third of the nursing home residents are admitted to the homes directly from hospitals, while 13% are transfers from other nursing homes. The remaining residents are admitted directly from their own residences. Less than 50% of the residents are fully ambulatory: 55% are impaired and 33% are incontinent. Only 20% of nursing home residents return to their own homes at some point (Moss & Halmandaris, 1977).

It is clear that long-term care institutions are increasingly being used for the care of very old patients, most of whom have some physical or mental impairment and many of whom have no close family on whom to rely. Long-term care institutions are closer to being chronic disease hospitals for physically and mentally impaired elderly than care centers and homes for ambulatory aged who are not self-sufficient (Tobin & Lieberman, 1976). This change has occurred in part because there are community and quasi-institutional options for those who are reasonably self-sufficient. Because of the change in the residential population of nursing homes, the care has become increasingly more medical, rather than social and psychological. However, "the loss of physical or psychological self-sufficiency does not automatically mean the loss of social needs; the consequences will indeed be dire if we retreat to warehousing these most needy elderly and do not make every effort to provide life-sustaining social as well as physical supports" (Tobin & Lieberman, 1976, p. 236).

Types of Long-term Care Institutions

There are many different types of long-term care facilities for the elderly. However, until the creation of national funding legislation in the mid-1960s, there were no national standards governing the types of care in any given facility. As a result of the Medicare and Medicaid legislation, extended care facilities (ECFs), skilled nursing home services, and intermediate care facilities (ICFs) were identified and defined in terms of standards of care. Since that time, many of the long-term care institutions have adjusted their services to meet the outlined criteria in order to be eligible for reimbursements. Even so, both more extensive care (such as that provided in chronic care hospitals) and less extensive care (such as that provided in domiciliary care facilities) are still under regulations as defined by individual states and, therefore, are more difficult to define nationally.

Extended Care Facilities

ECFs are defined almost entirely in terms of Medicare reimbursement. In actual operation, they differ very little, if at all, from skilled nursing services:

> The extended care facility is a short-term convalescent care facility specifically arranged to take care of carefully selected patients coming from hospitals. . . . It involves aspects of rehabilitation, social work, high-quality medical and nursing care, and supportive services—that is,

those services usually associated with long-term care of high quality
(Cohen, 1974, p. 20).

Extended care is defined more in terms of the length of stay, origin
of the patient, and rehabilitative potential than in the type of services
that are actually given. Because Medicare defines eligibility for extended care so narrowly, there are very few ECF beds actually in use,
and the beds that are available are usually in skilled nursing facilities.
Currently, then, almost all long-term nursing-related care falls into
the other two categories: skilled nursing care and intermediate care.

Skilled Nursing Facilities

Skilled nursing facilities are required to provide certain services including "the emergency and ongoing services of a physician, nursing
care, rehabilitative services, pharmaceutical services, dietetic ser-
vices, laboratory and radiologic services, dental services, social ser-
vices, and activity services" (Glasscote et al., 1976, p. 34). Some of
these services must be a part of the facility itself, but rehabilitative,
laboratory, radiological, social, and dental services may be provided
by formal contractual agreement with outside resources.

There must be visits by attending physicians every 30 days of the
first 90 days of a patient's stay. After that time, if justified, the visits
can be reduced to every 60 days. A patient care plan should also be
prepared and reviewed regularly so that the patient is assured of
receiving services that are needed and so that changing conditions
are being translated into appropriate care. Although there is no
statement about the amount of staff required in a skilled nursing
facility, states have defined nursing requirements as from 2 to 3
nursing hours per patient day. In general, between 1965 and 1974,
nursing home staffs (which include all paid employees) have increased from 4.7 employees for 10 patients to 6.6 employees for 10
patients (Glasscote et al., 1976). In skilled nursing facilities, nursing
services must be supervised by a full-time registered nurse. In addition, a registered nurse must be in charge on the day shift, and either
a registered or licensed practical nurse on the afternoon and night
shifts. Regular programs of activities, use and preparation of drugs,
physical facilities in relation to fire and safety codes are carefully
delineated for skilled nursing facilities. In general, skilled nursing
facilities can be characterized as medical institutions that care for
patients who are severely ill.

Intermediate Care Facilities

ICFs were defined in conjunction with the Medicaid legislation of the late 1960s. The definition evolved from the recognition that a large number of poor people were not ill enough to require full-time professional staff attention but did need health supervision and access to various health and rehabilitative components (Glasscote et al., 1976). This level of care is defined in terms of Medicaid reimbursement only. Those patients who are paying privately pay a fee which is established by the nursing home and are not involved in the definitions of levels of care.

Intermediate care can be provided not only in facilities that are set up for that purpose but in skilled care facilities, homes for the aged, hospitals, or personal care homes. In other words—as with skilled care—the definition of intermediate care is of the level of care provided rather than the facility providing that care.

Many regulations are the same as for skilled nursing facilities:

> Regulations for construction, sanitation, safety, and the handling of drugs are very similar. Theoretically and philosophically the difference is that the SNF is a "medical" institution and the ICF is a "health" institution. In the ICF, social and recreational policy is to be given near equal emphasis with medical policy" (Glasscote et al., 1976, p. 39).

In addition, there are lesser requirements for supervisory personnel. For example, on the day shift nursing services must be supervised full-time by either a registered nurse or a licensed practical nurse. This is a less sophisticated nursing requirement than that of the skilled nursing facility.

The federal regulations for both skilled nursing facilities and ICFs leave room for interpretation, new regulations, and elaboration (Glasscote et al., 1976). This is important because it allows the states, who administer, supervise, and control the nursing home program, to build an improved program based on their own particular needs and resources. It is also the states that set the criteria of who is eligible for which level of care. Potential patients who are eligible for Medicare, must have their conditions reviewed by the locally designated authority to determine the appropriate level of care for each condition. The nursing home is then reimbursed for the designated level of care, with the intermediate level determination receiving less reimbursement than the skilled level. The levels of care must be separated, either by facility or by wings in a facility. Because of this requirement, if the condition of a patient already admitted to a nursing home should change to the extent that the required level of care changes, that patient will either be moved to another section of the nursing home or in some cases, be moved to another facility. A private paying patient who becomes eligible for Medicaid after admission will, at that time, be evaluated and assigned a level of care that might or might not require a physical change.

In 1974, the breakdown of nursing homes by level of care was as follows:

Skilled only	14%
Intermediate only	28%
Both skilled and intermediate in home	8%
Skilled and extended care	17%
Skilled, extended care, and intermediate	7%
Not federally certified for any level of care	17%

(Glasscote et al., 1976, p. 24)

Board and Care, Personal Care, and Domiciliary Care Homes

Because there are no national regulations governing this level of care, each state has adopted its own terminology and regulations which govern the type of care that is given. Probably the best definition for this general level of care is contained in the Colorado regulations:

An establishment operated and maintained to provide residential accommodation, personal services, and social care to individuals who are not related to the licensee, and who, because of impaired capacity for self-care, elect or require protective living accommodations but who do not have an illness, injury, or disability for which regular medical care and 24-hour nursing services are required. (Glasscote et al., 1976, p. 58)

In summary, this level of care is primarily personal and custodial. Usually this level of long-term care requires that:
- Local and fire safety codes be met.
- There be a full-time administrator responsible for the supervision of staff, residents, and safety.
- Nursing personnel be on call most of the time.
- There are facilities for occasional distribution of medication.

Residents are usually required to arrange for their own medical care and, in many instances, provide for their own social activities. In effect, this level of care provides a protected environment, meals, and some personal care services but does not restrict nor organize the activities of the residents.

Also in the category of board and care, personal care, and domiciliary care homes are the homes for the aged. These are primarily nonprofit and often church-sponsored homes that provide personal care but require that persons entering be healthy. These homes go well beyond the standards which are set by the various states in that they usually provide comprehensive activities, social services, and personal care programs. Many of the residents have private rooms, and rarely are there more than two people in each room. Residents can select activities which are offered and are free to come and go from the facility as desired. These facilities can be small, often accommodating as few as 50 residents, and in some cases large enough to accommodate as many as 300. Attached to many of these homes for the aged are intermediate care or skilled-care units to provide appropriate medical treatment for those who need such care. Depending on the size of the facility, the home will either be able to continue to care for a resident that needs medical care on a regular basis or will transfer that person to a regular skilled or intermediate care facility.

Mental Hospitals

Today, mental hospitals continue to care for the elderly on a long-term basis but not in as significant numbers as before. In 1959, 1% of the elderly aged 65 and over were in mental hospitals, but by 1975, the figure had dropped to .5% (Glasscote et al., 1976). The decline became significant following the Medicare and Medicaid legislation, which opened opportunities for mental hospital patients to be transferred to skilled or intermediate care facilities. Even more recently, this transfer has been to the personal care level of facilities.

Older persons in mental health hospitals are comprised of long-term residents who are now old or of older persons who have recently been admitted. There is great variability in admission criteria among mental hospitals, criteria that are further complicated by the difficulty of determining pyschotic conditions related to organic brain syndrome. Often the community initiates inappropriate admissions, and it becomes the responsibility of the hospital to determine what type of care the potential patient actually needs.

Funding

The funding system of long-term care facilities has been a major influence on the development of types of facilities and care that are available. The two most important sources, in terms of shaping the long-term care industry, are Medicare and Medicaid.

As indicated earlier, Medicare legislation, which was passed in 1965, authorized care in a long-term care institution for those patients who were hospitalized for at least 3 consecutive days, who needed skilled nursing care, and who were to be admitted to a Medicare-certified facility within 14 days of their discharge from the hospital. The patient had to be evaluated regularly and could stay in the long-term care facilities for no longer than 90 days under Medicare. This new funding source made ECFs very popular in the last half of the 1960s, as it was an excellent vehicle for shortening hospital stays. In 1969, the rapidly rising costs for the program led to a change in the regulations. New administrative regulations required that participants in the program have rehabilitative potential. In addition, nursing care was defined in more narrow terms, which included only a very limited number of diagnoses and therapeutic situations. The effect of these new regulations was to virtually cut off Medicare as a vehicle for nursing home care for the elderly (Moss & Halmandaris, 1977). Because many nursing homes were caught losing thousands of dollars in disallowed costs at the time the regulations changed, the number of nursing homes that even wanted to participate in the Medicare program dramatically decreased. However, the precedent of reimbursement for medical long-term care was set.

As an illustration of the minor part Medicare currently plays in the financing of long-term care, in 1976, Medicare paid only $275 million to nursing homes, or about 2% of all nursing home revenues. During this same year, only 8,300 patients out of over 1 million in nursing homes on any given day had their care paid for by Medicare (Moss & Halmandaris, 1977). This regulative change reaffirms Medicare's primary role in reimbursing acute rather than chronic care.

Legislation establishing Medicaid—a system of medical cost reimbursement for the poor—opened the greatest opportunity for funding nursing home care. In 1976, 38% of Medicaid's $15 billion total went to pay for nursing home care (Moss & Halmandaris, 1977). In addition, 60% of all nursing home care is covered through Medicaid.

Since Medicaid is a shared federal-state program, the federal government provides a basic set of requirements upon which the states build the program. The states determine their own definitions of needy; there is some flexibility from state to state as to who is eligible for Medicaid in long-term care institutions. States can include the categorically needy—those who are eligible for federally aided financial assistance—and the medically needy—those whose incomes are sufficient for daily living expenses but not enough to pay for medical expenses. Because of the nature of this definition, persons who might not be eligible while in the community could be eligible for Medicaid if entering a long-term care institution. Often the institutional Medicaid eligibility factors for long-term care institutions relate more to personal assets than monthly income, and so once the assets are liquidated, a person entering a nursing home can become eligible for Medicaid reimbursements.

Patients can also enter a home as private paying patients, and as their assets diminish, they become eligible for Medicaid. In a recent study in the Detroit area by Barney (1977), it was found that 48.2% of patients entering nursing homes came into the home as private paying patients; 2 years later, only 30% of those still in the home were on a private paying basis. The study also found that only 37% of the Medicaid admissions were actually on Medicaid prior to entering the nursing home. Thus the medical definition of eligibility is important as it affects the availability of long-term care for older persons.

Extensive publicity has been generated on potential abuses of Medicaid reimbursements. Nationally, 77% of all nursing homes are profit-making businesses, while 23% are nonprofit or public homes (Horn & Griesel, 1977). These figures represent a one-third increase in the number of profit-making homes during the last decade. As Moss and Halmandaris (1977) point out, conflicts between profits and quality of care are likely when services become a money-making operation. The conflicts will be greatest in firms that operate a number of homes, since they may attempt to maximize their profits by lowering the costs they incur at any one particular home.

State regulatory agencies, understanding the financial incentives of the nursing home industry, promulgate reimbursement regulations that are designed to encourage quality care and limit profits. There have been variations in the success of these regulations. There are basically four methods for determining reimbursements to nursing homes under Medicaid:

1. *The Flat-fee system.* Under this system, all nursing homes in the state get a flat fee for each patient in the home who is eligible for Medicaid reimbursement. The advantages are that this system

provides a way of controlling the costs and fixes precise limits on the level of state obligations to nursing homes in any 1 year. Under this method, regardless of the cost to the home of a given patient, the home will get a predetermined fixed amount for each day the patient is in the nursing home. Two disadvantages to this system are that, first, the home will be encouraged to admit eligible patients who only require a minimum of care and, second, the home is encouraged to cut back on essential services, since what moneys are not spent on services become profit. For example, if the fixed reimbursement fee is $25 per patient per day and the home could cut services to $20 a day, the $5 difference would be profit.

2. *Cost-related reimbursement.* Under this system, the state reimburses the nursing home operators for reasonable costs expended, plus a profit margin, up to a certain maximum amount per patient per day. With this method, whatever the home spends is reimbursed, unless the home goes over the ceiling which has been imposed on the costs. For example, the state would reimburse a home for costs incurred, $23 a day plus 8% for profit. However, if the state ceiling on reimbursements was $30 and the home incurred $28 in expenses, the home would only be reimbursed an additional $2 for profit. Under this system, there is less incentive to keep costs down and the state has less control on the amount it should obligate from year to year. However, the advantage of this system is that there is less incentive to keep expenses down in order to widen profits.

3. *The point system.* In this system, the focus is on the patient who is assigned points for each item of patient disability. The greater the degree of disability, the more a nursing home is reimbursed. The advantage of this system is that it should encourage the home to accept those patients who are more difficult to care for. The disadvantage is that the nursing home is not encouraged to take adequate care of the patient. For example, if each point is worth $6 and a bed sore is worth 8 points, then the more bed sores a patient has, the more money the home will be reimbursed.

In Connecticut, the point system is focused on the ability of the home to meet or exceed federal and state standards. Homes are assigned a certain number of points if they comply with particular standards; then points are deducted for violating regulations. The homes are then graded and put into categories based on their total performance. The advantage to this method is that exceeding the regulations can bring a higher reimbursement. The disadvantage lies in the determination of just what earns points. Some services that relate very little to patient care and are relatively inexpensive can bring a high point count. Therefore a high point count does not necessarily reflect the quality of care (Moss & Halmandaris, 1977).

The method of determining Medicaid reimbursement is crucial to the quality of care of the patients and to the availability of beds to those patients most needing nursing home care. Unfortunately, the system has not yet been found that encourages quality care, ensures a modest profit, and provides incentives for the nursing homes to accept the hard-to-care-for patient.

In a study of nursing home Medicaid reimbursement patterns in 1975, it was found that daily reimbursements for skilled care ranged from $16.08 in Denver to $43.71 in New York City. Reimbursements for intermediate care ranged from $12.27 in Arkansas to $32.00 in New York City (Glasscote et al., 1976). In 1979, Maryland reimbursed up to $33.31 a day for skilled and intermediate care, which, for reimbursement purposes, have been combined.

As part of the Medicaid regulations, all costs are to be included in the reimbursement fee, and the patient is not to be charged extra for services given.

For all patients in nursing homes under Medicaid, each is eligible for at least $25 a month in spending money which can be spent for anything the patient wants, including cigarettes, haircuts, clothes, and magazines. This spending money is in exchange for the fact that any income the patient is receiving, such as social security, is to be paid to the home and subtracted from the amount of the Medicaid reimbursement. For those patients who can personally handle the money, the program is successful. However, for those patients who cannot manage their own resources, there has been potential for abuse in the use of the money, since it can come under the supervision of the nursing home administration.

Private Payments

A significant minority of nursing home payments come directly from the patients or their families. As mentioned earlier, a patient may have significant assets and enter the institution as a private paying patient. Then as these assets diminish—as they could in an extended stay in the nursing home—the patient becomes eligible for Medicaid reimbursements. At an average cost of $35 a day (low figure for private nursing home patients), the patient would be paying the home over $12,000 a year for care. Unlike reimbursements under Medicaid, the home can charge the patient for extra services which may be required for care. For example, extra padding, extra toileting time, extra time for feeding, could all result in extra charges. Private paying patients usually cannot predict the exact costs of the home and have no recourse if they object to the prices charged except to find another nursing home.

Much of the care which is provided under board and care, personal care, and domiciliary care homes is paid directly by the residents of the facilities. SSI and social security checks are turned over to the facility in exchange for personal care services that are rendered.

State and Local Funding

State funding, which covers about one-half (it varies slightly from state to state) of the Medicaid reimbursement, reimburses the board and care, personal care, and domiciliary care facilities when personal income is inadequate to cover the allowed daily reimbursement rate. It also covers the costs of individual care in mental hospitals, and in these settings the total cost of patient care is paid. One of the reasons for the increase in the number of elderly who are being transferred to nursing homes and personal care facilities from state hospitals is the states' desire to develop a situation where the federal government is paying at least part of the cost of caring for the elderly.

Long-term care facilities provide an excellent example of how the funding mechanisms have shaped the types of services and the amount of service available for the elderly. In addition, long-term care is unique in that the majority of care is being provided by profit-making organizations—a factor that both influences and is influenced by the funding available for this particular type of service.

Personnel and Programming

Staffing Patterns

Staffing patterns of long-term care institutions are closely related to reimbursement rates. Homes attempt to meet state regulations regarding personnel while at the same time keeping costs in line with reimbursement allowances, including profit. Unfortunately, the end result is generally an inadequate and poorly trained staff. Of the 722,000 nursing home personnel in the country, only 7% are regis-

tered nurses and 8% are licensed practical nurses. Aides and orderlies perform between 80 and 90% of all nursing care actually given
patients (Horn & Griesel, 1977). Most aides and orderlies receive no
training for their jobs. Of those applying for jobs in nursing homes,
53% have had no previous experience and only half of them have
completed high school. The turnover rate is 75% each year (Moss &
Halmandaris, 1977). One important reason for the lack of trained and
committed staff is the salary, which is usually at or just above minimum wage. This is a disincentive to produce a commitment to the
job, to seek additional training, or even to stay on the job for any
length of time beyond that of getting enough experience to get
another, perhaps better paying, job. However, any job training
beyond the minimal in-service programs required by the homes
would up the demands for higher wages, which in turn would reflect
directly on the Medicaid reimbursement figures. Community colleges are beginning to offer special training for aides, which in certain situations could help provide stability to staffing patterns.

The number of staff (including aides) actually on the floor of a
nursing home influences the quality and amount of care given. The
state minimum requirement, which varies from state to state, usually
says that a certain amount (2–3 hours) of nursing care is required per
patient per day. However, when this is translated to personnel, it
could be actual on-floor nursing care, or on-floor care except for
lunches and breaks, absences, and vacations. For the latter, the actual
on-floor care is ½ hour below that required. The interpretation
affects the care, the cost, the reimbursement rate, and the profit
margin. Some states have been reluctant to interpret such regulations precisely until they can generate a Medicaid reimbursement
rate that can pay for actual staffing requirements.

In addition to the basic nursing and support staff, homes are
required to have access to certain types of professional staff. The
extent to which the home actually hires the professional person required as opposed to responding to the need through contractual
agreements affects the quality of care in the home. For example,
actually hiring a social worker, a dietician, an occupational therapist,
and a full-time physician brings more services to the home than using
these people a few hours a week on a contract basis. The size of the
home, the relationship of the individual home to a larger organizational structure (the individual hired by a chain of homes can work
in two or three facilities), and the type of reimbursement mechanism
influence the extent to which the home actually hires the additional
personnel required.

Programming and Advocacy

Beyond having an activity director whose responsibility is to provide some activity for patients, state regulations do not stipulate the types of programming for nursing homes. The result is that there is a tremendous variety of programmed activities available in long-term care institutions. Some homes make only the minimum number of programs available, while others establish links with the community to ensure that those programs most appropriate to the patients' needs are presented.

Sensory training, reality orientation, and remotivation are essential components of nursing home programming. Reorientation of the patient to the larger world, heightening the patient's sensory sensitivity, and reestablishing earlier interests all help to improve the patients' daily functioning. As in other major services the range of activities that may be well received by patients runs the gamut from picnics, dance, theatre, and crafts to movies and guest speakers. Some nursing homes have links with senior centers, adult daycare centers, and nutrition programs in order to provide ways of getting patients into other settings and of bringing community people into the nursing homes. Volunteer organizations from the community also provide special services for patients in many community nursing homes.

Programming that has a purpose and recreates the interests and talents of the patients is the most successful. Many patients have little opportunity to share their experiences and even themselves with others when they enter a nursing home. Programming can create these opportunities if it is seen by the patient as being meaningful. In a study by Dudley and Hillery (1977), long-term care institutions had the highest scores on alienation and high scores on deprivation of freedom when compared to several other types of residential organizations. The level of alienation in part results from the practice of placing restrictions on the residents' ability to make decisions. Programming on a voluntary basis, with a variety of activities from which the patients may choose and which, from time to time, they suggest can have the effect of reducing the sense of alienation that comes with the institutional process, particularly, in nursing homes.

Families can also be built into the programming for the home. As Miller and Beer (1977) point out, familial friendships are the most meaningful and the most enduring of all preexisting resident relationships. There are no substitutes for positive family relationships. However, if a patient has only minimal family ties, the nursing home can create an atmosphere of the extended family through its programming by bringing in volunteers and using other patients, when appropriate.

Two advocacy programs in recent years have focused on the special needs of patients in long-term care settings, particularly nursing homes, and on how to get those needs vocalized in a way which produces a response. One, the patients' rights movement, began in the early 1970s when several states passed patients' rights legislation in response to the belief that the personal rights and liberties of patients were being lost with the institutional process (Wilson, 1978). In 1974, HEW developed regulations which established a set of patients' rights for patients in skilled and intermediate care facilities. These rights, which relate to individual liberties and dignities, are readily displayed, explained to the patients, and assigned to nursing home personnel for enforcement. Some of the rights covered in the regulations include being informed of the services available in the facility, being informed of one's medical condition and the plan of treatment, being encouraged and assisted throughout the stay in the nursing home, being able to manage personal financial affairs, being free from mental and physical abuse, being assured of confidential treatment of personal and medical records, being able to retain use of personal clothing and possessions as space permits, and being assured privacy for visits by one's spouse. Unfortunately, there are conditional clauses that make enforcement difficult, and the only disciplinary tool available is decertification of the facility, a recourse that is too severe for individual violations. Despite the difficulties of enforcement, HEW, working through the states, has made a firm commitment to enforce the patients' rights.

The second advocacy program created to respond to specific needs of patients is the ombudsman program, which is designed to examine complaints by patients and, through investigations, give patients a voice in determining their own individual circumstances. Begun in 1972, five ombudsman programs were funded nationally as models of the ways that the program could be most effective. Two more programs were added in 1973. Today, the ombudsman programs are affiliated with the state units on aging and work through the Area Agencies on Aging. They still retain the objective of being the focal point for complaints regarding nursing home care, but they also act as a nursing home referral service, an organizer of friendly visiting programs, and a center for educating patients and the community of the rights of nursing home patients (U.S. Administration on Aging, 1977).

Quality in Long-term Care Institutions

How well the long-term care institution is carrying out its mandate, meeting requirements, and providing the level of care agreed to under its contract with the funding sources, is evaluated through the inspection system. The federal government provides the regulative substructure on which the states build specific codes for operation. The states then divide the inspection responsibilities between local fire and safety agencies. The result is a series of inspections of the homes for different purposes, which are, at times, in conflict with one another. The two biggest problems with the current inspection system are: (1) Inspections are primarily to evaluate the physical plant rather than to evaluate the actual quality of care; because actual quality of care is very difficult to measure, long lists of physical requirements become the substitute; and (2) There is essentially no weapon for noncompliance except revoking the license to operate— a very difficult step, in many cases inappropriate to the situation, both because the need for nursing home beds is so acute and because shutting down a home and moving patients is traumatic; hence a state or local enforcement body will not usually impose such a step until after years of flagrant abuse.

Basically, most states have four components to their inspection systems: (1) sanitation and environment, (2) meals, (3) fire safety, and (4) patient care. This means that there is a visit by a sanitarian, a dietician, a professional review team, and a fire inspector (Moss & Halmandaris, 1977). In most states, at least two of the inspections are to be unannounced, although this is not always the case. Until the inspection procedures become better organized and develop more effective ways of measuring the actual quality of care, the inspection system will not be the best answer to improving the care in long-term care institutions.

Long-term care facilities thus remain one of the most troublesome elements in the system of services now available for the elderly. Americans seem ambivalent about whether it is best to provide this form of care or more advantageous to have the older person remain in the community. This ambivalence has allowed the number of beds in long-term care institutions to increase but resulted in a failure to provide the resources necessary to produce quality care for elderly in these settings. Until both the need for long-term care facilities is accepted and adequate resources are provided, the situation of low-quality care that exists in many long-term facilities is not likely to change. At this point we expect too much from these settings while providing too little.

References

Barney, J. The perogative of choice in long-term care. *Gerontologist*, 1977, *17*, 309–314.

Cohen, E. An overview of long-term care facilities. In E. Brody (Ed.), *A social work guide for long-term care facilities*. Rockville, Md.: National Institute of Mental Health, 1974.

Drake, J. *The aged in American society*. New York: Ronald, 1958.

Dudley, C., & Hillery, G. Freedom and alienation in homes for the aged. *Gerontologist*, 1977, *17*, 140–145.

Glasscote, R., et al. *Old folks at homes*. Washington, D.C.: American Psychiatric Association and the Mental Health Association, 1976.

Gottesman, L., & Hutchinson, E. Characteristics of the institutionalized elderly. In E. Brody (Ed.), *A social work guide for long-term care facilities*. Rockville, Md.: National Institute of Mental Health, 1974.

Horn, L., & Griesel, E. *Nursing homes*. Boston: Beacon, 1977.

Ingram, D., & Barry, J. National statistics on deaths in nursing homes. *Gerontologist*, 1977, *17*, 303–308.

Miller, D., & Beer, S. Patterns of friendship among patients in a nursing home setting. *Gerontologist*, 1977, *17*, 269–275.

Moss, F., & Halmandaris, V. *Too old, too sick, too bad*. Germantown, Md.: Aspen Systems Corp., 1977.

Tobin, S., & Lieberman, M. *Last home for the aged*. San Francisco: Jossey-Bass, 1976.

U.S. Administration on Aging. *Nursing home ombudsman program: A fact sheet and program directory*. Washington, D.C.: U.S. Government Printing Office, 1977.

Wershow, H. The four percent fallacy. *Gerontologist*, 1976, *16* (Pt. 1), 52–55.

Wilson, S. Nursing home patients' rights: Are they enforceable? *Gerontologist*, 1978, *18*, 255–261.

Winston, W., & Wilson, A. *Ethical considerations in long-term care*. St. Petersburg, Fla.: Eckerd College Gerontology Center, 1977.

16
The Future of Aging Programs and Services

In order to develop training and service priorities, social welfare program analysts continually engage in prognostications about the future. To attempt predictions about the course of aging programs and services necessitates some reflections on the underpinnings of support for services for the elderly and the changes among the present and future aged populations. Based on this discussion we will then attempt to outline trends in programs and services over the next 50 years.

The Elderly Voting Block

It is currently popular to attribute much of the growth of aging programs and services to the political activism of the elderly and the organizational efforts of such groups as the Gray Panthers. The data in support of this view are not conclusive. The basic problem with this approach is its tendency to characterize the elderly as a group with solidarity of concerns. Judging from the economic and social diversity within the over-60 population, there is little reason to expect the elderly to vote as a block. A more realistic view is that older adults form a large group whose views range from conservative to radical. Different age cohorts among the elderly have strongly differing values and political attitudes that were formed during childhood and carried through into adulthood. The carryover of these attitudes into old age has now been amply demonstrated by research. The thesis that individuals become politically conservative as they grow older is basically unfounded. In some instances, such as the election of senators in Florida in 1972, older voters appear to have had an impact (Butler, 1975). Organized efforts by senior citizen groups in 1965 also helped to promote the long-delayed passage of Medicare legislation. On the other hand, elderly voters in many states have shown that their negative feelings about expenditures of public funds for social and health services are deep seated, even when these expenditures are for programs that may benefit them at some later time.

The aged have yet to evidence a cohesive self-consciousness. Many elderly who correctly perceive "old age" as a stigmatized status in American society will continue to consciously avoid identification with their age peers. The efforts of organizers such as Maggie Kuhn are focused as much on changing the attitudes of the older person as they are on organizing. As Binstock (1972) has argued, it is not enough for a group to have an influence on the outcome of an election by balloting. Power at the polls must be translated into the types of lobbying and advocacy efforts that result in legislation and funds. The organizational coherence required for these efforts has only recently been shown by the aged.

General Support for Aging Programs and Services

Even if the elderly have not been as politically effective as their increasing numbers would suggest, the changing shape of the American age pyramid has made it difficult for legislators to ignore the needs of older adults. Unfortunately, younger groups are indicating an increased negativism about what they regard as burdensome costs required for support of older populations. The most dramatic example is the debate that arose in the 1970s about the potential solvency of the social security program and the need for younger workers to pay increasing amounts of money into the social security trust fund to support benefits for retirees. As of now, 25% of the federal budget is devoted to health care and social security for older adults. If this figure rises as predicted to 40% by 2025 (*Older American Reports,* 1979), we can expect a lessening of the present political support for aging programs.

Even with positive attitudes among the public toward at-risk populations, there is no guarantee that varied and large-scale programs are going to be instituted. This was evident in the response to racism and poverty attempted by the Kennedy and Johnson administrations in the 1960s. The Office of Economic Opportunity (OEO) programs that were part of the War on Poverty were never adequate to meet the real needs of the millions of poor in the United States. The Vietnam War, and public and bureaucratic antagonism toward OEO and the Model Cities program resulted in a 1970s reorganization of these programs into a less ambitious and threatening form. A similar reaction has not yet taken place in the field of aging. Aging programs and services contrast sharply with the poverty programs of the 1960s. As we can see in the following discussion, an examination of these two efforts provides a basis for understanding differences in public attitudes toward the War on Poverty and assistance for the elderly.

Basic Nature of Services

Many of the programs and services provided by Area Agencies on Aging (AAAs) and other organizations are basic in nature. Rather than dealing with issues such as self-esteem, the focus is on elementary survival needs: food, clothing, shelter, and companionship. Little emphasis has been placed on reshaping the values of the elderly. In contrast, under some War on Poverty programs, efforts were geared toward resocializing individuals and groups who did not seem to fit the industrial capitalistic model.

The types of basic programs offered to the elderly have two major advantages: (1) They provide tangible and accountable results; (2) They allow the provision of programs to a group that is noncontroversial and provide a shift in public focus away from stigmatized "minority" populations. The number of meals served, the number of housing units built, and the medical services provided is easily quantified. Legislators needing evidence of their concern for constituents' needs relish the opportunity to point to the type of concrete services provided to the aged.

For the majority of the American public, the elderly represent a passive and undemanding group. They are thus viewed as a contrast to threatening ethnic and minority groups. Housing for the elderly has thus become a popular means for many white communities to deal with requirements that they place a specific proportion of their federal housing funds into low-income projects. Housing for the elderly enabled these communities to serve a low-income population with some assurance that the low-income elderly would also be white.

Growth of Interest in Aging

As the population of elderly has grown and the birth rate declined to new lows, the median age of the general population has increased. This increase means that a vast number of individuals are at a point in midlife where they can envision themselves as aged. For the 30- and 40-year-old man or woman, it does not take a great leap in logic to realize that the development of better living conditions for the present-day generation of elderly, including increased respect for the aged, cannot but enrich their own later years. Of course, many middle-aged adults find it difficult if not impossible to confront the reality of their own aging. For an increasing number of middle-aged individuals and their families, the challenge of providing economic, physical, and social support to their own parents or relatives has become a concern. As noted in Chapter 1, the likelihood of having two generations of elderly in the average family is increasing rapidly. As this generational configuration becomes common, the growth of services for the aged will garner increasing support from families facing increased burdens on already strained resources.

Nonthreatening Programs

We have already noted that elderly housing is supported by many communities because of their feeling that the aged are tolerable, if not welcome, neighbors. Programs for the aged are also seen as nonthreatening by legislators. Few aging services require major shifts in priorities. There are no demands for "community control" similar to those posed by residents in designated Model City neighborhoods of the 1960s. There are also no threats to businesses and agencies that now have a strong, if not controlling, influence in many local communities. In fact one of the major outcomes of the expansion of federal funding for the elderly has been the efforts by many established agencies to expand their programs and services for the aged. This expansion has helped to offset cuts in other programmatic areas.

New Jobs and Profits

The nursing home industry provides a major example of a service delivery system that has expanded as financing mechanisms have been developed. With the passage of Medicare legislation in 1965, the numbers of nursing homes increased dramatically. Opportunities for nursing home proprietors and other providers of services for the aging were aided by developments in related fields, particularly the emphasis on moving individuals out of large long-term care settings such as mental hospitals. Because of a lack of adequate community-based alternatives, many of the elderly individuals discharged to the community became residents of nursing homes. This discharged population, along with a renewed emphasis on maintaining the individual in the community if at all possible, has helped to foster the growth of nutrition programs, daycare centers, and multipurpose senior centers that began to quickly develop after 1973.

As aging programs and services grew, a corps of individuals dedicated to providing the services associated with these programs and services naturally came into existence. Because of the basic nature of many aging programs and services, the ratio of service providers to elderly clients can be very high. This is especially true among programs and services for the aging which work with elderly who have difficulties in daily functioning. As the proportion of the service sector dedicated to working with the elderly enlarges, the interest group having a stake in the retention and enlargement of these services also increases. These interest groups are making the step from the ballot box to the halls of the legislature that is required for programs to be enacted and funds appropriated. Because of its community empowerment ideology, the War on Poverty never generated the professional and paraprofessional constituency that might have enabled poverty programs to resist dismantling. When either authorization or appropriation legislation is being threatened, the professional service delivery cadre are highly visible and emphasize their support for the legislation by stating that they represent the aged.

Service Delivery Issues in Aging

All of the elements outlined would seem to point to a continued growth of appropriations for services for the elderly. It would be difficult to expect that the rate of increase in program growth will be anywhere near the pace exhibited in the middle 1970s. Programs that explode with infusions of massive amounts of money must necessarily soon begin to attract questions from the public about program efficiency and waste. This is especially true in periods when the economy's growth rate is slowed and inflation is a matter of concern. At these points, the demand by the public is for evaluation and consolidation, not expansion. A number of service delivery issues that need to be confronted by providers have already become apparent. These include coordination, cost effectiveness, and family-agency relationships. As Butler (1975) has sarcastically noted, the 1971 White House Conference on Aging posed the question to delegates:

> Issue: Should a system of coordinated personal-health services of both the short- and long-term care of the physically and mentally aging be developed, legislated and financed? Or, should the uncoordinated, generally fragmented health services as now provided be continued? (p. 333)

The obvious ludicrousness of this question does not necessarily mean that changes in the system are automatically produced. Providers of each of the services in this fragmented model have major stakes in seeing their particular program continued. It is also possible to place a particular service on the continuum of services for the aged, but more difficult to comparatively evaluate the relative impacts of each program or service model. If we cannot yet argue in favor of one aging program over another, we should at least be able to assess what available services are most appropriate to the needs of an older individual.

Cost-Effectiveness Issues

The availability of community-based services has helped to reduce the numbers of elderly in inappropriate long-term care placements. A reduction in inappropriate placements is related to the tightening of legal requirements for clearer definitions of the need of an individual for a restrictive environment. To some degree, the growth of community-based services has also rested on the premise that these services are cheaper than long-term institutional arrangements. This assumption has yet to be clearly proven, and the cost effectiveness of community programs will be a major agenda item for gerontologists in the future.

Family-Agency Issues

The growing antipathy to nursing home and hospital arrangements for the elderly has required increased participation of families in the care of the elderly. The resources of the family to provide this assistance are a source of continuing debate. At a Congressional hearing in 1978, Herman Brotman pointed to societal changes that have created difficulties for the family unit:

> In addition, with industrialization which has been mentioned and urbanization, people have moved close to their place of business. You have the construction of complicated dense urban areas where housing becomes very expensive, so you have smaller and smaller apartments with less multigeneration housing. (U.S. House of Representatives, 1978, p. 22)

While the lack of available space to house an elderly parent creates problems for adult children, a General Accounting Office study of the elderly in Cleveland found that 87% of the individuals interviewed claimed that they had someone to take care of them as long as needed (Comptroller General of the United States, 1977). Of this 87%, 42% mentioned their children, while 26% cited a spouse as a major source of assistance. Siblings, relatives, and friends were the remaining groups included as sources of assistance. Interviews in New York by the Community Service Society with 96 families caring for a "disabled elderly" person indicated that responsibility for care usually rested on the shoulders of one or two family members rather than being divided among the entire family network (Frankfather et al., 1979).

As family responsibility for elderly relatives becomes common, we can assume that many families will not be able to provide extensive services unless training and financial assistance is forthcoming. As argued previously (Fandetti & Gelfand, 1976), payments are now made to agencies to provide intimate services to the elderly when these services could be provided by some family members themselves if they were given these same funds.

Service Utilization

Even with additional support for families assisting the elderly, it is not realistic to expect that services now in place will not be needed. The influential Government Accounting Office report (Comptroller General of the United States, 1977) provides some indication of how effectively services are reaching the elderly with varying degrees of impairment. Unfortunately, the government researchers found that a higher percentage of their sample was living in neighborhoods with very limited services rather than in neighborhoods with extensive services. A large number of elderly were also not utilizing available services. As Table 16.1 indicates, the nonutilization rates ranged from 89% for public housing to 29% for Medicaid. Elderly who had come into contact with assessment and referral programs were receiving more services than their counterparts who had not.

Table 16.1   Rate of Nonutilization of Federal Programs
by Elderly in Cleveland, Ohio

Program	Number Eligible	Number Ineligible	Percentage of Eligible not Receiving
Public housing	1,078	954	89
Food stamps	566	433	77
Supplemental Security Income	146	76	52
Medicaid	77	22	29

Source: Adapted from Comptroller General of the United States, *Report to the Congress: The Well-being of Older People in Cleveland, Ohio*, 1977.

The Government Accounting Office findings will not surprise practitioners who have been working in aging for any length of time. It is clear that there are many elderly, at all economic levels and with varied needs, who still have to be reached by programs and services. Manney (1975) cited six major reasons why the elderly are not represented adequately in many service delivery areas: (1) unavailability of a particular service, (2) fragmentation of services, (3) lack of information about service availability, (4) inaccessibility of services, (5) bureaucratic red tape within the service delivery system, and (6) impersonalization of services. The Government Accounting Office report confirmed the existence of these problems.

Many of the elderly interviewed in Cleveland did not perceive that they needed any services. Homemaker services were perceived as important by the elderly classified by the investigators as having difficulty with these aspects of living. In contrast, over half of the individuals in need of financial aid expressed no need for financial assistance or food stamps. Only 21% of the older respondents classified as having impaired social functioning stated a need for "social recreational services" (Comptroller General of the United States, 1977). These findings indicate that outreach programs must involve a strong educational component. This education must stress that services are not "charity" and will not result in the older person being stigmatized by friends, neighbors, and family for accepting aid. Elderly persons who inquire about services must also be treated as respected individuals and not enmeshed in a sea of regulations and forms to determine their eligibility.

The Future of Programs for the Aged

Understanding the probable changes in aging programs over the next 50 years requires a brief examination of changes among the elderly themselves. As the data cited in Chapter 1 indicate, the elderly are becoming a more educated, more "resourceful" population. This reflects the aging of cohorts of individuals who have had more opportunities to attain advanced education. In 1990, approximately half of the population over 65 will have had some high school education, and over 17% will have completed college (Cutler & Haryootan, 1975). These figures refer to American-born individuals. Unless international crises produce increased flows of refugees to this country, the estimates are that immigration rates will be approximately 400,000 individuals annually. Of this number, 84,000 will be under 9 years of age; 75,900, between 10 and 20; 117,000 between 20 and 30. Over half of this immigrant group will therefore be under 30, with a large percentage young enough to attain advanced education and proficiency in English (U.S. Bureau of the Census, 1977). Thus the problems presently encountered by service providers with poorly educated elderly possessing only limited fluency in English will be lessening during the next few decades.

In the past, advanced education has connoted higher income levels. We have already cited the disturbing evidence of slow declines in poverty among females, minorities, and individuals living independently. Continued growth of these groups with slow changes in their economic status may mean the maintenance of a large underclass of elderly. What is needed to prevent an enlarged older poverty-level group is continued effort to ensure that economic opportunities are redistributed throughout the population. Otherwise we can expect a widening gap between a population of older adults with more adequate financial resources than previous generations, and an increased number of elderly who are at or below the poverty level. The effectiveness of present-day efforts to eradicate educational and job discrimination will thus be evident to service providers in future years.

For many middle-aged and younger populations among the aging cohorts of the 21st century, the financial picture is relatively promising. How promising may largely be based on inflation. Economic inflation not only makes it difficult for individuals to live on existing income, but it erodes the real value of savings that are accumulated over many years. Social security benefits may increase to meet inflationary pressures on a formula basis, but private pensions, which are becoming increasingly important, will not withstand an inflation rate of 8% or more. As inflation continues unabated, middle-income elderly will find they are having great difficulties meeting their expenses. One hedge against inflation for many families is that increasingly both spouses will work for their whole careers. Pension benefits will thus be available to both husband and wife. This is an important change from previous periods, where women did not work long enough to qualify for either social security or any available private pensions.

It would be unrealistic to expect that increased resources will alleviate the need for many of the programs discussed in this book. Instead, expanded resources will produce shifts in priorities and program orientations. What may be seen by the elderly of the next 50 years as appropriate services can be examined on a program-by-program basis:

1. *Income maintenance programs.*   These programs will be expanded, but resources to support them will be obtained from general revenue funds, not only from a specially earmarked trust fund. Private pensions will be increasingly important to support older individuals, and these pensions will be available through both employers and programs such as the individual Retirement Account and Keogh plans. Requirements for vesting and payments will be stiffened to ensure that the money paid in by workers becomes available to them when needed. Unfortunately these requirements may discourage many companies from developing adequate pension systems. Some stress will be taken off public income maintenance programs by an increase in the number of white-collar and professional workers who maintain their career lives past 65. Health insurance will be expanded to cover a wider range of conditions and community-based as well as hospital-based programs. Increased coverage for mental health services will be included.

2. *Information and referral.*   Information and referral programs will remain the link between the individual needing some type of assistance and the program or service that can best meet his

or her needs. However, the diversity among information and referral programs will also persist. As many multiservice agencies have access to information, they develop means for sharing this information with constituent groups. These informal programs will continue to work alongside the larger, more defined programs. As the senior centers continue to become a focal point for programs and services, it is quite possible that future information and referral for the elderly will be largely generated through these centers.

3. *Health and mental health.* Because of increased coverage by health insurance for chronic illnesses, larger numbers of professionals will be available to the elderly for medical and mental health problems. As more professionals become involved in treating the elderly, attribution of these problems as an inevitable consequence of "growing old" or "senility" will disappear. This change in attitude among health and mental health professionals will help to lessen the present stigma attached to aging in the United States.

4. *Transportation.* These programs will increasingly be coordinated through AAAs in order to meet ever-rising operating costs. The transportation needs of various programs and services will be met through a pooling of resources. Specially equipped minibuses and vans will thus make scheduled stops at a number of multipurpose senior centers, daycare centers, or nutrition sites. General transportation facilities will also serve the suburban and rural elderly with regularly scheduled minibuses traveling through the suburbs and rural areas. These minibuses will feed into regular buses operating along major arterial roads or newly expanded subways and light rail systems in major cities.

5. *Crime prevention and legal assistance.* A large number of programs will be developed to provide a variety of counseling and legal services. Crimes against elderly victims will become harshly punished in most states, and the victims will be compensated financially for their losses. Counseling for elderly victims will also be widely available.

Restrictions will be placed on protective services. Guardianship and institutionalization will be increasingly utilized only for individuals whose needs cannot possibly be met through any other arrangement or less restrictive environment. The definition of an individual's need for guardianship or institutionalization will be clarified in all states and be based on specific determinations of the individual's physical and mental functioning.

6. *Employment.* Retraining programs will grow in numbers, but this training will be matched by an increase in programs dedi-

cated to varied, part-time work. Many white-collar workers will elect to maintain their full-time jobs, but retired blue-collar workers will enroll in training programs to develop skills that were impossible for them to attain during their work years.

7. *Nutrition.* Many future elderly will have a greater knowledge of nutritional needs and greater resources to purchase good meals. What they will require is assistance in meal preparation. Congregate and home-delivered meals will continue to maintain their importance, but the variety of meals prepared will be increased for a more demanding clientele. The same will be true at nutrition sites where the elderly may express a willingness to spend more money on food that is imaginative and well served. Increasing numbers of the nutrition programs will be linked to senior centers.

8. *Senior centers.* Many senior centers will continue to gain in community importance and be designated as focal points for programs and services. Centers are becoming increasingly accepted by older adults because they can offer a variety of resources that address older persons' changing needs and interests and a physical location with which they can identify. This support from older persons will help to generate funds for centers and the programs they house. The long-term success of a center is related to the extent to which it becomes identified with the community. The extent of that identification will in large part determine the ability of a particular center to expand its offerings enough to be officially designated a community focal point.

9. *Housing.* Housing will continue to be a crucial component of services to the elderly. Because of rapidly rising costs of housing on the private market, government-supported housing, from total subsidy to mortgage guarantees, will remain the only adequate housing available to many limited-income older persons. Housing will be seen as a total environment, and those planning housing units will continue to reach out to combine community services with the housing structure. More housing units will also be available to the elderly with disabilities and chronic illnesses, making it easier to remain in the community. Designs and locations will reflect the diversity of the population served. The limitation of available housing for the elderly is related to funding from both national and local sources. If the government finds it feasible to develop alternate funding mechanisms that combine both public and private dollars, housing programs will be able to maximize their potential for expansion.

10. *In-home services.* As professionals in the field recognize the need to provide viable alternatives to institutionalization, the potential for developing in-home services to the chronically ill and disabled elderly will increase. Unfortunately, the most used funding mechanisms for in-home services do not allow payment for the services most needed: ongoing personal care for the chronically ill. Until there is a legislative change, in-home services will continue to be selective, and inappropriate institutionalization will remain a major problem. Verbal support without follow-up funding leaves both service providers and clients confused about what support can really be anticipated.

11. *Daycare.* These programs will grow and coordinate their services with homemaker programs so that a total package of services for the individual can be designed. The activities at the daycare centers will move toward educational formats designed to appeal to a population with more diverse experiences and higher educational levels. This will require the use of ancillary part-time staff to offer a variety of craft and educational programs. Some daycare programs will expand their hours of services to offer night care and in effect become 24-hour programs for families needing services at different intervals during the day.

12. *Nursing homes.* The number of nursing homes will continue to grow but at a slower rate than in the past 20 years. The majority of homes will still be under proprietary auspices, but regulations will produce increased standardization of homes in areas such as staffing and activities. The number of seniors inappropriately placed in nursing homes will be reduced, and some homes will begin to establish linkages with senior centers and daycare centers in order to augment their services.

Educational Programs

It is not possible to conclude a discussion of programs and services for the aging without devoting some attention to the educational programs for seniors that became available in the 1970s. These programs have been based in churches, senior centers, and most important, in community and 4-year colleges.

Educational opportunities for seniors have increased as institutions of higher education have recognized the potential for having adults of all ages on campus and the need to move some of their educational programming into the community. As the cohort aged 18–24 decreases, the opportunities for adults to fill their places in the classroom become more apparent.

Community Colleges

Community colleges have become community educational centers not only for people seeking Associate of Arts degrees but for individuals wanting to upgrade skills and explore new areas of learning. Responding to this interest, many colleges have developed extensive noncredit programs that are offered both at the college and at sites in the community. For example, reading, literature, history, and art classes are often taken into nursing homes, senior daycare centers, and nutrition centers. Many of these noncredit programs, freed from semester structure, can be offered on a flexible time schedule. They are geared to the older person and often designed in conjunction with groups of seniors.

Community colleges have also encouraged older persons to take courses on campus through tuition waivers, precampus counseling, and remedial supports. Dundalk Community College in Maryland offers a full semester of orientation for older persons. During this orientation, each department is visited, time is spent in the labs and with the faculty, and remedial materials are made available. The campus-based courses include some geared particularly for the elderly as well as regular offerings which can be taken for credit or audit. The tuition waiver can come either through the decisions of the college itself or as part of a city, county, or statewide program of tuition waivers. Because of the unique nature of the community college, it has done more to encourage older persons to become involved in education than any other educational group.

College and University Programs

Universities and 4-year colleges have also expanded their participation in educational programming for older persons. The most common way to expand opportunities is through tuition and fee reductions or waivers. Universities have provided everything from a minimum reduction in fees for audit only to full waiver of tuitions and fees for any course or program of study. This latter approach usually offers all courses, degrees, and recreational facilities without cost to any state resident 60 and over. The first 2 years of the program often offers a full range of courses with the strongest emphasis in languages. Evaluation of these programs is showing that seniors who participated in these programs integrated themselves into the overall student body and did not ask for any special orientation, group meetings, or activities at the time they enrolled or at any later time. The university programs also appear to be primarily attracting older adults with previous college experience.

The extent to which a college or university can offer free programs is dependent upon the size and status of the institution. For large state universities, the effect of 300 tuition-fee students on the overall class structure will be minimal. For a small college or university, 300 students could make a significant difference in the course offerings and the size of classes. It is partly for this reason that educational opportunities for older persons vary greatly.

ElderHostle

ElderHostle is a national educational program that is gaining in popularity among older persons and educational institutions. This educational program sponsors 1-week courses on college campuses during the summer months. ElderHostelers interested in participating in the program stay in dormitories with other summer students on the particular college campus during the week of courses. The purpose of the program is to create opportunities for ElderHostelers to live with other students, participate in campus activities, and take courses from regular campus faculty. The courses, designed for the 1-week program, are similar to those that would be offered during the school year and may include an introduction to music, special history courses, flora of New England, or introduction to astronomy. Three courses are offered in each of the 1-week segments. A campus can offer 1, 2, or 3 weeks of courses for ElderHostelers, depending on the resources available.

The ElderHostelers come from throughout the nation and can go from campus to campus across the country throughout the summer if desired. Each ElderHosteler must pay his or her own transportation and $65 toward the costs of the course, room, and board; there are no additional charges for the program. During 1979, there were close to 20,000 ElderHostelers participating in programs on over 200 campuses throughout the country. The enthusiasm among seniors for ElderHostle should not be surprising. As the numbers of older adults with extensive educational backgrounds continue to grow, there will be more demands on their part for advanced educational opportunities.

Programming and Flexibility

Our predictions about programs and services for the aged may be erroneous and not borne out by future events, but the process of reexamining program models and biases is important for policymakers, practitioners, and students. Effective advocacy for aging programs is going to be required over the next half-century, but advocates should be careful not to enshrine a system of programs and services that may become less relevant to the needs of the elderly as the characteristics and desires of the elderly themselves change.

At this point there is no question about the impressiveness of the programs and services that have become available to seniors. These programs and services seem even more impressive when we realize that funding under the OAA had been primarily limited until 1973 to demonstrations. The present array of programs and services can be confusing to practitioners. A comparable degree of confusion certainly exists among older individuals and their families who attempt to ascertain what services are appropriate to their needs, where they are available, and their requirements. Information and referral and outreach must thus become a mainstay of the aging network. Correct referral must be reinforced, however, by treatment from providers which indicates to an older adult that they are not receiving charity and are valued individuals. In the end, this form of respect and attentiveness will turn out to be as important to the older person as any of the programs and services we have discussed.

References

Binstock, R. Responsibility for the care of the geriatric patient: Legal, psychological and ethical issues. *Journal of Geriatric Psychiatry*, 1972, *5*, 146–159.

Butler, R. Why survive? New York: Harper and Row, 1975.

Comptroller General of the United States. *Report to the Congress: The well-being of older people in Cleveland, Ohio.* Washington, D.C.: U.S. Government Printing Office, 1977.

Cutler, N., & Haryootan, R. Demography of the aged. In D. Woodruff & J. Birren (Eds.), *Aging: Scientific perspectives and social issues.* New York: D. Van Nostrand, 1975.

Fandetti, D., & Gelfand, D. Care of the aged: Attitudes of white ethnic families. *Gerontologist*, 1976, *16*, 544–549.

Frankfather, D., Smith, M., & Capers, O. *Family maintenance of the disabled elderly.* Paper presented at the 56th Annual Meeting of the American Orthopsychiatric Association, Washington, D.C., April, 1979.

Manney, J. *Aging in American society.* Ann Arbor, Michigan: Institute of Gerontology, 1975.

Older American Reports, 1979, 3(3), 1–6.

U.S. Bureau of the Census. *Projections of the population of the United States, 1977 to 2050.* (Current Population Reports, Series P-25, No. 704). Washington, D.C.: U.S. Government Printing Office, 1977.

U.S. House of Representatives, Select Committee on Population. *Consequences of changing U.S. population: Demographics of aging.* Washington, D.C.: U.S. Government Printing Office, 1978.

Appendixes

A

The Older Americans Act of 1978

Public Law 89–73 (July 14, 1965), as amended by
Public Law 90–42 (July 1, 1967),[1]
Public Law 91–69 (September 17, 1969),[2]
Public Law 92–258 (March 22, 1972),[3]
Public Law 93–29 (May 3, 1973),[4]
Public Law 93–351 (July 12, 1974),[5]
Public Law 94–135 (November 28, 1975),[6]
Public Law 95–65 (July 11, 1977),[7] and
Public Law 95–478 (October 18, 1978)[8]

𝕬n 𝕬ct

To provide assistance in the development of new or improved programs to help older persons through grants to the States for community planning and services and for training, through research, development, or training project grants, and to establish within the Department of Health, Education, and Welfare an operating agency to be designated as the "Administration on Aging".

---

[1] Hereinafter referred to as the "1967 Amendments".

[2] Hereinafter referred to as the "1969 Amendments".

[3] Hereinafter referred to as the "1972 Amendments".

[4] Hereinafter referred to as the "1973 Amendments".

[5] Hereinafter referred to as the "1974 Amendments".

[6] Hereinafter referred to as the "1975 Amendments".

[7] Hereinafter referred to as the "1977 Amendments".

[8] Hereinafter referred to as the "1978 Amendments". Sec. 504 states, "This Act, and the amendments made by this Act, shall take effect at the close of September 30, 1978."

Source: Reprinted from Administration on Aging, Office of Human Development Services, Older Americans Act of 1965, as Amended: History and Related Acts, Washington, D.C.: U.S. Department of Health, Education, and Welfare, 1979, pp. 1–85.

Be it enacted by the Senate and House of Representatives of the United
States of America in Congress assembled, That this Act may be cited as the
"Older Americans Act of 1965".

TITLE I—DECLARATION OF OBJECTIVES:

DEFINITIONS

DECLARATION OF OBJECTIVES FOR OLDER AMERICANS

SEC. 101. The Congress hereby finds and declares that, in keeping with
the traditional American concept of the inherent dignity of the individual
in our democratic society, the older people of our Nation are entitled to,
and it is the joint and several duty and responsibility of the governments
of the United States and of the several States and their political subdivisions to assist our older people to secure equal opportunity to the full and
free enjoyment of the following objectives:

(1) An adequate income in retirement in accordance with the American standard of living.

(2) The best possible physical and mental health which science can
make available and without regard to economic status.

(3) Suitable housing, independently selected, designed and located
with reference to special needs and available at costs which older
citizens can afford.

(4) Full restorative services for those who require institutional care.

(5) Opportunity for employment with no discriminatory personnel
practices because of age.

(6) Retirement in health, honor, dignity—after years of contribution to
the economy.

(7) Pursuit of meaningful activity within the widest range of civic,
cultural, and recreational opportunities.

(8) Efficient community services, including access to low-cost transportation,[1] which provide a choice in supported living arrangements
and[2] social assistance in a coordinated manner and which are readily
available when needed.

---

[1] The 1973 Amendments, sec. 102, inserted ", including access to low-cost
transportation, ".

[2] The 1978 Amendments, sec. 101, inserted, "a choice in supported living
arrangements and".

(9) Immediate benefit from proven research knowledge which can sustain and improve health and happiness.

(10) Freedom, independence, and the free exercise of individual initiative in planning and managing their own lives.[3]

DEFINITIONS

SEC. 102. For the purposes of this Act—

(1) The term "Secretary" means the Secretary of Health, Education, and Welfare, other than for purposes of title V.[4]

(2) The term "Commissioner" means, unless the context otherwise requires,[5] the Commissioner of the Administration on Aging.

---

[3] *In addition to the Declaration of Objectives of the Older Americans Act, embodied in sec. 101, the 1973 Amendments stated their objectives, as follows:*

"SEC. 101. The Congress finds that millions of older citizens in this Nation are suffering unnecessary harm from the lack of adequate services. It is therefore the purpose of this Act, in support of the objectives of the Older Americans Act of 1965, to—

(1) make available comprehensive programs which include a full range of health, education, and social services to our older citizens who need them,

(2) give full and special consideration to older citizens with special needs in planning such programs, and, pending the availability of such programs for all older citizens, give priority to the elderly with the greatest economic and social need,

(3) provide comprehensive programs which will assure the coordinated delivery of a full range of essential services to our older citizens, and, where applicable, also furnish meaningful employment opportunities for many individuals, including older persons, young persons, and volunteers from the community, and

(4) insure that the planning and operation of such programs will be undertaken as a partnership of older citizens, community agencies, and State and local governments, with appropriate assistance from the Federal Government."

[4] *The 1978 Amendments, sec. 503(a)(1), added ", other than for purposes of title V".*

[5] *The 1967 Amendments, sec. 5(a)(1) inserted, ", unless the context otherwise requires,".*

(3) The term "State" includes the District of Columbia, the Virgin Islands, Puerto Rico, Guam, American Samoa, and the Trust Territory of the Pacific Islands.[6]

(4) The term "nonprofit" as applied to any agency, institution, or organization means an agency, institution, or organization which is, or is owned and operated by,[7] one or more corporations or associations no part of the net earnings of which inures, or may lawfully inure, to the benefit of any private shareholder or individual.

(5) [8] The term "Indian" means a person who is a member of an Indian tribe.

(6)[8] The term "Indian tribe" [9] means any tribe, band, nation, or other organized group or community of Indians (including any Alaska Native village or regional or village corporation as defined in or established pursuant to the Alaska Native Claims Settlement Act (Public Law 92–203; 85 Stat. 688)) which (A) is recognized as eligible for the special programs and services provided by the United States to Indians because of their status as Indians; or (B) is located on, or in proximity to, a Federal or State reservation or rancheria.

(7) [8] The term "tribal organization" [9] means the recognized governing body of any Indian tribe, or any legally established organization of Indians which is controlled, sanctioned, or chartered by such governing body. In any case in which a contract is let or grant made to an organization to perform services benefiting more than one Indian tribe, the approval of each such Indian tribe shall be a prerequisite to the letting or making of such contract or grant.

---

[6] *The 1969 Amendments, sec. 10(a) added ", and the Trust Territory of the Pacific Islands".*

[7] *The 1967 Amendments, sec. 5(a)(2) deleted "The term 'non-profit institution or organization' means an institution or organization which is owned and operated by" and inserted "The term 'nonprofit' as applied to any agency, institution, or organization means an agency, institution, or organization which is, or is owned and operated by,".*

[8] *The 1975 Amendments, sec. 104(b) added the definitions in these paragraphs.*

[9] *Compare with the definition of "Indian tribe" and "tribal organization" in sec. 602(b).*

TITLE II—ADMINISTRATION ON AGING

ESTABLISHMENT OF ADMINISTRATION ON AGING [1]

SEC. 201. (a) There is established in the Office of the Secretary an Administration on Aging (hereinafter in this Act referred to as the "Administration") which shall be headed by a Commissioner on Aging (hereinafter in this Act referred to as the "Commissioner"). Except for title V, the Administration shall be the principal agency for carrying out this Act. In the performance of his functions, the Commissioner shall be directly responsible to the Office of the Secretary. The Secretary shall not approve any delegation of the functions of the Commissioner to any other officer not directly responsible to the Commissioner.

(b) The Commissioner shall be appointed by the President by and with the advice and consent of the Senate.

FUNCTIONS OF ADMINISTRATION

SEC. 202. (a) It shall be the duty and function of the Administration to—

(1) [2] serve as the effective and visible advocate for the elderly within the Department of Health, Education, and Welfare and with other departments, agencies, and instrumentalities of the Federal Government by maintaining active review and commenting responsibilities over all Federal policies affecting the elderly;

(2) serve as a clearinghouse for information related to problems of the aged and aging;

(3) assist the Secretary in all matters pertaining to problems of the aged and aging;

(4) administer the grants provided by this Act;

---

[1] *The 1973 Amendments, sec. 201(a), completely revised sec. 201, by (a) requiring that the Administration on Aging be in the Office of the Secretary, (b) requiring that AoA, with exceptions, be the principal agency for carrying out this Act, (c) requiring that the Commissioner, in the performance of his functions, be directly responsible to the Office of the Secretary, and (d) prohibiting approval by the Secretary of any delegation of the Commissioner's functions to "any other officer not directly responsible to the Commissioner", unless the Secretary took certain actions. However, the 1974 Amendments, sec. 2, changed this to an absolute prohibition against such delegation.*

[2] *The 1978 Amendments, sec. 102(a)(1) inserted paragraph 1.*

(5) [3] develop plans, conduct and arrange for research in the field of aging, and assist in the establishment of and carry out programs designed to meet the needs of older individuals for social services, including nutrition, hospitalization, preretirement training, continuing education, low-cost transportation and housing, and health services;

(6) provide technical assistance and consultation to States and political subdivisions thereof with respect to programs for the aged and aging;

(7) prepare, publish, and disseminate educational materials dealing with the welfare of older individuals;

(8) gather statistics in the field of aging which other Federal agencies are not collecting;

(9) stimulate more effective use of existing resources and available services for the aged and aging;

(10) [4] develop basic policies and set priorities with respect to the development and operation of programs and activities conducted under authority of this Act;

(11) provide for the coordination of Federal programs and activities related to such purposes;

(12) coordinate, and assist in, the planning and development by public (including Federal, State, and local agencies) and nonprofit private organizations of programs for older individuals, with a view to the establishment of a nationwide network of comprehensive, coordinated services and opportunities for such individuals;

(13) convene conferences of such authorities and officials of public (including Federal, State, and local agencies) and nonprofit private organizations concerned with the development and operation of programs for older individuals as the Commissioner deems necessary or proper for the development and implementation of policies related to the purposes of this Act;

(14) develop and operate programs providing services and opportunities as authorized by this Act which are not otherwise provided by existing programs for older individuals;

(15) carry on a continuing evaluation of the programs and activities related to the purposes of this Act, with particular attention to the impact of medicare and medicaid, the Age Discrimination in Employment Act of 1967, and the programs of the National Housing Act relating to housing for the elderly and the setting of standards for the

---

[3] *The 1973 Amendments, sec. 201(b)(1), revised paragraph (5). It previously read: "develop plans, conduct and arrange for research and demonstration programs in the field of aging;".*

[4] *The 1973 Amendments, sec. 201(b)(2), added paragraphs (10) through (17).*

licensing of nursing homes, intermediate care homes, and other facilities providing care for older people;

(16) provide information and assistance to private nonprofit organizations for the establishment and operation by them of programs and activities related to the purposes of this Act; and

(17) develop, in coordination with other agencies, a national plan for meeting the needs for trained personnel in the field of aging, and for training persons for carrying out programs related to the purposes of this Act, and conduct and provide for the conducting of such training.

(b) [5] In order to strengthen the involvement of the Administration in the development of policy alternatives in long-term care and to insure that the development of community alternatives is given priority attention, the Commissioner shall—

(1) develop planning linkages with health systems agencies designated under section 1515 of the Public Health Service Act (42 U.S.C. 300 1-4);

(2) participate in all departmental and interdepartmental activities which concern issues of institutional and noninstitutional long-term health care services development; and

(3) review and comment on all departmental regulations and policies regarding community health and social service development for the elderly.

(c) [6] In executing his duties and functions under this Act and carrying out the programs and activities provided for by this Act, the Commissioner, in consultation with the Director of Action, shall take all possible steps to encourage and permit voluntary groups active in social services, including youth organizations active at the high school or college levels, to participate and be involved individually or through representative groups in such programs or activities to the maximum extent feasible, through the performance of advisory or consultative functions, and in other appropriate ways.

FEDERAL AGENCY CONSULTATION [7]

SEC. 203. (a) The Commissioner, in carrying out the purposes and provisions of this Act, shall advise, consult, and cooperate with the head

---

[5] *The 1978 Amendments, sec. 102(a)(2) inserted subsection (b).*

[6] *The 1973 Amendments, sec. 201(b)(3) added this as a new subsection of sec. 202.*

[7] *The 1978 Amendments, sec. 102(b), completely revised sec. 203, which was added by the 1973 Amendments, sec. 201(c), as a new section of Title II. Between 1973 and 1978, it read as follows:*
Footnotes continued on next page

of each Federal agency or department proposing or administering programs or services substantially related to the purposes of this Act, with
respect to such programs or services. The head of each Federal agency
or department proposing to establish programs and services substantially
related to the purposes of this Act shall consult with the Commissioner
prior to the establishment of such programs and services. The head of
each Federal agency administering any program substantially related to
the purpose of this Act, particularly administering any program set forth
in subsection (b), shall, to achieve appropriate coordination, consult and
cooperate with the Commissioner in carrying out such program.

(b) For the purposes of subsection (a), programs related to the purpose
of this Act shall include—

(1) the Comprehensive Employment and Training Act of 1973,

(2) title II of the Domestic Volunteer Service Act of 1973,

(3) titles XVIII, XIX, and XX of the Social Security Act,

(4) sections 231 and 232 of the National Housing Act,

(5) the United States Housing Act of 1937,

(6) section 202 of the Housing Act of 1959,

(7) title I of the Housing and Community Development Act of 1974,

(8) section 222(a)(8) of the Economic Opportunity Act of 1964,

(9) the community schools program under the Elementary and
Secondary Education Act of 1965, and

(10) sections 3, 5, 9, and 16 of the Urban Mass Transportation Act of
1964.

THE NATIONAL INFORMATION AND RESOURCE CLEARING HOUSE FOR THE AGING [8]

SEC. 204. (a) The Commissioner is authorized and directed to establish
and operate a National Information and Resource Clearing House for the
Aging which shall—

(1) collect, analyze, prepare, and disseminate information related to the
needs and interests of older individuals, including information related to

---

Footnotes continued from last page

"SEC. 203. *Federal agencies proposing to establish programs substantially
related to the purposes of this Act shall consult with the Administration on
Aging prior to the establishment of such services, and Federal agencies
administering such programs shall cooperate with the Administration on
Aging in carrying out such services.*"

[8] *The 1973 Amendments, sec. 201(c), added this as a new section of Title
II.*

transportation services for older individuals offered by Federal, State, and local public agencies; [9]

(2) obtain information concerning older individuals from public and private agencies and other organizations serving the needs and interests of older individuals and furnish, upon request, information to such agencies and organizations, including information developed by Federal, State, and local public agencies with respect to programs of such agencies designed to serve the needs and interests of older individuals;

(3) encourage the establishment of State and local information centers and provide technical assistance to such centers, including sources established under section 304(c)(3) [10] and section 305(a)(7), [10] to assist older individuals to have ready access to information; and

(4) carry out a special program for the collection and dissemination of information relevant to consumer interests of older individuals in order that such older individuals may more readily obtain information concerning goods and services needed by them.

(b) The Commissioner shall take whatever action is necessary to achieve coordination of activities carried out or assisted by all departments, agencies, and instrumentalities of the Federal Government with respect to the collection, preparation, and dissemination of information relevant to older individuals. To the extent practicable, the Commissioner shall carry out his functions under this subsection through the National Information and Resource Clearing House for the Aging.

(c) There are authorized to be appropriated to carry out the provisions of this section, for fiscal years 1979, 1980, and 1981, such sums as may be necessary.[11]

FEDERAL COUNCIL ON THE AGING [12]

SEC. 205. (a) There is established a Federal Council on the Aging to be composed of fifteen members appointed by the President with the advice

---

[9] *The 1978 Amendments, sec. 102(c), inserted the phrase, "including information related to transportation services for older individuals offered by Federal, State, and local public agencies".*

[10] *These references are to section numbers before the 1978 Amendments. The corresponding sections now are secs. 306(a)(4) and 307(a)(9).*

[11] *The 1978 Amendments, sec. 102(d), revised sec. 204(c).*

[12] *The 1973 Amendments, sec. 201(c) added this as a new section of Title II. Sec. 202 of those Amendments repealed Title VIII of the Act, sec. 801 of which previously authorized an Advisory Committee on Older Americans and such technical advisory committees as the Secretary deemed appropriate for advising him in carrying out his functions under the Act.*

and consent of the Senate for terms of three years without regard to the provisions of title 5, United States Code. Members shall be appointed so as to be representative of rural and urban [13] older Americans, national organizations with an interest in aging, business, labor, and the general public. At least five of the members shall themselves be older individuals. No full-time officer or employee of the Federal Government may be appointed as a member of the Council. [13]

(b)(1) Of the members first appointed, five shall be appointed for a term of one year, five shall be appointed for a term of two years, and five shall be appointed for a term of three years, as designated by the President at the time of appointment.

(2) Any member appointed to fill a vacancy occurring prior to the expiration of the term for which his predecessor was appointed shall be appointed only for the remainder of such term. Members shall be eligible for reappointment and may serve after the expiration of their terms until their successors have taken office.

(3) Any vacancy in the Council shall not affect its powers, but shall be filled in the same manner by which the original appointment was made.

(4) Members of the Council shall, while serving on business of the Council, be entitled to receive compensation at a rate not to exceed the daily rate specified for grade GS-18 in section 5332 of title 5, United States Code, including traveltime, and while so serving away from their homes or regular places of business, they may be allowed travel expenses, including per diem in lieu of subsistence, in the same manner as the expenses authorized by section 5703(b) of title 5, United States Code, for persons in the Government service employed intermittently.

(c) The President shall designate the Chairman from among the members appointed to the Council. The Council shall meet at the call of the Chairman but not less often than four times a year. [14]

(d) The Council shall—

(1) advise and assist the President on matters relating to the special needs of older Americans;

(2) assist the Commissioner in making the appraisal of needs required by section 402;

(3) review and evaluate, on a continuing basis, Federal policies regarding the aging and programs and other activities affecting the aging conducted or assisted by all Federal departments and agencies for the

---

[13] *The 1978 Amendments, sec. 102(e)(1) inserted "rural and urban" and added the last sentence of sec. 205(a).*

[14] *The 1978 Amendments, sec. 102(e)(2), struck the final sentence of sec. 205(c), which read as follows: "The Secretary and the Commissioner on Aging shall be ex officio members of the Council."*

purpose of appraising their value and their impact on the lives of older Americans;

(4) serve as a spokesman on behalf of older Americans by making recommendations to the President, to the Secretary, the Commissioner, and to the Congress with respect to Federal policies regarding the aging and federally conducted or assisted programs and other activities relating to or affecting them;

(5) inform the public about the problems and needs of the aging, in consultation with the National Information and Resource Clearing House for the Aging, by collecting and disseminating information, conducting or commissioning studies and publishing the results thereof, and by issuing publications and reports; and

(6) provide public forums for discussing and publicizing the problems and needs of the aging and obtaining information relating thereto by conducting public hearings, and by conducting or sponsoring conferences, workshops, and other such meetings.

(e) [15] The Council shall have staff personnel, appointed by the Chairman, to assist it in carrying out its activities. The head of each Federal department and agency shall make available to the Council such information and other assistance as it may require to carry out its activities.

(f) Beginning with the year 1974 the Council shall make such interim reports as it deems advisable and an annual report of its findings and recommendations to the President not later than March 31 of each year. The President shall transmit each such report to the Congress together with his comments and recommendations.

(g)[16] (1) The Council shall undertake a thorough evaluation and study of programs conducted under this Act.

---

[15] *The 1978 Amendments, sec. 102(e)(3) substituted the new subsection (e) for the former subsection (e), which between 1973 and 1978 read as follows:*

"(e) The Secretary and the Commissioner shall make available to the Council such staff, information, and other assistance as it may require to carry out its activities."

[16] *The 1978 Amendments, sec. 102(e)(4), added a new subsection (g) to replace subsections (g), (h), and (i), which between 1973 and 1978 read as follows:*

"(g) The Council shall undertake a study of the interrelationships of benefit programs for the elderly operated by Federal, State, and local government agencies. Following the completion of this study, but no later than January 1, 1976, the President shall submit to Congress recommendations for bringing about greater uniformity of eligibility standards, and for eliminating the negative impact that one program's standards may have on another.

Footnotes continued on next page

(2) The study required in this subsection shall include—

(A) an examination of the fundamental purposes of such programs, and the effectiveness of such programs in attaining such purposes;

(B) an analysis of the means to identify accurately the elderly population in greatest need of such programs; and

(C) an analysis of numbers and incidence of low-income and minority participants in such programs.

(3) The study required under this subsection may include—

(A) an exploration of alternative methods for allocating funds under such programs to States, State agencies on aging, and area agencies on aging in an equitable and efficient manner, which will accurately reflect current conditions and insure that such funds reach the areas of greatest current need and are effectively used for such areas;

(B) an analysis of the need for area agencies on aging to provide direct services within the planning and service area; and

(C) an analysis of the number of nonelderly handicapped in need of home delivered meal services.

(h) [17] There are authorized to be appropriated to carry out the provisions of this section, for fiscal years 1979, 1980, and 1981, such sums as may be necessary.

Footnotes continued from last page

"(h) *The Council shall undertake a study of the combined impact of all taxes on the elderly—including but not limited to income, property, sales, social security taxes. Upon completion of this study, but no later than January 1, 1976, the President shall submit to Congress, and to the Governor and legislatures of the States, the results thereof and such recommendations as he deems necessary.*

"(i) *The Council shall undertake a study or studies concerning the effects of the formulae specified in section 303 for allotment among the States of sums appropriated for area planning and social service programs authorized under title III of this Act. Upon completion of this study, but no later than January 1, 1975, the results of such study, together with recommendations for such changes, if any, in such formulae as may be determined to be desirable and the justification for any changes recommended, shall be submitted to the Commissioner, the Secretary of Health, Education, and Welfare, the Committee on Labor and Public Welfare of the Senate and the Committee on Education and Labor of the House of Representatives.*"

[17] *The 1978 amendments, sec. 102(e)(4) added this as a new subsection* (h).

ADMINISTRATION OF THE ACT [18]

Sec. 206. (a) In carrying out the purposes of this Act, the Commissioner [19] is authorized to:

(1) provide consultative services and technical assistance to public or nonprofit private agencies and organizations; [20]

(2) provide short-term training and technical instruction;

(3) conduct research and demonstrations;

(4) collect, prepare, publish, and disseminate special educational or informational materials, including reports of the projects for which funds are provided under this Act; and

(5) provide staff and other technical assistance to the Federal Council on the Aging.[21]

(b) [22] The Commissioner shall prepare and submit to the Congress not later than September 30, 1980 a report on the effectiveness of programs conducted under part B of title III relating to legal services and an analysis of the need for a separate program of legal services under this Act and of factors which may prohibit the funding of legal services under this Act without such a separate program, together with such recommendations, including recommendations for additional legislation, as the Commissioner deems appropriate.

(c) In administering his [23] functions under this Act, the Commissioner [19] may utilize the services and facilities of any agency of the Federal Government and of any other public or nonprofit agency or organization, in accordance with agreements between the Commissioner and the head thereof, and is authorized to pay therefor, in advance or by way of reimbursement, as may be provided in the agreement.

----

[18] *The 1973 Amendments, sec. 201(c) added this as a new section of Title II. Sec. 202 of those Amendments repealed Title VIII of the Act, sec. 802 of which contained provisions similar in many respects to sec. 206. Differences between the two are discussed in footnotes 19, 20, and 24, below.*

[19] *Sec. 802, which was superseded by the new sec. 206, used the word, "Secretary" at this point.*

[20] *Sec. 802, which was superseded by the new sec. 206, used the words "agencies, organizations, and institutions" at this point.*

[21] *The 1967 Amendments, sec. 5(e) added "and to provide staff and other technical assistance to the President's Council on Aging" to sec. 802, which was superseded by sec. 206.*

[22] *The 1978 Amendments, sec. 102(f), inserted this as a new subsection (b).*

[23] *The 1967 Amendments, sec. 5(f), deleted "their respective" and inserted "his" in sec. 802, which was superseded by sec. 206.*

(d) [24] For the purpose of carrying out this section, there are authorized to be appropriated such sums as may be necessary.

EVALUATION [25]

SEC. 207. (a) The Secretary shall measure and evaluate the impact of all programs authorized by this Act, their effectiveness in achieving stated goals in general, and in relation to their cost, their impact on related programs, and their structure and mechanisms for delivery of services, including, where appropriate, comparisons with appropriate control groups composed of persons who have not participated in such programs. Evaluations shall be conducted by persons not immediately involved in the administration of the program or project evaluated.

(b) The Secretary may not make grants or contracts under section 308 [26] or title IV of this Act until he has developed and published general standards to be used by him in evaluating the programs and projects assisted under such section or title.[27] Results of evaluations conducted pursuant to such standards shall be included in the reports required by section 208.

(c) In carrying out evaluations under this section, the Secretary shall, whenever possible, arrange to obtain the opinions of program and project participants about the strengths and weaknesses of the programs and projects, and conduct, where appropriate, evaluations which compare the effectiveness of related programs in achieving common objectives.[28]

---

[24] *Sec. 802, which was superseded by sec. 206, contained no language comparable to subsection (d).*

[25] *The 1973 Amendments, sec. 201(c), added this as a new section of Title II. Sec. 202 of those amendments repealed Title VIII of the Act, sec. 804 of which contained provisions similar in some respects to sec. 207—though much briefer and less detailed than the latter. The 1969 Amendments, sec. 12 had added sec. 804 to the Act.*

[26] *This reference is to the section number before the 1978 Amendments. The corresponding section now is sec. 421.*

[27] *These "general standards" were published in the Federal Register for Thursday, June 28, 1973 (p. 17030, Vol. 38 No. 124).*

[28] *The 1978 Amendments, sec. 102(g)(1), added "and conduct, where appropriate, evaluations which compare the effectiveness of related programs in achieving common objectives".*

(d) The Secretary shall annually publish summaries and analyses [29] of the results of evaluative research and evaluation of program and project impact and effectiveness, the full contents of which shall be transmitted to Congress and be accessible to the public.[29]

(e) The Secretary shall take the necessary action to assure that all studies, evaluations, proposals, and data produced or developed with Federal funds shall become the property of the United States.

(f) Such information as the Secretary may deem necessary for purposes of the evaluations conducted under this section shall be made available to him, upon request, by the departments and agencies of the executive branch.

(g) The Secretary is authorized to use such sums as may be required, but not to exceed 1 per centum of the funds appropriated under this Act, or $1,000,000 whichever is greater, to conduct program and project evaluations (directly, or by grants or contracts) as required by this title. In the case of allotments from such an appropriation, the amount available for such allotments (and the amount deemed appropriated therefor) shall be reduced accordingly.

REPORTS [30]

SEC. 208. Not later than one hundred and twenty days after the close of each fiscal year, the Commissioner shall prepare and submit to the President for transmittal to the Congress a full and complete report on the activities carried out under this Act. Such annual reports shall include statistical data reflecting services and activities provided individuals during the preceding fiscal year.

---

[29] *The 1978 Amendments, sec. 102(g)(2) inserted "and analyses" and added requirements that the full contents of evaluations be "transmitted to Congress and be accessible to the public."*

[30] *The 1973 Amendments, sec. 201(c) added this as a new section of Title II. There was previously no comparable provision in the Act. Sec. 207(b) requires the results of certain evaluations to be included in the reports required by this section.*

JOINT FUNDING OF PROJECTS [31]

SEC. 209. Pursuant to regulations prescribed by the President, and to the extent consistent with the other provisions of this Act,[32] where funds are provided for a single project by more than one Federal agency to any agency or organization [33] assisted under this Act, the Federal agency principally involved [34] may be designated to act for all in administering the funds provided. In such cases, a single non-Federal share requirement may be established according to the proportion of funds advanced by each Federal agency, and any such agency may waive any technical grant or contract requirement (as defined by such regulations) which is inconsistent with the similar requirements of the administering agency or which the administering agency does not impose.[35]

ADVANCE FUNDING [36]

SEC. 210. (a) For the purpose of affording adequate notice of funding available under this Act, appropriations under this Act are authorized to be included in the appropriation Act for the fiscal year preceding the fiscal year for which they are available for obligation.

(b) In order to effect a transition to the advance funding method of timing appropriation action, the amendment made by subsection (a) shall apply notwithstanding that its initial application will result in the enactment in the same year (whether in the same appropriation Act or otherwise) of two separate appropriations, one for the then current fiscal year and one for the succeeding fiscal year.

---

[31] *The 1973 Amendments, sec. 201(c) added this as a new section of Title II. Sec. 202 of those Amendments repealed Title VIII of the Act, sec. 805 of which was similar in many respects to the new sec. 209. Differences between the two are discussed in footnotes 32 through 34, below. Sec. 805 had been added to the Act by sec. 13 of the 1969 amendments. As to the applicability to this section of the Joint Funding Simplification Act of 1974 (P.L. 93–510), see Sec. 211 of this Act.*

[32] *The phrase ", and to the extent consistent with the other provisions of this Act" was not in sec. 805, which was superseded by the new sec. 209.*

[33] *Sec. 805, which was superseded by the new sec. 209, used the words "agency, organization, institution, or person" at this point.*

[34] *Sec. 805, which was superseded by the new sec. 209, used the words "any one Federal agency" at this point, instead of "the Federal agency principally involved."*

[35] *As to joint funding, see also secs. 211 and 306(c), this Act.*

[36] *The 1973 Amendments, sec. 201(c) added this as a new section of Title II. There was previously no comparable provision in the Act.*

SEC. 211. (a) The provisions and requirements of the Act of December 5, 1974 (Public Law 93–510; [38] 88 Stat. 1604), and of title V of the Act of October 15, 1977 (Public Law 95–134; 91 Stat. 1164),[39] shall not apply to the administration of the provisions of this Act or to the administration of any program or activity under this Act.

(b) [40] No part of the costs of any project under any title of this Act may be treated as income or benefits to any eligible individual (other than any wage or salary to such individual) for the purpose of any other program or provision of Federal or State law.

REDUCTION OF PAPERWORK [41]

SEC. 212. In order to reduce unnecessary, duplicative, or disruptive demands for information, the Commissioner, in consultation with State agencies designated under section 305(a)(1), and other appropriate agencies and organizations, shall continually review and evaluate all requests by the Administration on Aging for information under this Act and take

---

[37] *The 1975 Amendments, sec. 102, added this as a new section of Title II.*

[38] *P.L. 93–510 is the Joint Funding Simplification Act of 1974, which was enacted Dec. 5, 1974. As to joint funding, see also sec. 209, above, and sec. 306(c).*

[39] *The 1978 Amendments, sec. 102(h)(2) inserted ", and of title V of the Act of October 15, 1977 (Public Law 95–134; 91 Stat. 1164)". That title reads, in pertinent part, as follows:*

"SEC. 501. In order to minimize the burden caused by existing application and reporting procedures for certain grant-in-aid programs available to the Virgin Islands, Guam, American Samoa, the Trust Territory of the Pacific Islands, and the Government of the Northern Mariana Islands (hereafter referred to as "Insular Areas") it is hereby declared to be the policy of the Congress that:

"(a) Notwithstanding any provision of law to the contrary, any department or agency of the Government of the United States which administers any Act of Congress which specifically provides for making grants to any Insular Area under which payments received may be used by such Insular Area only for certain specified purposes (other than direct payments to classes of individuals) may, acting through appropriate administrative authorities of such department or agency, consolidate any or all grants made to such area for any fiscal year or years."

[40]*The 1978 Amendments, sec. 102(h)(1), added subsection (b).*

[41]*The 1978 Amendments, sec. 102(i), added the final three sections of Title II. There were previously no comparable provisions in the Act.*

such action as may be necessary to reduce the paperwork required under this Act. The Commissioner shall request only such information as the Commissioner deems essential to carry out the purposes and provisions of this Act.

CONTRACTING AND GRANT AUTHORITY [41]

SEC. 213. None of the provisions of this Act shall be construed to prevent a recipient of a grant or a contract from entering into an agreement, subject to the approval of the State agency, with a profitmaking organization, where such organization demonstrates clear superiority with respect to the quality of services covered by such contract to carry out the provisions of this Act and of the appropriate State plan.

SURPLUS PROPERTY ELIGIBILITY [41]

SEC. 214. Any State or local government agency, and any nonprofit organization or institution, which receives funds appropriated for programs for older individuals under this Act, under title IV or title XX of the Social Security Act, or under the Economic Opportunity Act of 1964, shall be deemed eligible to receive for such programs, property which is declared surplus to the needs of the Federal Government in accordance with laws applicable to surplus property.

TITLE III—GRANTS FOR STATE AND COMMUNITY PROGRAMS ON AGING [1]

PART A—GENERAL PROVISIONS

PURPOSE; ADMINISTRATION

SEC. 301. (a) It is the purpose of this title to encourage and assist State and local agencies to concentrate resources in order to develop greater

---

[1] *The 1978 Amendments, sec. 103(b) completely revised Title III, although there are similarities between the revised title and the former title. The principal changes were the consolidation into Title III of programs previously*
Footnotes continued on next page

capacity and foster the development of comprehensive and coordinated service systems to serve older individuals by entering into new cooperative arrangements in each State with State and local agencies, and with the providers of social services, including nutrition services and multipurpose senior centers, for the planning for the provision of, and for the provision of, social services, nutrition services, and multipurpose senior centers, in order to—

(1) secure and maintain maximum independence and dignity in a home environment for older individuals capable of self care with appropriate supportive services;

(2) remove individual and social barriers to economic and personal independence for older individuals; and

(3) provide a continuum of care for the vulnerable elderly.

(b)(1) In order to effectively carry out the purpose of this title, the Commissioner [2] shall administer programs under this title through the Administration on Aging.

(2) In carrying out the provisions of this title, the Commissioner may request the technical assistance and cooperation of the Department of Labor, the Community Services Administration, the Department of Housing and Urban Development, the Department of Transportation, and such other agencies and departments of the Federal Government as may be appropriate.

DEFINITIONS

SEC. 302. For the purpose of this title—

(1) The term "comprehensive and coordinated system" means a system for providing all necessary social services, including nutrition services, in a manner designed to—

(A) facilitate accessibility to, and utilization of, all social services and nutrition services provided within the geographic area served by such system by any public or private agency or organization;

Footnotes continued from last page
authorized by Title III ("Social Services"), Title V ("Multi-purpose Senior Centers") and Title VII ("Nutrition Services"), and providing two separate authorizations for Congregate Nutrition Services and Home Delivered Nutrition Services. Title III had been extensively revised by the 1973 Amendments, sec. 301.

[2] *The 1973 Amendments throughout Title III named the Commissioner as the responsible official. From 1965 until then, the Secretary had been named.*

(B) develop and make the most efficient use of social services and nutrition services in meeting the needs of older individuals; and

(C) use available resources efficiently and with a minimum of duplication.

(2) The term "information and referral source" means a location where the State or any public or private agency or organization—

(A) maintains current information with respect to the opportunities and services available to older individuals, and develops current lists of older individuals in need of services and opportunities; and

(B) employs a specially trained staff to inform older individuals of the opportunities and services which are available, and to assist such individuals to take advantage of such opportunities and services.

(3) The term "long-term care facility" means any skilled nursing facility, as defined in section 1861(j) of the Social Security Act, any intermediate care facility, as defined in section 1905(c) of the Social Security Act, any nursing home, as defined in section 1908(e) of the Social Security Act, and any other similar adult care home.

(4) The term "legal services" means legal advice and representation by an attorney (including, to the extent feasible, counseling or other appropriate assistance by a paralegal or law student under the supervision of an attorney), and includes counseling or representation by a nonlawyer where permitted by law, to older individuals with economic or social needs.

(5) The term "planning and service area" means an area specified by a State agency under section 305(a)(1)(E).

(6) The term "State" means each of the several States, the District of Columbia, the Commonwealth of Puerto Rico, Guam, American Samoa, the Virgin Islands, the Trust Territory of the Pacific Islands and the Northern Mariana Islands.

(7) The term "State agency" means the State agency designated by a State under section 305(a)(1).

(8) The term "unit of general purpose local government" means—

(A) a political subdivision of the State whose authority is general and not limited to only one function or combination of related functions; or

(B) an Indian tribal organization.

AUTHORIZATION OF APPROPRIATIONS; USES OF FUNDS

SEC. 303. (a) There are authorized to be appropriated $300,000,000 for fiscal year 1979, $360,000,000 for fiscal year 1980, and $480,000,000 for fiscal year 1981 for the purpose of making grants under part B of this title (relating to social services).

(b)(1) There are authorized to be appropriated $350,000,000 for fiscal year 1979, $375,000,000 for fiscal year 1980, and $400,000,000 for fiscal year 1981 for the purpose of making grants under subpart 1 of part C of this title (relating to congregate nutrition services).

(2) There are authorized to be appropriated $80,000,000 for fiscal year 1979, $100,000,000 for fiscal year 1980, and $120,000,000 for fiscal year 1981 for the purpose of making grants under subpart 2 of part C of this title (relating to home delivered nutrition services).

(c) Grants made under parts B and C of this title may be used for paying part of the cost of—

(1) the administration of area plans by area agencies on aging designated under section 305(a)(2)(A), including the preparation of area plans on aging consistent with section 306 and the evaluation of activities carried out under such plans; and

(2) the development of comprehensive and coordinated systems for social services, congregate and home delivered nutrition services, the development and operation of multipurpose senior centers, and the delivery of legal services.

ALLOTMENT; FEDERAL SHARE

SEC. 304. (a)(1) From the sums appropriated under parts B and [3] C for fiscal years 1979, 1980, and 1981, each State shall be alloted an amount which bears the same ratio to such sums as the population aged 60 or older in such State bears to the population aged 60 or older in all States, except that (A) no State shall be allotted less than one-half of 1 percent of the sum appropriated for the fiscal year for which the determination is made; (B) Guam, the Virgin Islands, and the Trust Territory of the

---

[3] *From the enactment of the Act in 1965 until the 1973 Amendments, the statutory formula for allotting Title III formula grant funds required that each State be allotted one percent of the amount appropriated, each of the other jurisdictions named be allotted one-half of one percent, and that from the remainder of each year's appropriation each State and other jurisdiction be allotted an additional amount which bore "the same ratio to such remainder as the population aged sixty-five or over in such State bears to the population aged sixty-five or over in all the States. . . ." The 1973 Amendments, for the first time, based the allotment formula on the population aged 60 and over (instead of 65 and over). Except as indicated in footnote 6, the 1978 Amendments made no change in the formula.*

Pacific Islands,[4] shall each be allotted not less than one-fourth of 1 percent of the sum appropriated for the fiscal year for which the determination is made; (C) American Samoa [6] and the Northern Mariana Islands [5] shall each be allotted not less than one-sixteenth of 1 percent of the sum appropriated for the fiscal year for which the determination is made; and (D) no State shall be allotted an amount less than the State received for fiscal year 1978.[6] For the purpose of the exception contained in clause (A) only, the term "State" does not include Guam, American Samoa, the Virgin Islands, the Trust Territory of the Pacific Islands,[4] and the Northern Mariana Islands.[5]

(2) The number of individuals aged 60 or older in any State and in all States shall be determined by the Commissioner on the basis of the most recent satisfactory data available to him.

(b) Whenever the Commissioner determines that any amount allotted to a State under part B or C for a fiscal year under this section will not be used by such State for carrying out the purpose for which the allotment was made, he shall make such allotment available for carrying out such purpose to one or more other States to the extent he determines that such other States will be able to use such additional amount for carrying out such purpose. Any amount made available to a State from an appropriation for a fiscal year in accordance with the preceding sentence shall, for purposes of this title, be regarded as part of such State's allotment (as determined under subsection (a)) for such year, but shall remain available until the end of the succeeding fiscal year.

(c) If the Commissioner finds that any State has failed to qualify under the State plan requirements of section 307, the Commissioner shall withhold the allotment of funds to such State referred to in subsection (a). The Commissioner shall disburse the funds so withheld directly to any public or private nonprofit institution or organization, agency, or political subdivision of such State submitting an approved plan under section 307, which includes an agreement that any such payment shall be matched in the proportion determined under subsection (d)(1)(B) for such State, by funds for in-kind resources from non-Federal sources.

---

[4] *The 1969 Amendment, sec. 10(b), added "the Trust Territory of the Pacific Islands" to the list of jurisdictions other than States which are entitled to share in Title III allotments.*

[5] *The 1978 Amendments added "the Northern Mariana Islands" to that list.*

[6] *Between the 1973 Amendments and the 1978 Amendments, it was provided that each State's allotment could not be less than it received for fiscal year 1973, and that American Samoa was entitled to a minimum allotment of ¼ of 1%.*

(d)(1) From any State's allotment under this section for any fiscal year—

(A) such amount as the State agency determines, but not more than 8.5 percent thereof, shall be available for paying such percentage as the agency determines, but not more than 75 percent, of the cost of administration of area plans; and

(B) the remainder of such allotment shall be available to such State only for paying such percentage as the State agency determines, but not more than 90 percent in fiscal years 1979 and 1980, and 85 percent in fiscal year 1981, of the cost of social services and nutrition services authorized under parts B and C provided in the State as part of a comprehensive and coordinated system in planning and service areas for which there is an area plan approved by the State agency.

(2) [7] The non-Federal share shall be in cash or in kind. In determining the amount of the non-Federal share, the Commissioner may attribute fair market value to services and facilities contributed from non-Federal sources.

ORGANIZATION

SEC. 305. (a) In order for a State to be eligible to participate in programs of grants to States from allotments under this title—

(1) the State shall, in accordance with regulations of the Commissioner, designate a State agency as the sole State agency [8] to—

(A) develop a State plan to be submitted to the Commissioner for approval under section 307;

---

[7] *This provision was not in Title III before it was revised by the 1978 Amendments.*

[8] *Sec. 204 of the "Intergovernmental Cooperation Act of 1968" (P.L. 90–577) provided: "204. Notwithstanding any other Federal law which provides that a single State agency or multimember board or commission must be established or designated to administer or supervise the administration of any grant-in-aid program, the head of any Federal department or agency administering such program may, upon request of the Governor or other appropriate executive or legislative authority of the State responsible for determining or revising the organizational structure of State government, waive the single State agency or multimember board or commission provision upon adequate showing that such provision prevents the establishment of the most effective and efficient organizational arrangements within the State government and approve other State administrative structure or arrangements: Provided, That the head of the Federal department or agency determines that the objectives of the Federal statute authorizing the grant-in-aid program will not be endangered by the use of such other State structure or arrangements".*

(B) administer the State plan within such State;

(C) be primarily responsible for the coordination of all State activities related to the purposes of this Act;

(D) [7] serve as an effective and visible advocate for the elderly by reviewing and commenting upon all State plans, budgets, and policies which affect the elderly and providing technical assistance to any agency, organization, association, or individual representing the needs of the elderly; and

(E) divide the State into distinct areas, in accordance with guidelines issued by the Commissioner, after considering the geographical distribution of individuals aged 60 and older in the State, the incidence of the need for social services, nutrition services, multipurpose senior centers, and legal services, the distribution of older individuals who have low incomes residing in such areas, the distribution of resources available to provide such services or centers, the boundaries of existing areas within the State which were drawn for the planning or administration of social services programs, the location of units of general purpose local government within the State, and any other relevant factors; and

(2) the State agency designated under clause (1) shall—

(A) determine for which planning and service area an area plan will be developed, in accordance with section 306, and for each such area designate, after consideration of the views offered by the unit or units of general purpose local government in such area, a public or private nonprofit agency or organization as the area agency on aging for such area;

(B) provide assurances, satisfactory to the Commissioner, that the State agency will take into account, in connection with matters of general policy arising in the development and administration of the State plan for any fiscal year, the views of recipients of social services or nutrition services, or individuals using multipurpose senior centers provided under such plan;

(C) develop a formula, in accordance with guidelines issued by the Commissioner, for the distribution within the State of funds received under this title, taking into account, to the maximum extent feasible, the best available statistics on the geographical distribution of individuals aged 60 and older in the State, and publish such formula for review and comment;

(D) submit its formula developed under subclause (C) to the Commissioner for review and comment; and

(E) provide assurances that preference will be given to providing services to older individuals with the greatest economic or social needs and include proposed methods of carrying out the preference in the State plan.

(b)(1) In carrying out the requirement of clause (1) of subsection (a), the State may designate as a planning and service area any unit of general purpose local government which has a population of 100,000 or more. In any case in which a unit of general purpose local government makes application to the State agency under the preceding sentence to be designated as a planning and service area, the State agency shall, upon request, provide an opportunity for a hearing to such unit of general purpose local government. A State may designate as a planning and service area under clause (1) of subsection (a), any region within the State recognized for purposes of areawide planning which includes one or more such units of general purpose local government when the State determines that the designation of such a regional planning and service area is necessary for, and will enhance, the effective administration of the programs authorized by this title. The State may include in any planning and service area designated under clause (1) of subsection (a) such additional areas adjacent to the unit of general purpose local government or regions so designated as the State determines to be necessary for, and will enhance the effective administration of the programs authorized by this title.

(2) The State is encouraged in carrying out the requirement of clause (1) of subsection (a) to include the area covered by the appropriate economic development district involved in any planning and service area designated under such clause, and to include all portions of an Indian reservation within a single planning and service area, if feasible.

(3) The chief executive officer of each State in which a planning and service area crosses State boundaries, or in which an interstate Indian reservation is located, may apply to the Commissioner to request redesignation as an interstate planning and service area comprising the entire metropolitan area or Indian reservation. If the Commissioner approves such an application, he shall adjust the State allotments of the areas within the planning and service area in which the interstate planning and service area is established to reflect the number of older individuals within the area who will be served by an interstate planning and service area not within the State.

(4) Whenever a unit of general purpose local government, a region, a metropolitan area or an Indian reservation is denied designation under the provisions of clause (1) of subsection (a), such unit of general purpose local government, region, metropolitan area, or Indian reservation may appeal the decision of the State agency to the Commissioner. The Commissioner shall afford such unit, region, metropolitan area, or Indian reservation an opportunity for a hearing. In carrying out the provisions of this paragraph, the Commissioner may approve the decision of the State agency, disapprove the decision of the State agency and require the State agency to designate the unit, region, area, or Indian reservation

appealing the decision as a planning and service area, or take such other action as the Commissioner deems appropriate.

(c) An area agency on aging designated under subsection (a) shall be—

(1) an established office of aging which is operating within a planning and service area designated under subsection (a);

(2) any office or agency of a unit of general purpose local government, which is designated for the purpose of serving as an area agency by the chief elected official of such unit;

(3) any office or agency designated by the appropriate chief elected officials of any combination of units of general purpose local government to act on behalf of such combination for such purpose; or

(4) any public or nonprofit private agency in a planning and service area which is under the supervision or direction for this purpose of the designated State agency and which can engage in the planning or provision of a broad range of social services, or nutrition services within such planning and service area;

and shall provide assurance, determined adequate by the State agency, that the area agency will have the ability to develop an area plan and to carry out, directly or through contractual or other arrangements, a program in accordance with the plan within the planning and service area. In designating an area agency on aging within the planning and service area or within any unit of general purpose local government designated as a planning and service area the State shall give preference to an established office on aging, unless the State agency finds that no such office within the planning and service area will have the capacity to carry out the area plan.

AREA PLANS[9]

SEC. 306. (a) Each area agency on aging designated under section 305(a)(2)(A) shall, in order to be approved by the State agency, prepare and develop an area plan for a planning and service area for a 3-year period[10] with such annual adjustments as may be necessary. Each such

---

[9] *Sec. 209, Housing and Urban Development Act of 1974 (P.L. 93–383, Aug. 22, 1974) requires that low-income housing for the elderly and handicapped provide quality services and management consistent with the needs of the occupants, and that such projects be "in support of and supported by the applicable State plans for comprehensive services pursuant to . . . State and area plans pursuant to Title III of the Older Americans Act of 1965."*

[10] *From 1973, when provision was first made for area plans, until the 1978 Amendments, area plans were required to be developed annually.*

plan shall be based upon a uniform format for area plans within the State prepared in accordance with section 307(a)(1). Each such plan shall—

(1) provide, through a comprehensive and coordinated system, for social services, nutrition services, and, where appropriate, for the establishment, maintenance, or construction of multipurpose senior centers, within the planning and service area covered by the plan, including determining the extent of need for social services, nutrition services, and multipurpose senior centers in such area (taking into consideration, among other things, the number of older individuals with low incomes residing in such area), evaluating the effectiveness of the use of resources in meeting such need, and entering into agreements with providers of social services, nutrition services, or multipurpose senior centers in such area, for the provision of such services or centers to meet such need;

(2) [11] provide assurances that at least 50 percent of the amount allotted for part B to the planning and service area will be expended for the delivery of—

(A) services associated with access to services (transportation, outreach, and information and referral);

(B) in-home services (homemaker and home health aide, visiting and telephone reassurance, and chore maintenance); and

(C) legal services;

and that some funds will be expended for each such category of services;

(3) [11] designate, where feasible, a focal point for comprehensive service delivery in each community to encourage the maximum collocation and coordination of services for older individuals, and give special consideration to designating multipurpose senior centers as such focal point;

(4) provide for the establishment and maintenance of information and referral services in sufficient numbers to assure that all older individuals within the planning and service area covered by the plan will have reasonably convenient access to such services;

(5) [11] (A) provide assurances that preference will be given to providing services to older individuals with the greatest economic or social needs and include proposed methods of carrying out the preference in the area plan; and

(B) assure the use of outreach efforts that will identify individuals eligible for assistance under this Act, with special emphasis on rural elderly, and inform such individuals of the availability of such assistance;

(6) provide that the area agency on aging will—

(A) conduct periodic evaluations of activities carried out under the area plan;

---

[11]*There was no provision comparable to this in Title III before it was revised by the 1978 Amendments.*

(B) furnish appropriate technical assistance to providers of social services, nutrition services, or multipurpose senior centers in the planning and service area covered by the area plan;

(C) [12] take into account in connection with matters of general policy arising in the development and administration of the area plan, the views of recipients of services under such plan;

(D) [11] serve as the advocate and focal point for the elderly within the community by monitoring, evaluating, and commenting upon all policies, programs, hearings, levies, and community actions which will affect the elderly;

(E) where possible, enter into arrangements with organizations providing day care services for children so as to provide opportunities for older individuals to aid or assist on a voluntary basis in the delivery of such services to children;

(F) where possible, enter into arrangements with local educational agencies, institutions of higher education, and nonprofit private organizations, to use services provided for older individuals under the community schools program under the Elementary and Secondary Education Act of 1965;

(G) establish an advisory council consisting of older individuals who are participants or who are eligible to participate in programs assisted under this Act, representatives of older individuals, local elected officials, and the general public, to advise continuously the area agency on all matters relating to the development of the area plan, the administration of the plan and operations conducted under the plan;

(H) [11] develop and publish methods by which priority of services is determined, particularly with respect to the delivery of services under clause (2); and

(I) establish effective and efficient procedures for coordination between the programs assisted under this title and programs described in section 203(b).

(b)(1) [11] Each State, in approving area agency plans under this section, may, for fiscal years 1979 and 1980, waive any particular requirement relating to the delivery of services or the establishment or operation of multipurpose senior centers which such agency cannot meet because of the consolidation authorized by the Comprehensive Older Americans

---

[12] *From 1973 until 1975, this was subparagraph (D), following a subparagraph (C) which was deleted by the 1975 Amendments, sec. 105(a). The deleted subparagraph (C) read as follows: "(C) where necessary and feasible, enter into arrangements, consistent with the provisions of the area plan, under which funds under this title may be used to provide legal services to older persons in the planning and service area carried out through federally assisted programs or other public or nonprofit agencies;"*

Act Amendments of 1978, except that the State agency may grant such a waiver only if the area agency demonstrates to the State agency that it is taking steps to meet the requirements of this title, but in any event the State agency may not grant a waiver for any requirement of this Act in effect on September 30, 1978.

(2) [11] Each State, in approving area agency plans under this section, may waive the requirement described in clause (2) of subsection (a) for any category of services described in such clause if the area agency on aging demonstrates to the State agency that services being furnished for such category in the area are sufficient to meet the need for such services in such area. If the State agency grants a waiver under the preceding sentence with respect to any category, then the area agency shall expend under clause (2) of subsection (a) a percentage of the amount allotted for part B to the planning and service area, for the categories with respect to which such waiver does not apply, that is agreed upon by the State agency and the area agency.

(c) [13] (1) Subject to regulations prescribed by the Commissioner, an area agency on aging designated under section 305(a)(2)(A) or, in areas of a State where no such agency has been designated, the State agency, may enter into agreements with agencies administering programs under the Rehabilitation Act of 1973,[14] and titles XIX [15] and XX [16] of the Social Security Act for the purpose of developing and implementing plans for meeting the common need for transportation services of individuals receiving benefits under such Acts and older individuals participating in programs authorized by this title.

(2) In accordance with an agreement entered into under paragraph (1), funds appropriated under this title may be used to purchase transportation services for older individuals and may be pooled with funds made available for the provision of transportation services under the Rehabilitation Act of 1973, and titles XIX and XX of the Social Security Act.

STATE PLANS [17]

SEC. 307. (a) Except as provided in section 309(a), each State, in order to be eligible for grants from its allotment under this title for any fiscal

---

[13] *This subsection was added by the 1975 Amendments, sec. 105(b).*
[14] *See footnote 1, p. 145.*
[15] *See footnote 2, p. 150.*   page numbers refer to original source
[16] *See footnote 4, p. 152.*
[17] *See footnote 9.*

444

year, shall submit to the Commissioner a State plan for a 3-year period,[18] with such annual revisions as are necessary, which meets such criteria as the Commissioner may by regulation prescribe. Each such plan shall—

(1) [11] contain assurances that the State plan will be based upon area plans developed by area agencies on aging within the State designated under section 305(a)(2)(A) and that the State will prepare and distribute a uniform format for use by area agencies in developing area plans under section 306;

(2) provide that each area agency on aging designated under section 305(a)(2)(A) will develop and submit to the State agency for approval an area plan which complies with the provisions of section 306;

(3)(A) provide that the State agency will evaluate the need for social services (including legal services), nutrition services, and multipurpose senior centers within the State and determine the extent to which existing public or private programs meet such need; and

(B)[11] provide assurances that the State agency will spend in each fiscal year, for services to older individuals residing in rural areas in the State assisted under this title, an amount equal to not less than 105 percent of the amount expended for such services (including amounts expended under title V and title VII) in fiscal year 1978;

(4) provide for the use of such methods of administration (including methods relating to the establishment and maintenance of personnel standards on a merit basis, except that the Commissioner shall exercise no authority with respect to the selection, tenure of office, or compensation of any individual employed in accordance with such methods) as are necessary for the proper and efficient administration of the plan, and, where necessary, provide for the reorganization and reassignment of functions to assure such efficient administration; [19]

(5) [11] provide that the State agency will afford an opportunity for a hearing upon request to any area agency on aging submitting a plan under this title, to any provider of a service under such a plan, or to any applicant to provide a service under such a plan;

(6) provide that the State agency will make such reports, in such form, and containing such information, as the Commissioner may require, and comply with such requirements as the Commissioner may impose to insure the correctness of such reports;

(7) [11] provide satisfactory assurance that such fiscal control and fund accounting procedures will be adopted as may be necessary to assure

---

[18] *From 1973 until the 1978 Amendments, State plans were required to be developed annually.*

[19] *The 1978 Amendments added, ", and, where necessary, provide for the reorganization and reassignment of functions to assure such efficient administration."*

proper disbursement of, and accounting for, Federal funds paid under this title to the State, including any such funds paid to the recipients of a grant or contract;

(8) provide that the State agency will conduct periodic evaluations of activities and projects carried out under the State plan;

(9) provide for establishing and maintaining information and referral services in sufficient numbers to assure that all older individuals in the State who are not furnished adequate information and referral services under section 306(a)(4) will have reasonably convenient access to such services;

(10) provide that no social services, including nutrition services, will be directly provided by the State agency or an area agency on aging, except where, in the judgment of the State agency, provision of such services by the State agency or an area agency on aging is necessary to assure an adequate supply of such services;

(11) provide that subject to the requirements of merit employment systems of State and local governments, preference shall be given to individuals aged 60 or older for any staff positions (full time or part time) in State and area agencies for which such individuals qualify;

(12) [20] provide assurances that the State agency will—

(A) establish and operate, either directly or by contract or other arrangement with any public agency or other appropriate private non-profit organization which is not responsible for licensing or certifying long-term care services in the State or which is not an association (or an affiliate of such an association) of long-term care facilities (including any other residential facility for older individuals), a long-term care ombuds-man program which will—

(i) investigate and resolve complaints made by or on behalf of older individuals who are residents of long-term care facilities relating to administrative action which may adversely affect the health, safety, welfare, and rights of such residents;

(ii) monitor the development and implementation of Federal, State, and local laws, regulations, and policies with respect to long-term care facilities in that State;

(iii) provide information as appropriate to public agencies regarding the problems of older individuals residing in long-term care facilities;

---

[20] *Before the 1978 Amendments, there was no specific provision for using Title III formula grant funds for long-term care ombudsman services, although such use may have been permissible. Nevertheless, ombudsman services were provided throughout the Nation by using Model Project funds. Paragraph (16) of this subsection provides for use of a minimum portion of a State's social services allotment for "carrying out the provisions of" this paragraph (12).*

(iv) provide for training volunteers and promote the development of citizen organizations to participate in the ombudsman program; and

(v) carry out such other activities as the Commissioner deems appropriate;

(B) establish procedures for appropriate access by the ombudsman to long-term care facilities and patients' records, including procedures to protect the confidentiality of such records and ensure that the identity of any complainant or resident will not be disclosed without the written consent of such complainant or resident, or upon court order;

(C) establish a statewide uniform reporting system to collect and analyze data relating to complaints and conditions in long-term care facilities for the purpose of identifying and resolving significant problems, with provision for submission of such data to the agency of the State responsible for licensing or certifying long-term care facilities in the State and to the Commissioner on a regular basis; and

(D) establish procedures to assure that any files maintained by the ombudsman program shall be disclosed only at the discretion of the ombudsman having authority over the disposition of such files, except that the identity of any complainant or resident of a long-term care facility shall not be disclosed by such ombudsman unless—

(i) such complainant or resident, or his legal representative, consents in writing to such disclosure; or

(ii) such disclosure is required by court order;

(13) [21] provide with respect to nutrition services that—

(A) each project providing nutrition services will be available to individuals aged 60 or older, and to their spouses;

(B) each project will provide meals in a congregate setting, except that each such project may provide home delivered meals based upon a determination of need made by the recipient of a grant or contract entered into under this title;

(C)(i) each project will permit recipients of grants or contracts to charge participating individuals for meals furnished in accordance with guidelines established by the Commissioner, taking into consideration the income ranges of eligible individuals in local communities and other

---

[21] *Before the 1978 Amendments, there was no specific provision for using Title III formula grant funds for nutrition programs for the elderly, although this could be and was done, particularly before enactment in 1972 of the Title VII "Nutrition Program for the Elderly." The 1978 Amendments consolidated the Title VII program into Title III, repealing Title VII and enacting as new provisions of Title III this paragraph (13) State plan requirement, Part C of this Title III, and sec. 311, regarding surplus commodities.*

sources of income of the recipients of a grant or contract; and (ii) such charges will be used to increase the number of meals served by the project involved;

(D) a site for such services and for comprehensive social services is furnished in as close proximity to the majority of eligible individuals' residences as feasible, with particular attention upon a multipurpose senior center, a school, a church, or other appropriate community facility, preferably within walking distance where possible, and where appropriate, transportation to such site is furnished or home delivered meals are furnished to eligible individuals who are homebound;

(E) each project will establish outreach activities which assure that the maximum number of eligible individuals may have an opportunity to participate;

(F) each project may establish and administer the nutrition project with the advice of persons competent in the field of service in which the nutrition project is being provided, older individuals who will participate in the program, and of persons who are knowledgeable with regard to the needs of older individuals;

(G) each project will provide special menus, where feasible and appropriate, to meet the particular dietary needs arising from the health requirements, religious requirements, or ethnic backgrounds of eligible individuals;

(H) [11] each area agency will give consideration, where feasible, in the furnishing of home delivered meals to the use of organizations which (i) have demonstrated an ability to provide home delivered meals efficiently and reasonably; and (ii) furnish assurances to the area agency that such an organization will maintain efforts to solicit voluntary support and that funds made available under this title to the organization will not be used to supplant funds from non-Federal sources; and

(I) [22] each State agency may, only for fiscal years 1979 and 1980, use not to exceed 20 percent of the amounts allotted under part C to the State for supportive services, including recreational activities, informational services, health and welfare counseling, and referral services, directly related to the delivery of congregate or home delivered meals, except that the Commissioner may approve an application from a State to use not to exceed 50 percent of its amount allotted under part C in areas with unusually high supportive services costs;

---

[22] *Subparagraph (I) is similar in some respects to clause (iii) of sec. 705(a)(2)(A) of the Act prior to the 1978 Amendments, except that sec. 705(a)(2)(A) contained no percentage limitation.*

(14) [23] provide, with respect to the acquisition (in fee simple or by lease for 10 years or more), alteration, or renovation of existing facilities (or the construction [24] of new facilities in any area in which there are no suitable structures available, as determined by the State agency, after full consideration of the recommendations made by area agencies, to be a focal point for the delivery of services assisted under this title) to serve as multipurpose senior centers, that—

(A) [25] the plan contains or is supported by reasonable assurances that (i) for not less than 10 years after acquisition, or not less than 20 years after the completion of construction, the facility will be used for the purpose for which it is to be acquired or constructed, unless for unusual circumstances the Commissioner waives the requirement of this division; (ii) sufficient funds will be available to meet the non-Federal share of the cost of acquisition or construction of the facility; (iii) sufficient funds will be available when acquisition or construction is completed, for effective use of the facility for the purpose for which it is being acquired or constructed; and (iv) the facility will not be used and is not intended to be used for sectarian instruction or as a place for religious worship;

---

[23] *The 1973 Amendments, sec. 501, inserted into the Act a new Title V, entitled "Multipurpose Senior Centers". Before the 1978 Amendments, there was no specific provision for using Title III formula grant funds for acquisition, alteration, renovation, or construction of facilities for use as senior centers. The 1978 Amendments consolidated the Title V program into Title III, repealing Title V and enacting as new provisions of Title III this paragraph (14) State plan requirement, sec. 312 ("Recapture of Payments"), and sec. 321(b), permitting use of Title III Social Services formula grant funds for this purpose. In addition, sections on mortgage insurance and annual interest grants, which were in Title V before it was repealed, were reenacted in Title IV, Part D. The 1978 Amendments, sec. 501, in repealing Title V, authorized the Commissioner to complete any project which was undertaken with Title V funds before it was repealed with funds obligated but unspent on the effective date of the repeal, September 30, 1978.*

[24] *The 1978 Amendments, for the first time, authorize use of Older Americans Act funds for construction of facilities to be used as senior centers. The Act, as originally enacted in 1965 prohibited use of the Act's funds for "costs of construction, other than for minor alterations and repairs." Before the 1978 Amendments, Title V funds were authorized to be used only for "acquisition, alteration, or renovation" of centers, not for construction.*

[25] *The provisions of subparagraph (A) are comparable to those of the former sec. 502(a)(1).*

(B) [26] the plan contains or is supported by reasonable assurances that, in the case of purchase or construction, there are no existing facilities in the community suitable for leasing as a multipurpose senior center;

(C) [27] the plans and specifications for the facility are in accordance with regulations relating to minimum standards of construction, promulgated with particular emphasis on securing compliance with the requirements of the Act of August 12, 1968, commonly known as the Architectural Barriers Act of 1968;

(D) [28] the plan contains or is supported by adequate assurance that any laborer or mechanic employed by any contractor or subcontractor in the performance of work on the facility will be paid wages at rates not less than those prevailing for similar work in the locality as determined by the Secretary of Labor in accordance with the Act of March 3, 1931 (40 U.S.C. 276a—276a-5; commonly known as the Davis-Bacon Act), and the Secretary of Labor shall have, with respect to the labor standards specified in this clause, the authority and functions set forth in reorganization plan numbered 14 of 1950 (15 F.R. 3176; 64 Stat. 1267), and section 2 of the Act of June 13, 1934 (40 U.S.C. 276c); and

(E) [29] the plan contains assurances that the State agency will consult with the Secretary of Housing and Urban Development with respect to the technical adequacy of any proposed alteration or renovation;

(15) [30] provide that with respect to legal services—

(A) the plan contains assurances that area agencies on aging will (i) enter into contracts with providers of legal services which can demonstrate the experience or capacity to deliver legal services; (ii) include in any such contract provisions to assure that any recipient of funds under division (i) will be subject to specific restrictions and regulations promulgated under the Legal Services Corporation Act (other than restrictions and regulations governing eligibility for legal assistance under such Act and governing membership of local governing boards) as determined appropriate by the Commissioner; and (iii) attempt to involve the private bar in legal services activities authorized under this title, including

---

[26] *The provisions of subparagraph (B) are comparable to those of the former sec. 502(a)(2).*

[27] *The provisions of subparagraph (C) are comparable to those of the former sec. 502(a)(3).*

[28] *The provisions of subparagraph (D) are comparable to those of the former sec. 502(a)(4).*

[29] *The provisions of subparagraph (E) are comparable to those of the former sec. 502(b)(2).*

[30] *Although there were provisions in Title III regarding legal services before the 1978 Amendments, the language of this paragraph (15) is almost entirely that of the 1978 Amendments.*

groups within the private bar furnishing services to older individuals on a pro bono and reduced fee basis;

(B) the plan contains assurances that no legal services will be furnished unless the grantee—

(i) is a recipient of funds under the Legal Services Corporation Act; or

(ii) administers a program designed to provide legal services to all older individuals with social or economic need and has agreed to coordinate its services with existing Legal Services Corporation projects in the area in order to concentrate the use of funds provided under this title on individuals with the greatest such need but who are not eligible for legal assistance under the Legal Services Corporation Act;

and the area agency makes a finding after assessment, pursuant to standards for service promulgated by the Commissioner, that any grantee selected is the entity best able to provide the particular services;

(C) the State agency will provide for the coordination of the furnishing of legal services to older individuals within the State, and provide advice and technical assistance in the provision of legal services to older individuals within the State and support the furnishing of training and technical assistance for legal services for older individuals; and

(D) the plan contains assurances, to the extent practicable, that legal services furnished under the plan will be in addition to any legal services for older individuals being furnished with funds from sources other than this Act and that reasonable efforts will be made to maintain existing levels of legal services for older individuals; and

(16) provide that the State agency, from funds allotted under section 304(a) for part B will use an amount equal to an amount not less than 1 percent of such allotment or $20,000, whichever is greater, for the purpose of carrying out the provisions of clause (12), except that (A) the requirement of this clause shall not apply in any fiscal year in which a State spends from State or local sources an amount equal to the amount required to be spent by this clause; and (B) the provisions of this clause shall not apply to American Samoa, Guam, the Virgin Islands, the Trust Territory of the Pacific Islands, and the Northern Mariana Islands.

(b)(1) The Commissioner shall approve any State plan which he finds fulfills the requirements of subsection (a).

(2) The Commissioner, in approving any State plan under this section may, for the fiscal years 1979 and 1980, waive any particular requirement relating to the delivery of services or the establishment or operation of multipurpose senior centers which the State agency cannot meet because of the consolidation authorized by the Comprehensive Older Americans Act Amendments of 1978 or because meeting such requirement would

reduce or jeopardize the quality of services under this Act, except that the Commissioner may grant such a waiver only if the State agency demonstrates that it is taking steps to meet the requirements of this title, but in any event the Commissioner may not grant a waiver for any requirement of this Act in effect on September 30, 1978. The Commissioner may not disapprove any State plan under paragraph (1) solely on the ground that a State requested a waiver under the preceding sentence.

(3) The Commissioner, in approving any State plan under this section, may waive the requirement described in clause (3)(B) of subsection (a) if the State agency demonstrates to the Commissioner that the service needs of older individuals residing in rural areas in the State are being met, or that the number of older individuals residing in such rural areas is not sufficient to require the State agency to comply with the requirement described in clause (3)(B) of subsection (a).

(c) [31] The Commissioner shall not make a final determination disapproving any State plan, or any modification thereof, or make a final determination that a State is ineligible under section 305, without first affording the State reasonable notice and opportunity for a hearing.

(d) [31] Whenever the Commissioner, after reasonable notice and opportunity for a hearing to the State agency, finds that—

(1) the State is not eligible under section 305,

(2) the State plan has been so changed that it no longer complies substantially with the provisions of subsection (a), or

(3) in the administration of the plan there is a failure to comply substantially with any such provision of subsection (a),

the Commissioner shall notify such State agency that no further payments from its allotments under section 304 and section 308 will be made to the State (or, in his discretion, that further payments to the State will be limited to projects under or portions of the State plan not affected by such failure), until he is satisfied that there will no longer be any failure to comply. Until he is so satisfied, no further payments shall be made to such State from its allotments under section 304 and section 308 (or payments shall be limited to projects under or portions of the State plan not affected by such failure). The Commissioner shall, in accordance with regulations he shall prescribe, disburse the funds so withheld directly to any public or nonprofit private organization or agency or

---

[31] *Provisions substantially similar to subsections (c), (d), and (e) have been in the Act since it was first enacted in 1965, with changes discussed in footnotes 32, 34, and 35, below. These subsections correspond to subsections (d), (e), and (f) of sec. 305 of the Act before the 1978 Amendments.*

political subdivision of such State [32] submitting an approved plan in accordance with the provisions of section 307. Any such payment shall be matched in the proportions specified in section 304.

(e) [31] (1) A State which is dissatisfied with a final action [33] of the Commissioner under subsection (b), (c), or (d) may appeal to the United States court of appeals for the circuit in which the State is located, by filing a petition with such court within 30 [34] days after such final action. A copy of the petition shall be forthwith transmitted by the clerk of the court to the Commissioner, or any officer designated by him for such purpose. The Commissioner thereupon shall file in the court the record of the proceedings on which he based his action, as provided in section 2112 of title 28, United States Code.

(2) Upon the filing of such petition, the court shall have jurisdiction to affirm the action of the Commissioner or to set it aside, in whole or in part, temporarily or permanently, but until the filing of the record, the Commissioner may modify or set aside his order. The findings of the Commissioner as to the facts, if supported by substantial evidence, shall be conclusive, but the court, for good cause shown, may remand the case to the Commissioner to take further evidence, and the Commissioner shall, within 30 days,[35] file in the court the record of those further proceedings. Such new or modified findings of fact shall likewise be conclusive if supported by substantial evidence. The judgment of the court affirming or setting aside, in whole or in part, any action of the Commissioner shall be final, subject to review by the Supreme Court of the United States upon certiorari or certification as provided in section 1254 of title 28, United States Code.

---

[32] *The 1973 Amendments first authorized disbursement of a State's allotment to an entity other than the State agency on aging, where there has been a compliance failure.*

[33] *In Alabama Commission on Aging v. Finch, 430 F. 2d 667 (U. S. Court of Appeals, 1970), held that redistribution among other States, whose plans had been approved, of funds previously allotted to Alabama did not constitute "final action" such as would confer jurisdiction upon Court of Appeals to review such action, where dispute over approval or disapproval of Alabama's plan remained unresolved, despite (unheeded) advice to that State Commission on Aging that it had only to request hearing to secure final action on its plan.*

[34] *Until the 1978 Amendments, sixty days was allowed for filing a petition for judicial review.*

[35] *Until the 1978 Amendments, there was no specified limit on the time within which the Commissioner could file the record of further proceedings.*

(3) The commencement of proceedings under this subsection shall not, unless so specifically ordered by the court, operate as a stay of the Commissioner's action.

PLANNING, COORDINATION, EVALUATION, AND ADMINISTRATION OF STATE PLANS [36]

SEC. 308. (a)(1) Amounts appropriated under section 303 may be used to make grants to States for paying such percentages as each State agency determines, but not more than 75 percent,[37] of the cost of the administration of its State plan, including the preparation of the State plan, the evaluation of activities carried out under such plan, the collection of data and the carrying out of analyses related to the need for social services, nutrition services, and multipurpose senior centers within the State, and dissemination of information so obtained, the provision of short-term training to personnel of public or nonprofit private agencies and organizations engaged in the operation of programs authorized by this Act, and the carrying out of demonstration projects of statewide significance relating to the initiation, expansion, or improvement of services assisted under this title.

(2) Any sums received by a State under this section for part of the cost of the administration of its State plan which the State determines is not needed for such purpose may be used by the State to supplement the amount available under section 304(d)(1)(A) to cover part of the cost of the administration of area plans.

(3) Any State which has designated a single planning and service area under section 305(a)(1)(E) covering all, or substantially all, of the older individuals in such State, as determined by the Commissioner, may elect to pay part of the costs of the administration of State and area plans either out of sums received under this section or out of sums made available for the administration of area plans under section 304(d)(1)(A), but shall not pay such costs out of sums received or allotted under both such sections.

(b)(1) From the sums appropriated for any fiscal year under section 303 for carrying out the purposes of this section, each State shall be

---

[36] *This section is substantially similar to sec. 306 of the Act before the 1978 Amendments, with few changes, some of which are discussed in the footnotes which follow.*

[37] *The Act as originally enacted in 1965, sec. 304, limited the Federal matching percentage for State plan administration to 50 percent. The 1969 Amendments, sec. 4(b), raised this limit to 75 percent, where it has since remained.*

allotted [38] an amount which bears the same ratio to such sums as the population aged 60 or older in such State bears to the population aged 60 or older in all States, except that (A) no State shall be allotted less than one-half of 1 percent of the sum appropriated for the fiscal year for which the determination is made, or $300,000,[39] whichever is greater; and (B) Guam, American Samoa, the Virgin Islands, the Trust Territory of the Pacific Islands,[40] and the Northern Mariana Islands[41] shall be each allotted no less than one-fourth of 1 percent of the sum appropriated for the fiscal year for which the determination is made, or $75,000,[42] whichever is greater. For the purpose of the exception contained in clause (A), the term "State" does not include Guam, American Samoa, the Virgin Islands, the Trust Territory of the Pacific Islands, and the Northern Mariana Islands.

(2) [43] (A) Any State which desires to receive amounts, in addition to amounts allotted to such State under paragraph (1), to be used in the administration of its State plan in accordance with subsection (a) may transmit an application to the Commissioner in accordance with this paragraph. Any such application shall be transmitted in such form, and according to such procedures, as the Commissioner may require, except that such application may not be made as part of, or as an amendment to, the State plan.

(B) The Commissioner may approve any application transmitted by a State under subparagraph (A) if the Commissioner determines, based upon a particularized showing of need, that—

(i) the State will be unable to fully and effectively administer its State plan and to carry out programs and projects authorized by this title unless such additional amounts are made available by the Commissioner;

---

[38] *See footnote 3, this title.*

[39] *The 1965 Act, sec. 304, provided a minimum of $15,000 per State for State plan administration, which was increased to $25,000 by the 1967 Amendments, sec. 3, to $75,000 by the 1969 Amendments, sec. 4(b), to $160,000 by the 1973 Amendments, to $200,000 by the 1975 Amendments, sec. 107(a), and, finally, to $300,000 by the 1978 Amendments.*

[40] *See footnote 4, this title.*

[41] *See footnote 5, this title.*

[42] *The 1965 Act, sec. 304, provided a minimum of $15,000 for State plan administration, including administration of plans of U.S. jurisdictions other than States. The minimum was increased to $25,000 by the 1967 Amendments, sec. 3, to $50,000 for the named jurisdictions other than States by the 1973 Amendments, to $62,500 by the 1975 Amendments, sec. 107(a), and, finally, to $75,000 by the 1978 Amendments.*

(ii) the State is making full and effective use of its allotment under paragraph (1) and of the personnel of the State agency and area agencies designated under section 305(a)(2)(A) in the administration of its State plan in accordance with subsection (a); and

(iii) the State agency and area agencies of such State designated under section 305 are carrying out, on a full-time basis, programs and activities which are in furtherance of the purposes of this Act.

(C) The Commissioner may approve that portion of the amount requested by a State in its application under subparagraph (A) which he determines has been justified in such application.

(D) Amounts which any State may receive in any fiscal year under this paragraph may not exceed three-fourths of 1 percent of the sum of the amounts allotted under section 304(a) to such State to carry out the State plan for such fiscal year.

(E) No application by a State under subparagraph (A) shall be approved unless it contains assurances that no amounts received by the State under this paragraph will be used to hire any individual to fill a job opening created by the action of the State in laying off or terminating the employment of any regular employee not supported under this Act in anticipation of filling the vacancy so created by hiring an employee to be supported through use of amounts received under this paragraph.

(3) [43] Each State shall be entitled to an allotment under this section for any fiscal year in an amount which is not less than the amount of the allotment to which such State was entitled under paragraph (1) for the fiscal year ending June 30, 1975.

(4) The number of individuals aged 60 or older in any State and in all States shall be determined by the Commissioner on the basis of the most recent satisfactory data available to him.

(5) [44] Notwithstanding any other provision of this title, with respect to funds received under section 303(b)(1) and (2), a State may elect in its plan under section 307(a)(13) regarding part C of this title, to transfer a portion of the funds appropriated between subpart 1 and subpart 2 of part C, for use as the State considers appropriate to meet the needs of the area served. The Commissioner shall approve any such transfer unless he determines that such transfer is not consistent with the purposes of this Act.

---

[43] *Paragraphs (2) and (3) were inserted by the 1975 Amendments, sec. 107 (b), and reenacted by the 1978 Amendments.*

[44] *Prior to the 1978 Amendments, there was no provision in the Act comparable to paragraph (5).*

(c) [45] The amounts of any State's allotment under subsection (b) for any fiscal year which the Commissioner determines will not be required for that year for the purposes described in subsection (a)(1) shall be available to provide services under part B or part C, or both, in the State.

PAYMENTS

SEC. 309. (a) Payments of grants or contracts under this title may be made (after necessary adjustments resulting from previously made over-payments or underpayments) in advance or by way of reimbursement, and in such installments, as the Commissioner may determine.[46] From a State's allotment for a fiscal year which is available under section 308 the Commissioner may pay to a State which does not have a State plan approved under section 307 such amounts as he deems appropriate for the purpose of assisting such State in developing a State plan.[47]

(b)(1) [48] For each fiscal year, not less than 25 percent of the non-Federal share of the total expenditures under the State plan which is required by section 304(d) shall be met from funds from State or local public sources.

---

[45] *The 1978 Amendments substituted the new subsection (c) for the subsection (c) which was added by the 1969 Amendments, and which read as follows:*

"(c) The amounts of any State's allotment under subsection (b) for any fiscal year which the Commissioner determines will not be required for that year shall be reallotted, from time to time and on such dates during such year as the Commissioner may fix, to other States in proportion to the original allotments to such States under subsection (b) for that year, but with such proportionate amount for any of such other States being reduced to the extent it exceeds the sum the Commissioner estimates such State needs and will be able to use for such year; and the total of such reductions shall be similarly reallotted among the States whose proportionate amounts were not so reduced. Such reallotments shall be made on the basis of the State plan so approved, after taking into consideration the population aged sixty or over. Any amount reallotted to a State under this subsection during a year shall be deemed part of its allotment under subsection (b) for that year."

[46] *The first sentence of sec. 309(a) has been in the Act since it was first enacted during 1965.*

[47] *The 1973 Amendments added the second sentence of sec. 309(a).*

[48] *The 1973 Amendments added paragraph (1) to the Act, effective with fiscal year 1975.*

(2) [49] Funds required to meet the non-Federal share required by section 304(d)(1)(B), in amounts exceeding the non-Federal share required prior to fiscal year 1981, shall be met from State sources.

(c) [49] A State's allotment under section 304 for a fiscal year shall be reduced by the percentage (if any) by which its expenditures for such year from State sources under its State plan approved under section 307 are less than its expenditures from such sources for the preceding fiscal year.

DISASTER RELIEF REIMBURSEMENTS [50]

SEC. 310. (a)(1) The Commissioner may provide reimbursements to any State, upon application for such reimbursement, for funds such State makes available to area agencies in such State for the delivery of social services during any major disaster declared by the President in accordance with the Disaster Relief Act of 1974.

(2) Total payments to all States under paragraph (1) in any fiscal year shall not exceed 5 percent of the total amount appropriated and available for carrying out the purposes of section 421.

(b)(1) At the beginning of each fiscal year the Commissioner shall set aside, for payment to States under subsection (a), an amount equal to 5 percent of the total amount appropriated and available for carrying out the purposes of section 421.

(2) Amounts set aside under paragraph (1) which are not obligated by the end of the third quarter of any fiscal year shall be made available for carrying out the purposes of section 421.

(c) Nothing in this section shall be construed to prohibit expenditures by States for disaster relief for older individuals in excess of amounts reimbursable under this section, by using funds made available to them under other sections of this Act or under other provisions of Federal or State law, or from private sources.

AVAILABILITY OF SURPLUS COMMODITIES [51]

SEC. 311. (a)(1) Agricultural commodities and products purchased by the Secretary of Agriculture under section 32 of the Act of August 24,

---

[49] *Before the 1978 Amendments, there were no provisions in the Act comparable to paragraph (2) and subsection (c).*

[50] *The 1978 Amendments inserted sec. 310.*

[51] *This section (311) is similar in most respects to sec. 707 of Title VII before that title was repealed by the 1978 Amendments. Sec. 707 was in Title VII as it was added to the Act by the 1972 Amendments, but this section was revised by the 1973 Amendments.*

1935 (7 U.S.C. 612c), shall [52] be donated to a recipient of a grant or contract to be used for providing nutrition services in accordance with the provisions of this title.

(2) The Commodity Credit Corporation shall [52] dispose of food commodities under section 416 of the Agricultural Act of 1949 (7 U.S.C. 1431) by donating them to a recipient of a grant or contract to be used for providing nutrition services in accordance with the provisions of this title.

(3) Dairy products purchased by the Secretary of Agriculture under section 709 of the Food and Agriculture Act of 1965 (7 U.S.C. 1446a-1) shall [52] be used to meet the requirements of programs providing nutrition services in accordance with the provisions of this title.

(4) [53] In donating commodities under this subsection, the Secretary of Agriculture shall maintain an annually programmed level of assistance of not less than 15 cents per meal during fiscal year 1976, 25 cents per meal during fiscal year 1977 and fiscal year 1978,[54] and 30 cents per meal during the three succeeding fiscal years. The amount specified in this paragraph shall be adjusted on an annual basis for each fiscal year after June 30, 1975, to reflect changes in the series for food away from home of the Consumer Price Index published by the Bureau of Labor Statistics of the Department of Labor. Such adjustment shall be computed to the nearest one-fourth cent. Among the commodities delivered under this subsection, the Secretary shall give special emphasis to high protein foods, meat, and meat alternates. The Secretary of Agriculture, in consultation with the Commissioner, is authorized to prescribe the terms and conditions respecting the donating of commodities under this subsection.

(b)(1) During each of the fiscal years ending before October 1, 1981, the Secretary of Agriculture shall purchase high protein foods, meat, and meat alternates on the open market, at prices not in excess of market prices, out of funds appropriated under this section, as determined under paragraph (3), for distribution to recipients of grants or contracts to be used for providing nutrition services in accordance with the provisions of this title. High protein foods, meat, and meat alternates purchased by the Secretary of Agriculture under this subsection shall be grown and produced in the United States.

(2) High protein foods, meat, and meat alternates donated under this subsection shall not be considered donated commodities for purposes of

---

[52] The 1975 Amendments, sec. 111(c) substituted "shall" for "may".

[53] Paragraph (4) was added by the 1974 Amendments, sec. 5.

[54] The 25 cent minimum for fiscal year 1978 was added by the 1977 Amendments.

meeting the requirement of subsection (a)(4) with respect to the annually programmed level of assistance under subsection (a).

(3) There are authorized to be appropriated such sums as may be necessary in order to carry out the program established by paragraph (1).

(c) [55] (1) Notwithstanding any other provision of law, a State [56] may, for purposes of the programs authorized by this act, elect to receive cash payments in lieu of donated foods for all or any portion of its project.[57] In any case in which a State makes such an election, the Secretary of Agriculture shall make cash payments to such State in an amount equivalent in value to the donated foods which the State otherwise would have received if such State had retained its commodity distribution.

(2) When such payments are made, the State agency shall promptly and equitably disburse any cash it receives in lieu of commodities to recipients of grants or contracts. Such disbursements shall only [58] be used by such recipients of grants or contracts to purchase United States agricultural commodities and other foods for their nutrition projects.

(3) [59] Nothing in this subsection shall be construed to authorize the Secretary of Agriculture to require any State to elect to receive cash payments under this subsection.

MULTIPURPOSE SENIOR CENTERS: RECAPTURE OF PAYMENTS [60]

SEC. 312. If, within 10 years after acquisition, or within 20 years after the completion of construction,[61] of any facility for which funds have been paid under this title—

(1) the owner of the facility ceases to be a public or nonprofit private agency or organization; or

---

[55] *Subsection (c) was added by the 1975 Amendments, sec. 111(a).*

[56] *As enacted in 1975, this paragraph contained language restricting to States which had phased out commodity distribution facilities before June 30, 1974, the privilege of electing to receive cash payments. The 1977 Amendments, sec. 2(b)(1) eliminated that restrictive language.*

[57] *The words "for all or any portion of its project" were added by the 1978 Amendments.*

[58] *The 1977 Amendments, sec. 2(b)(2) added "only".*

[59] *Paragraph (3) was added by the 1978 Amendments.*

[60] *This section (312) is similar in most respects to sec. 504 of Title V before that title was repealed by the 1978 Amendments. Sec. 504 was in that title from the time when it was added to the Act by the 1973 Amendments.*

[61] *The phrase, "or within 20 years after the completion of construction," was added by the 1978 Amendments.*

(2) the facility ceases to be used for the purposes for which it was acquired (unless the Commissioner determines, in accordance with regulations, that there is good cause for releasing the applicant or other owner from the obligation to do so);

the United States shall be entitled to recover from the applicant or other owner of the facility an amount which bears to the then value of the facility (or so much thereof as constituted an approved project or projects) the same ratio as the amount of such Federal funds bore to the cost of the facility financed with the aid of such funds. Such value shall be determined by agreement of the parties or by action brought in the United States district court for the district in which such facility is situated.

AUDIT

SEC. 313. The Commissioner and the Comptroller General of the United States or any of their duly authorized representatives shall have access for the purpose of audit and examination to any books, documents, papers, and records that are pertinent to a grant or contract received under this title.

PART B—SOCIAL SERVICES [62]

PROGRAM AUTHORIZED

SEC. 321.[63] (a) The Commissioner shall carry out a program for making grants to States under State plans approved under section 307 for any of the following social services:

(1) health, continuing education, welfare, informational, recreational, homemaker, counseling, or referral services;

(2) transportation services to facilitate access to social services or nutrition services, or both;

(3) services designed to encourage and assist older individuals to use the facilities and services available to them;

---

[62] *Part B was inserted into Title III by the 1978 Amendments as part of its consolidation into this title of programs previously authorized by Title III ("Social Services"), Title V ("Multipurpose Senior Centers"), and Title VII ("Nutrition").*

[63] *Except as discussed in footnotes 64 and 65, below, subsection (a) is similar in most respects to sec. 302(1) of the Act before the 1978 Amendments, which defined the social services to be provided under Title III.*

(4) services designed to assist older individuals to obtain adequate housing, including residential repair and renovation projects designed to enable older individuals to maintain their homes in conformity with minimum housing standards or to adapt homes to meet the needs of older individuals suffering from physical disabilities;

(5) services designed to assist older individuals in avoiding institutionalization, including preinstitution evaluation and screening and home health services, homemaker services, shopping services, escort services, reader services, letter writing services, and other similar services designed to assist such individuals to continue living independently in a home environment;

(6) services designed to provide legal services and other counseling services and assistance, including tax counseling and assistance and financial counseling, to older individuals;

(7) services designed to enable older individuals to attain and maintain physical and mental well-being through programs of regular physical activity and exercise;

(8) [64] services designed to provide health screening to detect or prevent illness, or both, that occur most frequently in older individuals;

(9) [64] services designed to provide preretirement and second career counseling for older individuals;

(10) [64] services of an ombudsman at the State level to receive, investigate, and act on complaints by older individuals who are residents of long-term care facilities and to advocate the well-being of such individuals;

(11) [64] services which are designed to meet the unique needs of older individuals who are disabled; or

(12) any other services;

if such services meet standards prescribed by the Commissioner [65] and are necessary for the general welfare of older individuals.

(b) [66] (1) The Commissioner shall carry out a program for making grants to States under State plans approved under section 307 for the acquisition, alteration, or renovation of existing facilities, including

---

[64] *This paragraph was not included in the sec. 302(1) definition of social services before the 1978 Amendments.*

[65] *The requirement that "such services meet standards prescribed by the Commissioner" was inserted by the 1978 Amendments.*

[66] *The 1978 Amendments consolidated into Title III the multipurpose senior center program by repealing Title V (which previously contained provisions on this subject) and by inserting into Title III this subsection (b), paragraph (14) of sec. 307(a), and sec. 312.*

mobile units, and, where appropriate, construction of facilities [67] to serve as multipurpose senior centers which shall be community facilities for the organization and provision of a broad spectrum of services, including provision of health, social, nutritional, and educational services and provision of facilities for recreational activities for older individuals.

(2) [68] Funds made available to a State under this part may be used, for the purpose of assisting in the operation of multipurpose senior centers, to meet all or part of the costs of compensating professional and technical personnel required for the operation of multipurpose senior centers.

PART C—NUTRITION SERVICES [69]

Subpart 1—Congregate Nutrition Services

PROGRAM AUTHORIZED

SEC. 331. The Commissioner shall carry out a program for making grants to States under State plans approved under section 307 for the establishment and operation of nutrition projects—

(1) which, 5 or more days a week, provide at least one hot or other appropriate meal per day and any additional meals which the recipient of a grant or contract under this subpart may elect to provide, each of which assures a minimum of one-third of the daily recommended dietary allowances as established by the Food and Nutrition Board of the National Academy of Sciences-National Research Council;

(2) which shall be provided in congregate settings; and

---

[67] *The phrase, "including mobile units, and, where appropriate, construction of facilities" was not in Title V, which was repealed by the 1978 Amendments.*

[68] *Before the 1978 Amendments, sec. 511 authorized grants for initial staffing of senior centers, but that authorization was never funded.*

[69] *The 1978 Amendments consolidated into Title III the nutrition program for the elderly by repealing Title VII (which previously contained provisions on this subject) and by inserting into Title III this new Part C, paragraph (13) of sec. 307, and sec. 311. The 1978 Amendments, sec. 501, authorized the Commissioner to complete any project undertaken under Title VII before its repeal with funds obligated but unspent, and provided that Title VII projects would continue to receive funds under Part C, Title III.*

(3) which may include nutrition education services and other appropriate nutrition services for older individuals.

Subpart 2—Home Delivered Nutrition Services [70]

PROGRAM AUTHORIZED

SEC. 336. The Commissioner shall carry out a program for making grants to States under State plans approved under section 307 for the establishment and operation of nutrition projects for older individuals which, 5 or more days a week, provide at least one home delivered hot, cold, frozen, dried, canned, or supplemental foods (with a satisfactory storage life) meal per day and any additional meals which the recipient of a grant or contract under this subpart may elect to provide, each of which assures a minimum of one-third of the daily recommended dietary allowances as established by the Food and Nutrition Board of the National Academy of Sciences-National Research Council.

CRITERIA

SEC. 337. The Commissioner, in consultation with organizations of and for the aged, blind, and disabled, and with representatives from the American Dietetic Association, the Association of Area Agencies on Aging, the National Association of Title VII Project Directors, the National Association of Meals Programs, Incorporated, and any other appropriate group, shall develop minimum criteria of efficiency and quality for the furnishing of home delivered meal services for projects described in section 336. The criteria required by this section shall take into account the ability of established home delivered meals programs to continue such services without major alteration in the furnishing of such services.

---

[70] *There was no specific provision for home delivered meals in Title VII before its repeal by the 1978 Amendments, although such meals could be and were provided by grantees and contractors under that program.*

TITLE IV—TRAINING, RESEARCH, AND

DISCRETIONARY PROJECTS AND PROGRAMS [1]

PART A—TRAINING [2]

STATEMENT OF PURPOSE [3]

SEC. 401. (a) The purpose of this part is to develop and implement a national manpower policy for the field of aging. Such a policy shall reflect the present and future needs for training personnel, including personnel involved in advocacy and leadership, in all programs serving the elderly recognizing the unique health, transportation, and housing problems of the elderly, the continual growth of the elderly population of the United States, and the high incidence of disabilities within such population. The national manpower policy established under this part shall require that training programs shall give priority to training personnel responsible for carrying out projects relating to multipurpose senior

---

[1] *The 1978 Amendments, sec. 104(c)(2), changed the heading of Title IV, which was previously "TRAINING AND RESEARCH."*

[2] *From the 1965 Act until the 1973 Amendments, the provisions of the Act relating to Training were in Title V, which was devoted exclusively to that subject. The 1973 Amendments repealed Title V and devoted Part A, Title IV, to that subject. Before the 1973 Amendments, sec. 501 contained language somewhat comparable to that of sec. 404 as it presently reads. There was nothing in the former Title V comparable to the present sections 401, 402, and 403. The 1973 Amendments repealed sec. 503, which had been added by the 1967 Amendments, sec. 6. That section of the Act authorized the Secretary to study and report to the President and to the Congress concerning needs for trained personnel in aging. The study was conducted and the report was transmitted, as required.*

[3] *The 1978 Amendments completely revised sec. 401. Between 1973 and 1978 it read as follows:*

"SEC. 401. The purpose of this part is to improve the quality of service and to help meet critical shortages of adequately trained personnel for programs in the field of aging by (1) developing information on the actual needs for personnel to work in the field of aging, both present and long range; (2) providing a broad range of quality training and retraining opportunities, responsive to changing needs of programs in the field of aging; (3) attracting a greater number of qualified persons into the field of aging; and (4) helping to make personnel training programs more responsive to the need for trained personnel in the field of aging."

centers under part B of title III and for carrying out programs under part C of title III.

(b) The policy required by this title shall be developed and implemented by the Commissioner in cooperation with other departments and agencies of the Federal Government, including the Public Health Service, the Health Care Financing Administration, the Social Security Administration, the National Institutes of Health, and in particular the National Institute on Aging, the Administration for Public Services, the Rehabilitation Services Administration, the Veterans' Administration, the Department of Labor, the Department of Housing and Urban Development, and the Department of Transportation, State employment agencies, State and area agencies on aging, and other appropriate agencies.

APPRAISING PERSONNEL NEEDS IN THE FIELD OF AGING [4]

SEC. 402. (a) The Commissioner shall, at such times as he deems appropriate and in cooperation with representatives referred to in section 401(b), assess the Nation's existing and future personnel needs in the field of aging, including as part of such assessment, the needs for personnel in both institutional and non-institutional long-term care settings, and evaluate all programs, including institutional and non-institutional long-term care programs, serving the elderly at all levels of government recogniz-

----

[4] *The 1978 Amendments revised sec. 402, which previously read as follows:*

"SEC. 402. (a) The Commissioner shall from time to time appraise the Nation's existing and future personnel needs in the field of aging, at all levels and in all types of programs, and the adequacy of the Nation's efforts to meet these needs. In developing information relating to personnel needs in the field of aging, the Commissioner shall consult with, and make maximum utilization of statistical and other related information of the Department of Labor, the Veterans' Administration, the Office of Education, Federal Council on the Aging, the National Foundation on the Arts and Humanities, State educational agencies, other State and local public agencies and offices dealing with problems of the aging, State employment security agencies, and other appropriate public and private agencies.

"(b) The Commissioner shall prepare and publish annually as a part of the annual report provided in section 208 a report on the professions dealing with the problems of the aging, in which he shall present in detail his view on the state of such professions and the trends which he discerns with respect to the future complexion of programs for the aging throughout the Nation and the funds and the needs for well-educated personnel to staff such programs. The report shall indicate the Commissioner's plans concerning the allocation of Federal assistance under this title in relation to the plans and programs of other Federal agencies."

ing the continual growth of the elderly population. The assessment required by this section shall be conducted in accordance with the national manpower policy developed under section 401.

(b) The assessment required by this section shall be submitted biennially to the Congress. Each such report shall indicate the impact of the assessment on the national manpower policy and plans for the future.

ATTRACTING QUALIFIED PERSONS TO THE FIELD OF AGING

Sec. 403. In accordance with the requirements set forth in the national manpower policy,[5] the Commissioner may make grants to State agencies referred to in section 304, State or local educational agencies, institutions of higher education as defined in section 1201(a) of the Higher Education Act of 1965,[6] or other public or nonprofit private agencies, organizations, or institutions, and he may enter into contracts with any agency, institution, or organization for the purpose of—

(1) publicizing available opportunities for careers in the field of aging;

(2) encouraging qualified persons to enter or reenter the field of aging;

(3) encouraging artists, craftsmen, artisans, scientists, and persons from other professions and vocations and homemakers, to undertake assignments on a part-time basis or for temporary periods in the field of aging; or

(4) preparing and disseminating materials including audiovisual materials and printed materials, for use in recruitment and training of persons employed or preparing for employment in carrying out programs related to the field of aging.[7]

TRAINING PROGRAMS FOR PERSONNEL IN THE FIELD OF AGING

Sec. 404. (a) In accordance with the requirements set forth in the national manpower policy, the [8] Commissioner may make grants to any public or nonprofit private agency, organization, or institution or with State agencies referred to in section 304, or contracts with any agency,

---

[5] *The 1978 Amendments, sec. 104(a)(3) inserted, "In accordance with the requirements set forth in the national manpower policy,".*

[6] *The phrase ". . . as defined . . ." was inserted by the 1975 Amendments, sec. 109.*

[7] *The 1978 Amendments, sec. 104(a)(3)(B) struck "to the purposes of this Act" and inserted instead "to the field of aging."*

[8] *The 1978 Amendments, sec. 104(a)(4)(A)(i), inserted "In accordance with the requirements set forth in the national manpower policy,".*

organization, or institution, to assist them in training persons who are employed or preparing for employment in the field of aging—[9]

(1) [10] to coordinate the training efforts of all programs serving the elderly at the Federal, State, and local levels recognizing the continual growth of the elderly population,

(2) [11] to assist in paying the costs, in whole or in part, of short-term and inservice training courses, workshops, institutes and other activities designed to improve the capabilities of participants to provide services to older persons and to administer programs related to the field of aging,[12]

(3) [11] to assist in paying the costs, in whole or in part, of post-secondary education courses of training or study related to the purposes of this Act, including the payment of stipends to students enrolled in such courses,

(4) for establishing and maintaining fellowships to train persons to be supervisors or trainers of persons employed or preparing for employment in fields related to the purposes of this Act,

(5) for seminars, conferences, symposiums, and workshops in the field of aging, including the conduct of conferences and other meetings for the purposes of facilitating exchange of information and stimulating new approaches with respect to activities related to the purposes of this Act,

(6) [13] to assess future national personnel needs, including the need for training of advocates, with respect to the elderly with special emphasis on the needs of elderly minority group individuals and the need for the training of minority group individuals to meet such needs,

(7) [13] to assist in paying the costs, in whole or in part, of special courses of training designed to meet the needs of service providers in rural areas,

(8) for the improvement of programs for preparing personnel for careers in the field of aging, including design, development, and evalua-

---

[9] *The 1978 Amendments, sec. 104(a)(4)(A)(ii), substituted "the field of aging" for "fields related to the purposes of this Act".*

[10] *The 1978 Amendments, sec. 104(a)(4)(C), inserted paragraph (1).*

[11] *The 1975 Amendments, sec. 110(b) substituted the present paragraphs (2) and (3) for the previous paragraph (1), enacted by the 1973 Amendments, which read as follows: "(1) to assist in covering the cost of courses of training or study (including short-term or regular session institutes and other inservice and preservice training programs),"*

[12] *The 1978 Amendments, sec. 104(a)(4)(B), substituted "field of aging" for "purposes of the Act."*

[13] *The 1978 Amendments, sec. 104(a)(4)(D), inserted paragraphs (6) and (7).*

tion of exemplary training programs, introduction of high quality and more effective curricula and curriculum materials, and

(9) the provision of increased opportunities for practical experience.

(b) The Commissioner may include in the terms of any contract or grant under this part provisions authorizing the payment, to persons participating in training programs supported under this part, of such stipends (including allowances for subsistence and other expenses for such persons and their dependents) as he determines to be consistent with prevailing practices under comparable federally-supported programs. Where the Commissioner provides for the use of funds under this section for fellowships, he shall (in addition to stipends for the recipients) pay to colleges or universities in which the fellowship is being pursued such amounts as the Commissioner shall determine to be consistent with prevailing practices under comparable federally-supported programs.

(c) [14] The Commissioner may make grants under subsection (a) to assist in (1) the training of lawyers and paraprofessional persons who will (A) provide legal (including tax and financial) counseling and services to older persons; or (B) monitor the administration of any program by any public or private nonprofit institution, organization, or agency, or any State or political subdivision of a State, designed to provide assistance or services to older persons, including nursing home programs and other similar programs; and (2) the training of persons employed by or associated with public or private nonprofit agencies or organizations, including a State or political subdivision of a State, who will identify legal problems affecting older persons, develop solutions for such problems, and mobilize the resources of the community to respond to the legal needs of older persons.

PART B—RESEARCH AND DEVELOPMENT PROJECTS [15]

DESCRIPTION OF ACTIVITIES

SEC. 411.[16] (a) To support research efforts related to the implementation of this Act together with areas of concern relating to the living conditions of the elderly,[17] the Commissioner may make grants to any public or nonprofit private agency, organization, or institution and

---

[14] *The 1975 Amendments, sec. 110(c), added subsection (c).*

[15] *From the 1965 Act until the 1973 Amendments, Title IV was devoted exclusively to "Research and Development Projects."*

[16] *Sec. 411 is similar in most respects to sec. 401 of the Act as it read from the 1965 Act until the 1973 Amendments.*

[17] *The 1978 Amendments, sec. 104(b)(1)(B), inserted this clause.*

contracts with any [18] agency, organization, or institution or with any individual for the purpose of—

(1) studying current patterns and conditions of living of older individuals and identifying factors which are beneficial or detrimental to the wholesome and meaningful living of such persons;

(2) developing or demonstrating new approaches, techniques, and methods (including the use of multipurpose [19] centers) which hold promise of substantial contribution toward wholesome and meaningful living for older individuals;

(3) developing or demonstrating approaches, methods, and techniques for achieving or improving coordination of community services for older individuals;

(4) evaluating these approaches, techniques, and methods, as well as others which may assist older individuals to enjoy wholesome and meaningful lives and to continue to contribute to the strength and welfare of our Nation;

(5) [20] collecting and disseminating, through publications and other appropriate means, information concerning research findings, demonstration results, and other materials developed in connection with activities assisted under this part; or

(6) [20] conducting conferences and other meetings for the purposes of facilitating exchange of information and stimulating new approaches with respect to activities related to the purposes of this part.

(b) [21] In accordance with the purposes of this part, the Commissioner shall make grants to any public agency or nonprofit private organization or institution and contracts with any agency, organization, or institution or with an individual for the purpose of—

(1) conducting a study related to the problems experienced by State and area agencies on aging and other service providers in operating transportation services, with particular emphasis on the difficulties of continually rising insurance costs and restrictions being placed upon the operation of such services by insurance underwriters;

(2) revising existing Federal transportation programs for older individuals to—

---

[18] *The 1969 Amendments, sec. 7(a) deleted "any such agency" and substituted "any agency".*

[19] *The 1967 Amendments, sec. 5(b) deleted "activity" between "multipurpose" and "centers".*

[20] *The 1969 Amendments, sec. 7(b) added to sec. 401, as it then read, subsections (e) and (f), which were substantially identical to paragraphs (5) and (6) of the present sec. 411.*

[21] *The 1978 Amendments, sec. 104(b)(2), added subsections (b) and (c).*

(A) provide more coordinated and comprehensive services to such individuals;

(B) eliminate unnecessary duplication among such programs;

(C) eliminate disparities in eligibility requirements among Federal transportation programs for older individuals; and

(D) study the possibility of transferring to a single administrative unit the responsibility for the administration of all Federal transportation programs for older individuals; and

(3) conducting a study related to the differences in unit costs, service delivery, and access between rural areas and urban areas for services assisted under this Act and the special needs of the elderly residing in rural areas.

(c) [21] Upon completion of the studies described in subsection (b), but not later than 2 years after the date of the enactment of the Comprehensive Older Americans Act Amendments of 1978, the Commissioner shall submit to the Congress and make available through the National Information and Resource Clearing House for the Aging the results of the studies, together with such recommendations as he deems necessary.

PART C—DISCRETIONARY PROJECTS AND PROGRAMS [22]

DEMONSTRATION PROJECTS

SEC. 421. [23] (a) The Commissioner may, after consultation with the State agency in the State involved, make grants to any public agency or nonprofit private organization or enter into contracts with any agency or organization within such State for paying part or all of the cost of developing or operating nationwide, statewide, regional, metropolitan area, county, city, or community model projects which will demonstrate methods to improve or expand social services or nutrition services or otherwise promote the well-being of older individuals. The Commissioner shall give special consideration to the funding of rural area agencies on aging to conduct model projects devoted to the special needs of the rural elderly.[24] Such projects shall include alternative health care deliv-

---

[22] *The 1978 Amendments, sec. 104(c)(1)(C), inserted Part C into Title IV.*

[23] *Sec. 421 is similar in many respects to sec. 308 ("Model Projects") of the Act as it read before the 1978 Amendments. Major changes are discussed in the footnotes which follow. Sec. 308 was added to the Act by the 1973 Amendments.*

[24] *The 1978 Amendments added the last two sentences of sec. 421.*

ery systems, advocacy and outreach programs, and transportation services.[24]

(b) In making grants and contracts under this section, the Commissioner shall give special consideration to projects designed to—

(1) assist in meeting the special housing needs of older individuals by—

(A) providing financial assistance to such individuals, who own their own homes, necessary to enable them to make the repairs or renovations to their homes, which are necessary for them to meet minimum standards;

(B) studying and demonstrating methods of adapting existing housing, or construction of new housing, to meet the needs of older individuals suffering from physical disabilities; and

(C) demonstrating alternative methods of relieving older individuals of the burden of real property taxes on their homes;

(2) provide continuing education to older individuals designed to enable them to lead more productive lives by broadening the educational, cultural, or social awareness of such older individuals, emphasizing, where possible, free tuition arrangements with colleges and universities;

(3) provide preretirement education information, and relevant services (including the training of personnel to carry out such programs and the conducting of research with respect to the development and operation of such programs) to individuals planning retirement;

(4) provide services to assist in meeting the particular needs of physically and mentally impaired older individuals, including special transportation and escort services, homemaker, home health and shopping services, reader services, letter writing services, and other services designed to assist such individuals in leading more independent lives;

(5)[25] meet the special needs of, and improve the delivery of services to, older individuals who are not receiving adequate services under other provisions of this Act, with emphasis on the needs of low-income, minority, Indian, and limited English-speaking individuals and the rural elderly;

(6)[25] assist older individuals to remain within their communities and out of institutions and to maintain their independent living, in their own residences or in a family living arrangement, by—

----

[25] *Paragraphs (5) and (6)—before 1978 designated as (6) and (7)—were added to the former sec. 308 by the 1975 Amendments, sec. 108, together with a paragraph (5), omitted by the 1978 Amendments, which read as follows:*

(5) enable State agencies on aging and other public and private nonprofit organizations to assist in the promotion and development of omsbudsman services for residents of nursing homes;"

(A) providing financial assistance for the establishment and operation of senior ambulatory care day centers (providing a planned schedule of health, therapeutic, education, nutrition, recreational, rehabilitation, and social services at least 24 hours per week, transportation arrangements at low or no cost for participants to and from the center, a mid-day meal, outreach and public information programs, and opportunities for maximum participation of senior participants and senior volunteers in the planning and operation of the center); and

(B) maintaining or initiating arrangements (or providing reasonable assurances that such arrangements will be maintained or initiated) with any agency of the State involved which administers or supervises the administration of a State plan approved under titles XIX and XX of the Social Security Act, and with other appropriate social services agencies receiving, or reimbursed through, Federal financial assistance, for the payment of all or a part of the center's costs in providing services to eligible individuals;

(7) [26] meet the special needs of older individuals residing in rural areas; or

(8) [26] develop or improve methods of coordinating all available social services for the homebound elderly, blind, and disabled by establishing demonstration projects in 10 States, in accordance with subsection (c).

(c)(1) [27] The Commissioner shall consult with the Commissioner of the Rehabilitation Services Administration, the Commissioner of the Social Security Administration, and the Surgeon General of the Public Health Service, to develop procedures for—

(A) identifying elderly, blind, and disabled individuals who need social services;

(B) compiling a list in each community of all services available to the elderly, blind, and disabled; and

(C) establishing an information and referral service within the appropriate community agency to—

(i) inform those in need of the availability of such services; and

(ii) coordinate the delivery of such services to the elderly, blind, and disabled.

The Commissioner shall establish procedures for administering demonstration projects under subsection (b)(8) no later than 6 months after the effective date of this subsection. The Commissioner shall report to the Congress with respect to the results and findings of the demonstration

---

[26] *Paragraphs (7) and (8) were not in sec. 308, as it read before the 1978 Amendments.*

[27] *Paragraph (1) was not in sec. 308, as it read before the 1978 Amendments.*

projects at the end of fiscal year 1979. In such report, the Commissioner shall make such recommendation, based upon the findings, as may be appropriate to improve the delivery of social services to such elderly, blind, and disabled individuals.

(2)(A) There are authorized to be appropriated for fiscal years 1979, 1980, and 1981, such sums as may be necessary for the purpose of implementing the demonstration projects under subsection (b)(8).

(B) For the purpose of carrying out this subsection, there are authorized to be appropriated such sums as may be necessary for fiscal year 1979.

SPECIAL PROJECTS IN COMPREHENSIVE LONG-TERM CARE [28]

SEC. 422. (a)(1) The Commissioner may make grants to selected State agencies designated under section 305(a)(1), and, in consultation with State agencies, selected area agencies on aging designated under section 305(a)(2)(A), institutions of higher education, and other public agencies and private nonprofit organizations, associations, and groups to support the development of comprehensive, coordinated systems of community long-term care for older individuals, with special emphasis upon—

(A) services designed to support alternatives to institutional living; and

(B) the assessment of need, the development of a plan of care, and the referral of individuals, in the delivery of long-term care services, including non-institutional and institutional services, where appropriate.

(2) A grant under this section may be made to pay part or all of the estimated cost of a program (including start-up cost) for a period of not more than 3 years, except that no funds may be used to pay for direct services which are eligible for reimbursement under title XVIII, title XIX, or title XX of the Social Security Act.

(3) A grant made under this section shall be used for the development of programs which provide a full continuum of services. Such services may include—

(A) adult day health;

(B) monitoring and evaluation of service effectiveness;

(C) supported living in public and private nonprofit housing;

(D) family respite services;

(E) preventive health services;

---

[28] *There was nothing in the Act before the 1978 Amendments comparable to secs. 422, 423, 424, and 425.*

(F) home health, homemaker, and other rehabilitative and maintenance in-home services;

(G) geriatric health maintenance organizations; and

(H) other services which the Commissioner determines are appropriate, which were previously unavailable to the individuals to be served and which, at a minimum, provide for identification and assessment of the long-term care needs of older individuals, referral of such individuals to the appropriate services, and follow-up and evaluation of the continued appropriateness of such services with provision for re-referral as appropriate.

(4) A grant under this section may be used to encourage the development of manpower training programs designed to further the purposes described in paragraph (3).

(b)(1) In making grants to States under this section preference shall be given to applicants which demonstrate that—

(A) adequate State standards have been developed to ensure the quality of services provided;

(B) the State has made a commitment to carry out the program assisted under this section with the State agency responsible for the administration of title XIX of the Social Security Act or title XX of the Social Security Act, or both such agencies;

(C) the State will develop plans to finance the comprehensive program assisted under this section; and

(D) the State agency has a plan for statewide or designated regions of the State containing provisions designed to maximize access to older individuals for long-term care services.

(2) In awarding grants to agencies and organizations under this section, preference shall be given to applicants that—

(A) possess the capability to establish community-based long-term care programs; and

(B) demonstrate that a need exists for the establishment of such programs in the area to be served.

(3) Agencies and organizations assisted under this section shall establish procedures for evaluating the program assisted under this section, with respect to the benefits accruing to persons receiving assistance, the feasibility of the administrative model used for comprehensive coordination of services including coordination with other local programs, and the comparative costs and quality of services provided, and shall submit such evaluation to the Commissioner on a periodic basis.

(c) The Secretary shall involve appropriate Federal departments and agencies in carrying out the provisions of this section in order to assure coordination at the Federal level and to avoid duplication and shall report to the Congress annually on the impact of grants made, on the experiences of grantees in meeting the requirements of this section, and on the comparative benefits and costs of projects assisted under this section.

(d) Sums appropriated to carry out this section shall, to the extent feasible, be used to support programs equitably distributed throughout the Nation between urban and rural areas.

SPECIAL DEMONSTRATION PROJECTS ON LEGAL SERVICES FOR OLDER AMERICANS [28]

SEC. 423. (a) The Commissioner may make grants to and enter into contracts with public and private nonprofit agencies or organizations in order to—

(1) support legal research, technical assistance, training, information dissemination, and other support activities to agencies, organizations, institutions, and private law firms that are providing, developing, or supporting pro bono or reduced-fee legal services to older individuals; and

(2) support demonstration projects to expand or improve the delivery of legal services to older individuals with social or economic need.

(b) Any grants or contracts entered into under subsection (a)(2) shall contain assurances that the requirements of section 307(a)(15) are met.

(c) From the sums appropriated under section 451 for each fiscal year, not less than $5,000,000 shall be reserved to carry out the provisions of this section.

NATIONAL IMPACT DEMONSTRATIONS [28]

SEC. 424. (a) The Commissioner may carry out directly or through grants or contracts—

(1) innovation and development projects and activities of national significance which show promise of having substantial impact on the expansion or improvement of social services, nutrition services, or multipurpose senior centers or otherwise promoting the well-being of older individuals; and

(2) dissemination of information activities related to such programs.

(b) An amount not to exceed 15 percent of any sums appropriated under section 451 may be used for carrying out this section.

UTILITY AND HOME HEATING COST DEMONSTRATION PROJECTS [28]

SEC. 425. The Secretary may, after consultation with the appropriate State agency designated under section 305(a)(1), make grants to pay for part or all of the costs of developing model projects which show promise of relieving older individuals of the excessive burdens of high utility service and home heating costs. Any such project shall give special consideration to projects under which a business concern engaged in providing home heating oil to the public, or a public utility, provides home heating oil or utility services to low-income older individuals at a cost which is substantially lower than providing home heating oil or utility services to other individuals.

PART D—MORTGAGE INSURANCE AND INTEREST GRANTS FOR MULTIPURPOSE SENIOR CENTERS [29]

MORTGAGE INSURANCE AUTHORIZED

SEC. 431. (a) It is the purpose of this part to assist and encourage the provision of urgently needed facilities for programs for the elderly.

(b) For the purpose of this part the terms "mortgage", "mortgagor", "mortgagee", "maturity date", and "State" shall have the meanings respectively set forth in section 207 of the National Housing Act.[30]

---

[29] *Secs. 431 and 432 of this Part D are almost identical with secs. 506 and 507 of the Title V ("Multipurpose Senior Centers") which was repealed by the 1978 Amendments. The major difference is that the new sections permit construction of centers (as well as acquisition, alteration, and renovation), while the repealed sections did not permit construction.*

[30] *Sec. 207 of the National Housing Act defines these terms as follows:*
"Rental Housing Insurance

"Sec. 207. (a) As used in this section—"(1) The term "mortgage" means a first mortgage on real estate in fee simple, or on the interest of either the lessor or lessee thereof (A) under a lease for not less than ninety-nine years which is renewable or (B) under a lease having a period of not less than fifty years to run from the date the mortgage was executed, upon which there is located or upon which there is to be constructed a building or buildings designed principally for residential use or upon which there is located or to be constructed facilities for mobile homes; and the term "first mortgage" means such classes of first liens as are commonly given to secure advances (including but not being limited to advances during construction) on, or the unpaid purchase price of, real estate under the laws of the State in which the real

Footnotes continued on next page

(c) The Secretary of Health, Education, and Welfare is authorized to insure any mortgage (including advances on such mortgage during acquisition, alteration, renovation, or construction) in accordance with the provisions of this section upon such terms and conditions as he may prescribe and make commitments for insurance of such mortgage prior to the date of its execution or disbursement thereon.

(d) In order to carry out the purpose of this section, the Secretary is authorized to insure any mortgage which covers a new multipurpose senior center, including equipment to be used in its operation, subject to the following conditions:

(1) The mortgage shall be executed by a mortgagor, approved by the Secretary, who demonstrates ability successfully to operate one or more programs for the elderly. The Secretary may in his discretion require any such mortgagor to be regulated or restricted as to minimum charges and methods of financing, and in addition thereto, if the mortgagor is a corporate entity, as to capital structure and rate of return. As an aid to the regulation or restriction of any mortgagor with respect to any of the foregoing matters, the Secretary may make such contracts with and acquire for not to exceed $100 such stock interest in such mortgagor as he may deem necessary. Any stock or interest so purchased shall be paid for out of the Multipurpose Senior Center Insurance Fund, and shall be redeemed by the mortgagor at par upon the termination of all obligations of the Secretary under the insurance.

(2) The mortgage shall involve a principal obligation in an amount not to exceed $250,000 and not to exceed 90 percent of the estimated

---

Footnotes continued from last page

estate is located, together with the credit instrument or instruments, if any, secured thereby, and may be in the form of trust mortgages or mortgage indentures or deeds of trust securing notes, bonds, or other credit instruments.

"(2) The term "mortgagee" means the original lender under a mortgage, and its successors and assigns, and includes the holders of credit instruments issued under a trust mortgage or deed of trust pursuant to which such holders act by and through a trustee therein named.

"(3) The term "mortgagor" means the original borrower under a mortgage and its successors and assigns.

"(4) The term "maturity date" means the date on which the mortgage indebtedness would be extinguished if paid in accordance with the periodic payments provided for in the mortgage."

*   *   *   *   *

"(7) The term "State" includes the several States, and Puerto Rico, the District of Columbia, Guam, the Trust Territory of the Pacific Islands, and the Virgin Islands."

replacement cost of the property or project, including equipment to be used in the operation of the multipurpose senior center, when the proposed improvements are completed and the equipment is installed.

(3) The mortgage shall—

(A) provide for complete amortization by periodic payments within such term as the Secretary shall prescribe, and

(B) bear interest (exclusive of premium charges for insurance and service charges, if any) at not to exceed such per centum per annum on the principal obligation outstanding at any time as the Secretary finds necessary to meet the mortgage market.

(4) The Secretary shall not insure any mortgage under this section unless he has determined that the center to be covered by the mortgage will be in compliance with minimum standards to be prescribed by the Secretary.

(5) In the plans for such multipurpose senior center, due consideration shall be given to excellence of architecture and design, and to the inclusion of works of art (not representing more than 1 percent of the cost of the project).

(e) The Secretary shall fix and collect premium charges for the insurance of mortgages under this section which shall be payable annually in advance by the mortgagee, either in cash or in debentures of the Multipurpose Senior Center Insurance Fund issued at par plus accrued interest. In the case of any mortgage such charge shall not be less than an amount equivalent to one-fourth of 1 percent per annum nor more than an amount equivalent to 1 percent per annum of the amount of the principal obligation of the mortgage outstanding at any one time, without taking into account delinquent payments or prepayments. In addition to the premium charge provided for in this subsection, the Secretary is authorized to charge and collect such amounts as he may deem reasonable for the appraisal of a property or project during acquisition, alteration, or renovation; but such charges for appraisal and inspection shall not aggregate more than 1 percent of the original principal face amount of the mortgage.

(f) The Secretary may consent to the release of a part or parts of the mortgaged property or project from the lien of any mortgage insured under this section upon such terms and conditions as he may prescribe.

(g)(1) The Secretary shall have the same functions, powers, and duties (insofar as applicable) with respect to the insurance of mortgages under this section as the Secretary of Housing and Urban Development has with respect to the insurance of mortgages under title II of the National Housing Act.

(2) The provisions of subsections (e), (g), (h), (i), (j), (k), (l), and (n) of section 207 of the National Housing Act shall apply to mortgages

insured under this section; except that, for the purposes of their application with respect to such mortgages, all references in such provisions to the General Insurance Fund shall be deemed to refer to the Multipurpose Senior Center Insurance Fund, and all references in such provisions to "Secretary" shall be deemed to refer to the Secretary of Health, Education, and Welfare.

(h)(1) There is hereby created a Multipurpose Senior Center Insurance Fund which shall be used by the Secretary as a revolving fund for carrying out all the insurance provisions of this section. All mortgages insured under this section shall be insured under and be the obligation of the Multipurpose Senior Center Insurance Fund.

(2) The general expenses of the operations of the Department of Health, Education, and Welfare relating to mortgages insured under this section may be charged to the Multipurpose Senior Center Insurance Fund.

(3) Moneys in the Multipurpose Senior Center Insurance Fund not needed for the current operations of the Department of Health, Education, and Welfare with respect to mortgages insured under this section shall be deposited with the Treasurer of the United States to the credit of such fund, or invested in bonds or other obligations of, or in bonds or other obligations guaranteed as to principal and interest by, the United States. The Secretary may, with the approval of the Secretary of the Treasury, purchase in the open market debentures issued as obligations of the Multipurpose Senior Center Insurance Fund. Such purchases shall be made at a price which will provide an investment yield of not less than the yield obtainable from other investments authorized by this section. Debentures so purchased shall be canceled and not reissued.

(4) Premium charges, adjusted premium charges, and appraisal and other fees received on account of the insurance of any mortgage under this section, the receipts derived from property covered by such mortgages and from any claims, debts, contracts, property, and security assigned to the Secretary in connection therewith, and all earnings as the assets of the fund, shall be credited to the Multipurpose Senior Center Insurance Fund. The principal of, and interest paid and to be paid on, debentures which are the obligation of such fund, cash insurance payments and adjustments, and expenses incurred in the handling, management, renovation, and disposal of properties acquired or constructed in connection with mortgages insured under this section, shall be charged to such fund.

(5) There are authorized to be appropriated to provide initial capital for the Multipurpose Senior Center Insurance Fund, and to assure the soundness of such fund thereafter, such sums as may be necessary.

ANNUAL INTEREST GRANTS

SEC. 432. (a) To assist nonprofit private agencies to reduce the cost of borrowing from other sources for the acquisition, alteration, renovation, or construction of facilities for multipurpose senior centers, the Secretary may make annual interest grants to such agencies.

(b) Annual interest grants under this section with respect to any facility shall be made over a fixed period not exceeding forty years, and provision for such grants shall be embodied in a contract guaranteeing their payment over such period. Each such grant shall be in an amount not greater than the difference between (1) the average annual debt service which would be required to be paid, during the life of the loan, on the amount borrowed from other sources for the acquisition, alteration, renovation, or construction of such facilities, and (2) the average annual debt service which the institution would have been required to pay, during the life of the loan, with respect to such amounts if the applicable interest rate were 3 percent per annum, except that the amount on which such grant is based shall be approved by the Secretary.

(c)(1) There are hereby authorized to be appropriated to the Secretary such sums as may be necessary for payment of annual interest grants in accordance with this section.

(2) Contracts for annual interest grants under this section shall not be entered into in an aggregate amount greater than is authorized in appropriation Acts.

(d) Not more than 12½ per centum of the funds provided for in this section for grants may be used within any one State.

PART E—MULTIDISCIPLINARY CENTERS OF GERONTOLOGY [31]

SEC. 441. The Commissioner may make grants to public and private nonprofit agencies, organizations, and institutions for the purpose of establishing or supporting multidisciplinary centers of gerontology, and gerontology centers of special emphasis (including health, income maintenance, housing, service delivery and utilization, preretirement and retirement, and long-term care and alternatives).[32] A grant may be made under this section only if the application therefor—

---

[31] *The 1973 Amendments added this part to the Act.*

[32] *The 1978 Amendments, sec. 104(d)(1), added the phrase "and gerontology centers of special emphasis (. . .)".*

(1) provides satisfactory assurance that the applicant will expend the full amount of the grant to establish or support a multidisciplinary center of gerontology which shall—

(A) recruit and train personnel at the professional and subprofessional levels in accordance with the national manpower policy as described in section 401,[33]

(B) conduct basic and applied research on work, leisure, and education of older people, living arrangements of older people, social services for older people, the economics of aging, and other related areas,

(C) provide consultation to public and voluntary organizations with respect to the needs of older people and in planning and developing services for them,

(D) serve as a repository of information and knowledge with respect to the areas for which it conducts basic and applied research,

(E) stimulate the incorporation of information on aging into the teaching of biological, behavioral, and social sciences at colleges or universities,

(F) help to develop training programs on aging in schools of social work, public health, health care administration, education, and in other such schools at colleges and universities, and

(G) create opportunities for innovative, multidisciplinary efforts in teaching, research, and demonstration projects with respect to aging;

(2) provides for such fiscal control and fund accounting procedures as may be necessary to assure proper disbursement of and accounting for funds paid to the applicant under this section;

(3) provides for making such reports, in such form and containing such information, as the Commissioner may require to carry out his functions under this section, and for keeping such records and for affording such access thereto as the Commissioner may find necessary to assure the correctness and verification of such reports; and

(4) [34] provides for making biennial reports to the Commissioner summarizing the training, research, and special demonstration efforts of the centers which shall then be made available through the National Information and Resource Clearing House for the Aging, where appropriate.

---

[33] *The 1978 Amendments, sec. 104(d)(2), added the phrase, "in accordance with the national manpower policy as described in section 401".*

[34] *The 1978 Amendments, sec. 104(d)(3), added paragraph (4).*

PART F—AUTHORIZATION OF APPROPRIATIONS

AUTHORIZATION OF APPROPRIATIONS

SEC. 451.[35] (a) Except as otherwise specifically provided in this title, there are authorized to be appropriated to carry out the provisions of this title such sums as may be necessary for each fiscal year ending prior to October 1, 1981.

(b) [36] No funds appropriated under this section—

(1) may be transferred to any office or other authority of the Department of Health, Education, and Welfare which is not directly responsible to the Commissioner; or

(2) may be used for any research program or activity which is not specifically authorized by this title.

PAYMENTS OF GRANTS

SEC. 452.[37] (a) To the extent he deems it appropriate, the Commissioner shall require the recipient of any grant or contract under this title to contribute money, facilities, or services for carrying out the project for which such grant or contract was made.

(b) Payments under this title pursuant to a grant or contract may be made (after necessary adjustment, in the case of grants, on account of previously made overpayments or underpayments) in advance or by way of reimbursement, and in such installments and on such conditions, as the Commissioner may determine.

(c) [38] The Commissioner may make multicategorical grants or contracts under any or all sections of this title by making grants or contracts

---

[35] *From the 1965 Act until the 1973 Amendments, authorizations for Title IV (Research and Demonstrations) and Title V (Training) were provided in a section of the "General" Title. The 1973 Amendments repealed all of that Title (VIII), including its section (803) which contained authorizations for those programs, and substituted a new sec. 431, which was, in turn, superseded by sec. 451, as enacted by the 1978 Amendments.*

[36] *Before the 1978 Amendments, there was in the Act no provision comparable to subsection (b).*

[37] *The language of this section is substantially the same as that of secs. 402 and 502 of the Act before the 1973 Amendments, which sections related to payment of grants and contracts for research and development projects and training projects, respectively. Between 1973 and 1978, this was sec. 432.*

[38] *The 1978 Amendments, sec. 104 (e)(2), inserted paragraph (c).*

for the purpose of supporting extensive research and demonstration of particular areas of need.

(d) The Commissioner shall make no grant or contract under this title in any State which has established or designated a State agency for purposes of title III of this Act unless the Commissioner has consulted with such State agency regarding such grant or contract.

TITLE V [1]—COMMUNITY SERVICE

EMPLOYMENT FOR OLDER AMERICANS [2]

SHORT TITLE

SEC. 501. This title may be cited as the "Older American Community Service Employment Act".

OLDER AMERICAN COMMUNITY SERVICE EMPLOYMENT PROGRAM

SEC. 502. (a) In order to foster and promote useful part-time opportunities in community service activities for unemployed low-income persons who are fifty-five years old or older and who have poor employment prospects, the Secretary of Labor (hereinafter in this title referred to as the "Secretary") is authorized to establish an older American community service employment program.

(b)(1) In order to carry out the provisions of this title, the Secretary is authorized to enter into agreements with public or private nonprofit

---

[1] From 1965 until 1973, Title V was the title on "Training Projects". The 1973 Amendments transferred training provisions to Title IV, Part A, and enacted a new Title V on "Multipurpose Senior Centers". The 1978 Amendments amended the Act to deal with centers in sec. 307(a)(14), sec. 312, and Part D, Title IV, and to redesignate the previous Title IX ("Community Service Employment for Older Americans") as Title V.

[2] This title was added to the Act by the 1975 Amendments, sec. 113, as Title IX, and redesignated Title V by the 1978 Amendments. With minor differences it is identical with Title IX of The Older Americans Comprehensive Services Amendments of 1973 (P.L. 93–29–May 3, 1973). That title, as enacted in 1973, was a separate Act, in no way a part of the Older Americans Act of 1965, as Amended. The changes made in adding the new Title IX of the Older Americans Act, are discussed in the footnotes which follow. The 1975 Amendments, sec. 113, after adding Title IX to the Act, repealed Title IX of the 1973 Act.

agencies or organizations, including national organizations,[3] agencies of a State government or a political subdivision of a State (having elected or duly appointed governing officials), or a combination of such political subdivisions, or tribal organizations in order to further the purposes and goals of the program. Such agreements may include provisions for the payment of costs, as provided in subsection (c), of projects developed by such organizations and agencies in cooperation with the Secretary in order to make the program effective or to supplement the program. No payment shall be made by the Secretary toward the cost of any project established or administered by any such organization or agency unless he determines that such project—

(A) will provide employment only for eligible individuals, except for necessary technical, administrative, and supervisory personnel, but such personnel shall, to the fullest extent possible, be recruited from among eligible individuals;

(B) will provide employment for eligible individuals in the community in which such individuals reside, or in nearby communities;

(C) will employ eligible individuals in services related to publicly owned and operated facilities and projects, or projects sponsored by organizations, other than political parties, exempt from taxation under the provisions of section 501(c)(3) of the Internal Revenue Code of 1954, except projects involving the construction, operation, or maintenance of any facility used or to be used as a place for sectarian religious instruction or worship;

(D) will contribute to the general welfare of the community;

(E) will provide employment for eligible individuals whose opportunities for other suitable public or private paid employment are poor;

(F) (i) will result in an increase in employment opportunities over those opportunities which would otherwise be available, (ii) will not result in the displacement of currently employed workers (including partial displacement, such as a reduction in the hours of nonovertime work or wages or employment benefits), and (iii) will not impair existing contracts or result in the substitution of Federal funds for other funds in connection with work that would otherwise be performed;

(G) [4] will not employ or continue to employ any eligible individual to perform work the same or substantially the same as that performed by any other person who is on layoff;

(H) will utilize methods of recruitment and selection (including listing of job vacancies with the employment agency operated by any State or

---

[3] *The phrase, "including national organizations," was not in Title IX of the 1973 Act.*

[4] *Subparagraphs (G) and (N) were inserted into this title when it was added to the Act as Title IX by the 1975 Amendments.*

political subdivision thereof) which will assure that the maximum number of eligible individuals will have an opportunity to participate in the project;

(I) will include such training as may be necessary to make the most effective use of the skills and talents of those individuals who are participating, and will provide for the payment of the reasonable expenses of individuals being trained, including a reasonable subsistence allowance;

(J) will assure that safe and healthy conditions of work will be provided, and will assure that persons employed in community service jobs assisted under this title shall be paid wages which shall not be lower than whichever is the highest of (i) the minimum wage which would be applicable to the employee under the Fair Labor Standards Act of 1938, if section 6(a)(1) of such Act applied to the participant and if he were not exempt under section 13 thereof, (ii) the State or local minimum wage for the most nearly comparable covered employment, or (iii) the prevailing rates of pay for persons employed in similar public occupations by the same employer;

(K) will be established or administered with the advice of persons competent in the field of service in which employment is being provided, and of persons who are knowledgeable with regard to the needs of older persons;

(L) will authorize pay for necessary transportation costs of eligible individuals which may be incurred in employment in any project funded under this title, in accordance with regulations promulgated by the Secretary;

(M) will assure that, to the extent feasible, such project will serve the needs of minority, Indian, and limited English-speaking eligible individuals in proportion to their numbers in the State; and

(N) [4] will authorize funds to be used, to the extent feasible, to include individuals participating in such project under any State unemployment insurance plan.

(2) The Secretary is authorized to establish, issue, and amend such regulations as may be necessary to effectively carry out the provisions of this title.

(3) [5] The Secretary shall develop alternatives for innovative work modes and provide technical assistance in creating job opportunities through work sharing and other experimental methods to prime sponsors, labor organizations, groups representing business and industry and workers as well as to individual employers, where appropriate.

---

[5] *The 1978 Amendments, sec. 105(b) inserted paragraphs (3) and (4) of sec. 502(b) and added subsections (d) and (e).*

(4) [5] The Secretary may enter into an agreement with the Administrator of the Environmental Protection Agency to establish a Senior Environmental Employment Corps.

(c)(1) The Secretary is authorized to pay not to exceed 90 per centum of the cost of any project which is the subject of an agreement entered into under subsection (b), except that the Secretary is authorized to pay all of the costs of any such project which is (A) an emergency or disaster project, or (B) a project located in an economically depressed area, as determined by the Secretary in consultation with the Secretary of Commerce and the Director of the Community Services Administration.

(2) The non-Federal share shall be in cash or in kind. In determining the amount of the non-Federal share, the Secretary is authorized to attribute fair market value to services and facilities contributed from non-Federal sources.

(d)(1) [5] Whenever a national organization or other program sponsor conducts a project within a State such organization or program sponsor shall submit to the State agency on aging a description of such project to be conducted in the State, including the location of the project, 30 days prior to undertaking the project, for review and comment according to guidelines the Secretary shall issue to assure efficient and effective coordination of programs under this title.

(2) The Secretary shall review on his own initiative or at the request of any public or private nonprofit agency or organization, or an agency of the State government, the distribution of programs under this title within the State including the distribution between urban and rural areas within the State. For each proposed reallocation of programs within a State, the Secretary shall give notice and opportunity for a hearing on the record by all interested individuals and make a written determination of his findings and decision.

(e) [5] The Secretary, in addition to any other authority contained in this title, may enter into agreements designed to assure the transition of individuals employed in public service jobs under this title to employment opportunities with private business concerns. The Secretary, from amounts reserved under section 506(a)(1)(B) in any fiscal year, may pay all of the costs of any agreement entered into under the provisions of this subsection.

ADMINISTRATION

SEC. 503. (a) In order to effectively carry out the provisions of this title, the Secretary shall, through the Commissioner of the Administration on Aging, consult with the State agency on aging designated under section 305(a)(1) and the appropriate area agencies on aging established under section 305(a)(2) with regard to—[6]

(1) the localities in which community service projects of the type authorized by this title are most needed;

(2) consideration of the employment situations and the type of skills possessed by available local individuals who are eligible to participate; and

(3) potential projects and the number and percentage of eligible individuals in the local population.

(b) If the Secretary determines that to do so would increase job opportunities available to individuals under this title, the Secretary is authorized to coordinate the program assisted under this title with programs authorized under the Emergency Jobs and Unemployment Assistance Act of 1974, the Comprehensive Employment and Training Act of 1973, the Community Services Act of 1974, and the Emergency Employment Act of 1971. Appropriations under this Act may not be used to carry out any program under the Emergency Jobs and Unemployment Assistance Act of 1974, the Comprehensive Employment and Training Act of 1973, the Community Services Act of 1974, or the Emergency Employment Act of 1971. [7]

(c) In carrying out the provisions of this title, the Secretary is authorized to use, with their consent, the services, equipment, personnel, and facilities of Federal and other agencies with or without reimbursement, and on a similar basis to cooperate with other public and private agencies and instrumentalities in the use of services, equipment, and facilities.

(d) [7] Payments under this title may be made in advance or by way of reimbursement and in such installments as the Secretary may determine.

---

[6] *The introductory language of sec. 503 is substantially as provided in the 1975 Amendments. Between 1973 and 1975, it read as follows:*

"SEC. 903. (a) *In order to effectively carry out the purposes of this title, the Secretary is authorized to consult with agencies of States and their political subdivisions with regard to—*"

[7] *This sentence was added by the 1975 Amendments in lieu of the following sentence which was in effect between 1973 and 1975:*

"*In carrying out the provisions of this paragraph, the Secretary is authorized to make necessary arrangements to include projects and activities assisted under this title within a common agreement and a common application with projects assisted under this Act and other provisions of law such as the Economic Opportunity Act of 1964, the Manpower Development and Training Act of 1962, the Emergency Employment Act of 1971.*"

(e) The Secretary shall not delegate any function of the Secretary under this title to any other department or agency of the Federal Government.

(f) [8] In carrying out the provisions of this title, the Secretary may fund and expand projects concerning the Senior Environmental Employment Corps and energy conservation from sums appropriated under section 508 for such fiscal year.

PARTICIPANTS NOT FEDERAL EMPLOYEES

SEC. 504. (a) Eligible individuals who are employed in any project funded under this title shall not be considered to be Federal employees as a result of such employment and shall not be subject to the provisions of part III of title 5, United States Code.

(b) No contract shall be entered into under this title with a contractor who is, or whose employees are, under State law, exempted from operation of the State workmen's compensation law, generally applicable to employees, unless the contractor shall undertake to provide either through insurance by a recognized carrier, or by self-insurance, as authorized by State law, that the persons employed under the contract shall enjoy workmen's compensation coverage equal to that provided by law for covered employment.[9]

---

[8] *The 1978 Amendments, sec. 105(c)(3), added subsection (f).*

[9] *The 1975 Amendments deleted a second sentence of this subsection, which, between 1973 and 1975 read as follows:*

"The Secretary must establish standards for severance benefits, in lieu of unemployment insurance coverage, for eligible individuals who have participated in qualifying programs and who have become unemployed."

INTERAGENCY COOPERATION

SEC. 505. (a)[10] The Secretary shall consult with, and obtain the written views of, the Commissioner of the Administration on Aging prior to the establishment of rules or the establishment of general policy in the administration of this title.

(b)[10] The Secretary shall consult and cooperate with the Director of the Community Services Administration, the Secretary of Health, Education, and Welfare, and the heads of other Federal agencies carrying out related programs, in order to achieve optimal coordination with such other programs. In carrying out the provisions of this section, the Secretary shall promote programs or projects of a similar nature. Each Federal agency shall cooperate with the Secretary in disseminating information relating to the availability of assistance under this title and in promoting the identification and interests of individuals eligible for employment in projects assisted under this title.

(c)[11] In administering projects under this title concerning the Senior Environmental Employment Corps and energy conservation, the Secretary shall consult with the Administrator of the Environmental Protection Agency and the Secretary of Energy and shall enter into an agreement with the Administrator and the Secretary of Energy to coordinate programs conducted by them with such projects.

---

[10] *Subsections (a) and (b) are substantially as enacted in 1975. Between 1973 and 1975, sec. 905 of Title IX of the 1973 Amendments read as follows:*

"SEC. 905. The Secretary shall consult and cooperate with the Office of Economic Opportunity, the Administration on Aging, the Department of Health, Education, and Welfare, and any other related Federal agency administering related programs, with a view to achieving optimal coordination with such other programs and shall promote the coordination of projects under this title with other public and private programs or projects of a similar nature. Such Federal agencies shall cooperate with the Secretary in disseminating information about the availability of assistance under this title and in promoting the identification and interests of individuals eligible for employment in projects funded under this title."

[11] *The 1978 Amendments, sec. 105(d), added subsection (c).*

EQUITABLE DISTRIBUTION OF ASSISTANCE [12]

SEC. 506. (a)(1)(A). Subject to the provisions of paragraph (2),[13] from sums appropriated under this title for each fiscal year, the Secretary shall first reserve such sums as may be necessary for national grants or contracts with public agencies and public or private nonprofit organizations to maintain the level of activities carried on under such grants or

---

[12] *The 1975 amendments revised this section. From 1973 until 1975, the corresponding section (906) of Title IX of the 1973 Amendments read as follows:*

"SEC. 906. (a)(1) From the sums appropriated for any fiscal year under section 908 there shall be initially allotted for projects within each State an amount which bears the same ratio to such sum as the population, aged fifty-five or over in such State bears to the population aged fifty-five or over in all States, except that (A) no State shall be allotted less than one-half of 1 per centum of the sum appropriated for the fiscal year for which the determination is made; and (B) Guam, American Samoa, the Virgin Islands, and the Trust Territory of the Pacific Islands shall each be allotted an amount equal to one-fourth of 1 per centum of the sum appropriated for the fiscal year for which the determination is made. For the purpose of the exception contained in this paragraph, the term "State" does not include Guam, American Samoa, the Virgin Islands, and the Trust Territory of the Pacific Islands.

"(2) The number of persons aged fifty-five or over in any State and for all States shall be determined by the Secretary on the basis of the most satisfactory data available to him.

"(b) The amount allotted for projects within any State under subsection (a) for any fiscal year which the Secretary determines will not be required for that year shall be reallotted, from time to time and on such dates during such year as the Secretary may fix, to projects within other States in proportion to the original allotments to projects within such States under subsection (a) for that year, but with such proportionate amount for any of such other States being reduced to the extent it exceeds the sum the Secretary estimates that projects within such State need and will be able to use for such year; and the total of such reductions shall be similarly reallotted among the States whose proportionate amounts were not so reduced. Any amount reallotted to a State under this subsection during a year shall be deemed part of its allotment under subsection (a) for that year.

"(c) The amount apportioned for projects within each State under subsection (a) shall be apportioned among areas within each such State in an equitable manner, taking into consideration the proportion which eligible persons in each such area bears to such total number of such persons, respectively, in that State."

[13] *The 1978 Amendments, sec. 105 (e) (1)(B) inserted the phrase, "Subject to the provisions of paragraph (2),".*

contracts at least at the level of such activities supported under this title and under any other provision of Federal law relating to community service employment programs for older Americans in fiscal year 1978.[14] Preference in awarding such grants or contracts shall be given to national organizations of proven ability in providing employment services to older persons under this program and similar programs. The Secretary, in awarding grants and contracts under this section, shall, to the extent feasible, assure an equitable distribution of activities under such grants and contracts, in the aggregate, among the States, taking into account the needs of underserved States.

(B) [15] From sums appropriated under this title for each fiscal year after September 30, 1978, the Secretary may reserve an amount not to exceed one per centum of the amount appropriated in excess of the amount appropriated for fiscal year 1978 for the purpose of entering into agreements under section 502(e), relating to improved transition to private employment.

(2) [15] For each fiscal year in which the sums appropriated under this title exceed the amount appropriated for fiscal year 1978, the Secretary shall reserve not more than 45 per centum of such excess amount for the purpose described in paragraph (1). The remainder of such excess shall be allotted pursuant to paragraph (3).

(3) The Secretary shall allot for projects within each State the remainder of the sums appropriated for any fiscal year under section 508 so that each State will receive an amount which bears the same ratio to such remainder as the product of the number of persons aged fifty-five or over in the State and the allotment percentage of such State bears to the sum of the corresponding product for all States, except that (A) no State shall be allotted less than one-half of 1 per centum of the remainder of the sums appropriated for the fiscal year for which the determination is made, or $100,000, whichever is greater, and (B) Guam, American Samoa, the Virgin Islands, and the Trust Territory of the Pacific Islands shall each be allotted an amount which is not less than one-fourth of 1 per centum of the remainder of the sums appropriated for the fiscal year for which the determination is made, or $50,000, whichever is greater. For the purpose of the exception contained in this paragraph the term "State" does not include Guam, American Samoa, the Virgin Islands, and the Trust Territory of the Pacific Islands.

(4) For the purpose of this subsection—

---

[14] *The 1978 Amendments, sec. 105(e)(1)(C) inserted "1978" in lieu of "1975".*

[15] *The 1978 Amendments, sec. 105(e), inserted subparagraph (B) and paragraph (2).*

(A) the allotment percentage of each State shall be 100 per centum less that percentage which bears the same ratio to 50 per centum as the per capita income of such State bears to the per capita income of the United States, except that (i) the allotment percentage shall in no case be more than 75 per centum or less than 33⅓ per centum, and (ii) the allotment percentage for the District of Columbia, Puerto Rico, Guam, the Virgin Islands, American Samoa, and the Trust Territory of the Pacific Islands shall be 75 per centum;

(B) the number of persons aged fifty-five or over in any State and in all States, and the per capita income in any State and in all States, shall be determined by the Secretary on the basis of the most satisfactory data available to him; and

(C) for the purpose of determining the allotment percentage, the term "United States" means the fifty States and the District of Columbia.

(b) The amount allotted for projects within any State under subsection (a) for any fiscal year which the Secretary determines will not be required for such year shall be reallotted, from time to time and on such dates during such year as the Secretary may fix, to projects within other States in proportion to the original allotments to projects within such States under subsection (a) for such year, but with such proportionate amount for any of such other States being reduced to the extent it exceeds the sum the Secretary estimates that projects within such State need and will be able to use for such year; and the total of such reductions shall be similarly reallotted among the States whose proportionate amounts were not so reduced. Any amount reallotted to a State under this subsection during a year shall be deemed part of its allotment under subsection (a) for such year.

(c) The amount apportioned for projects within each State under subsection (a) shall be apportioned among areas within each such State in an equitable manner, taking into consideration (1) the proportion which eligible individuals in each such area bears to the total number of such individuals, respectively, in that State, and (2) the relative distribution of such individuals residing in rural and urban areas within the State.

DEFINITIONS

SEC. 507. As used in this title—

(1) the term "State" means any of the several States of the United States, the District of Columbia, Puerto Rico, the Virgin Islands, American Samoa, Guam, and the Trust Territory of the Pacific Islands;

(2) the term "eligible individual" means an individual who is fifty-five years old or over, who has a low income (including any such individual whose income is not more than 125 per centum of the poverty guidelines

established by the Bureau of Labor Statistics), and who has or would have difficulty in securing employment, except that, pursuant to regulations prescribed by the Secretary, any such individual who is sixty years old or over shall have priority for the work opportunities provided for under this title;

(3) the term "community service" means social, health, welfare, and educational services, legal and other counseling services and assistance, including tax counseling and assistance and financial counseling,[16] and library, recreational, and other similar services; conservation, maintenance, or restoration of natural resources; community betterment or beautification; antipollution and environmental quality efforts; economic development; and such other services essential and necessary to the community as the Secretary, by regulation, may prescribe; and

(4) the term "program" means the older American community service employment program established under this title.

AUTHORIZATION OF APPROPRIATIONS [17]

SEC. 508. There are authorized to be appropriated to carry out this title $100,000,000 for the fiscal year ending June 30, 1976, $37,500,000 for the period beginning July 1, 1976, and ending September 30, 1976, $150,000,000 for the fiscal year ending September 30, 1977, $200,000,000 for the fiscal year ending September 30, 1978, $350,000,000 for the fiscal year ending September 30, 1979, $400,000,000 for the fiscal year ending September 30, 1980, and $450,000,000 for the fiscal year ending September 30, 1981.

---

[16] *The phrase "legal and other counseling services . . . financial counseling," was not included in the definition of "community service" in Title IX of the 1973 Amendments, and was added by the 1975 Amendments.*

[17] *Title IX of the 1973 Amendments provided no authorizations for fiscal year 1976 and subsequent years. The 1975 Amendments, in adding that title as Title IX of the Act, added authorizations for 1976, 1977, and 1978. The 1978 Amendments, sec. 105(g), added authorizations for 1979, 1980, and 1981.*

TITLE VI [1]—GRANTS FOR INDIAN [2] TRIBES

STATEMENT OF PURPOSE

SEC. 601. It is the purpose of this title to promote the delivery of social services, including nutritional services, for Indians that are comparable to services provided under title III.

ELIGIBILITY

SEC. 602. (a) A tribal organization of an Indian tribe is eligible for assistance under this title only if—

(1) the tribal organization represents at least 75 individuals who have attained 60 years of age or older;

(2) the tribal organization demonstrates the ability to deliver social services, including nutritional services; and

(3) individuals to be served by the tribal organization will not receive for the year for which application under this title is made, services under title III.

(b) The terms "Indian tribe" and "tribal organization" for the purposes of this title are defined as in section 4 of the Indian Self-Determination and Education Assistance Act (25 U.S.C. 450b). [3]

---

[1] *From the enactment of the Act in 1965 until 1969, Title VI was the "General" title, containing sections on advisory committees, administration, and authorizations of appropriations for Title IV ("Research and Development Projects") and Title V ("Training Projects"). The 1969 Amendments, sec. 9, inserted a new Title VI ("National Older Americans Volunteer Program") and redesignated the former Title VI as Title VII. However, the new Title VI was repealed by the "Domestic Volunteer Service Act of 1973" (P. L. 93–113, enacted October 1, 1973), which incorporated most of the substance of the repealed Title VI of the Older Americans Act into Title II of that Act.*

[2] *For definition of "Indian" see paragraph (5) of sec. 102.*

[3] *Subsections (b) and (c) of sec. 4 of that Act (P.L. 93–638, Jan. 4, 1975) read as follows:*

"(b) 'Indian tribe' means any Indian tribe, band, nation, or other organized group or community, including any Alaska Native village or regional or village corporation as defined in or established pursuant to the Alaska Native Claims Settlement Act (85 Stat. 688) which is recognized as eligible for the special programs and services provided by the United States to Indians because of their status as Indians;

Footnotes continued on next page

GRANTS AUTHORIZED

SEC. 603. The Commissioner may make grants to eligible tribal organizations to pay all of the costs for delivery of social services and nutritional services for Indians who are aged 60 and older.

APPLICATIONS

SEC. 604. (a) No grant may be made under this title unless the eligible tribal organization submits an application to the Commissioner which meets such criteria as the Commissioner may by regulation prescribe. Each such application shall—

(1) provide that the eligible tribal organization will evaluate the need for social and nutritional services among older Indians to be represented by the tribal organization;

(2) provide for the use of such methods of administration as are necessary for the proper and efficient administration of the program to be assisted;

(3) provide that the tribal organization will make such reports in such form and containing such information, as the Commissioner may reasonably require, and comply with such requirements as the Commissioner may impose to assure the correctness of such reports;

(4) provide that a nonprofit private organization selected by the tribal organization will conduct periodic evaluation of activities and projects carried out under the application;

(5) establish objectives consistent with the purposes of this title toward which activities under the application will be directed, identify obstacles to the attainment of such objectives, and indicate the manner in which the tribal organization proposes to overcome such obstacles;

(6) provide for establishing and maintaining information and referral services to assure that older Indians to be served by the assistance made

---

Footnotes continued from last page

"(c) 'Tribal organization' means the recognized governing body of any Indian tribe; any legally established organization of Indians which is controlled, sanctioned, or chartered by such governing body or which is democratically elected by the adult members of the Indian community to be served by such organization and which includes the maximum participation of Indians in all phases of its activities: Provided, That in any case where a contract is let or grant made to an organization to perform services benefitting more than one Indian tribe, the approval of each such Indian tribe shall be a prerequisite to the letting or making of such contract or grant;"

Compare with definition of "Indian tribe" and "tribal organization" in paragraphs (6) and (7) of sec. 102.

available under this title will have reasonably convenient access to such services;

(7) provide a preference for Indians aged 60 and older for full- or part-time staff positions wherever feasible;

(8) provide assurances that either directly or by way of grant or contract with appropriate entities nutritional services will be delivered to older Indians represented by the tribal organization substantially in compliance with the provisions of part C of title III;

(9) contain assurances that the provisions of sections 307(a)(14)(A) (i) and (iii), 307(a)(14)(B), and 307(a)(14)(C) will be complied with whenever the application contains provisions for the acquisition, alteration, or renovation of facilities to serve as multipurpose senior centers;

(10) provide assurances that either directly or by way of grant or contract with appropriate entities legal and ombudsman services will be made available to older Indians represented by the tribal organization substantially in compliance with the provisions of title III relating to the furnishing of similar services; and

(11) provide satisfactory assurance that fiscal control and fund accounting procedures will be adopted as may be necessary to assure proper disbursement of, and accounting for, Federal funds paid under this title to the tribal organization, including any funds paid by the tribal organization to a recipient of a grant or contract.

(b) For the purpose of any application submitted under this title, the tribal organization may develop its own population statistics, with certification from the Bureau of Indian Affairs, in order to establish eligibility.

(c) The Commissioner shall approve any application which complies with the provisions of subsection (a).

(d) Whenever the Commissioner approves an application under this title he shall withhold from the allotment of the appropriate State made under section 304 an amount attributable to the Indians to be served under the application who were also counted for the purpose of allotments under title III. The Commissioner shall reallot sums withheld under this subsection in accordance with the provisions of section 304(b).

(e) Whenever the Commissioner determines not to approve an application submitted under subsection (a) he shall—

(1) state his objections in writing to the tribal organization within 60 days after such decision;

(2) provide to the extent practicable technical assistance to the tribal organization to overcome his stated objections; and

(3) provide the tribal organization with a hearing, under such rules and regulations as he may prescribe.

(f) Whenever the Commissioner approves an application of a tribal organization under this title, funds shall be awarded for not less than 12 months, during which time such tribal organization may not receive funds under title III.

ADMINISTRATION

SEC. 605. (a) In establishing regulations for the purpose of this title the Commissioner shall consult with the Secretary of the Interior.

(b) The Commissioner shall prescribe final regulations for the administration of this title not later than 90 days after the date of the enactment of the Comprehensive Older Americans Act Amendments of 1978.

SURPLUS EDUCATIONAL FACILITIES

SEC. 606. (a) Notwithstanding any other provision of law, the Secretary of the Interior through the Bureau of Indian Affairs shall make available surplus Indian educational facilities to tribal organizations, and nonprofit organizations with tribal approval, for use as multipurpose senior centers. Such centers may be altered so as to provide extended care facilities, community center facilities, nutritional services, child care services, and other social services.

(b) Each eligible tribal organization desiring to take advantage of such surplus facilities shall submit an application to the Secretary of the Interior at such time and in such manner, and containing or accompanied by such information, as the Secretary of the Interior determines to be necessary to carry out the provisions of this section.

PAYMENTS

SEC. 607. Payments may be made under this title (after necessary adjustments, in the case of grants, on account of previously made overpayments or underpayments) in advance or by way of reimbursement in such installments and on such conditions, as the Commissioner may determine.

AUTHORIZATION OF APPROPRIATIONS

SEC. 608. (a) Except as provided in subsection (c), there are authorized to be appropriated such sums as may be necessary for fiscal years 1979, 1980, and 1981, to carry out the provisions of this title.

(b) For any fiscal year in which less than $5,000,000 is appropriated under subsection (a) tribal organizations are authorized to receive assistance in accordance with the provisions of title III.

(c) There are authorized to be appropriated such sums as may be necessary for fiscal years 1979, 1980, and 1981, to carry out the provisions of section 606.

TITLE VI (Repealed)

From the enactment of the Act in 1965 until 1969, Title VI was the "General" title, containing sections on advisory committees, administration, and authorization of appropriations for Title IV ("Research and Development Projects") and Title V ("Training Projects"). The 1969 Amendments, sec. 9, inserted a new Title VI ("National Older Americans Volunteer Program") and redesignated the former Title VI as Title VII. From 1969 until July 1, 1971, the Retired Senior Volunteer Program and the Foster Grandparent Program, which were authorized by Title VI as it then read, were administered in the Administration on Aging. Effective on that date, the two programs were transferred to the new ACTION agency by the terms of the President's Reorganization Plan No. 1 of 1971; and Title VI was repealed by the "Domestic Volunteer Service Act of 1973" (P.L. 93–113, enacted October 1, 1973), which incorporated most of the substance of the repealed Title VI of the Older Americans Act into Title II of that Act. The text of Title II of the Domestic Volunteer Service Act of 1973 appears beginning on page 112 of this publication.

There was no Title VI in the Act from then until enactment of the present Title VI ("Grants for Indian Tribes") by the 1978 Amendments.

TITLE VII (Repealed)

NOTE: When the 1969 Amendments inserted a new Title VI, entitled "National Older American Volunteer Program", the former Title VI ("General") was redesignated Title VII (See footnote 1, Title VI). It remained as such from 1969 until 1972, when the 1972 Amendments added a new Title VII and redesignated the "General" title as Title VIII. From 1972 until 1978, Title VII was, therefore, entitled "Nutrition Program for the Elderly". The 1978 Amendments repealed Title VII, consolidating the nutrition program into Title III. Provisions previously in Title VII were reenacted as Sec. 307(a)(13), sec. 311, and Part C, Title III. In this connection, the 1978 Amendments, sec. 501, provided:

"SEC. 501. (a) Effective at the close of September 30, 1978, title V and title VII are repealed. The Commissioner on Aging may complete any project which was undertaken under either such title, or under title V, as so redesignated in section 105(a), before such date, and which is unfinished on such date, with funds obligated but unexpended on such date.

"(b) Any project receiving funds under title VII of the Older Americans Act of 1965, as in effect on the day before the effective date of this Act, shall continue to receive funds under part C of title III of such Act, as amended by this Act, if such project meets the requirements and criteria established in such title III, as amended by this Act, except that a State, pursuant to regulations prescribed by the Commissioner on Aging, shall not discontinue the payment of such funds to a project unless such State, after a hearing (if requested by the person responsible for administering such project), determines that such project has not carried out activities supported by such funds with demonstrated effectiveness."

TITLE VIII (Repealed)

NOTE: From 1965 until the 1973 Amendments, the last title of the Act was the "GENERAL" title. Beginning with the 1965 Act, it was Title VI. When the 1969 Amendments added a new Title VI ("National Older Americans Volunteer Program"), the "GENERAL" title became Title VII. When the 1972 Amendments added a new Title VII ("Nutrition Program for the Elderly"), the "GENERAL" title became Title VIII. The 1973 Amendments repealed Title VIII, but added new sections in Title II covering the same subjects as were in the sections of the former Title VIII. (See Title II's footnotes 12, 18, 25, and 31.)

TITLE IX (Repealed)

NOTE: The 1975 Amendments, sec. 113, added Title IX to the Act. With minor differences, it was identical with Title IX of The Older Americans Comprehensive Services Amendments of 1973 (P.L. 93–29). The 1978 Amendments, sec. 105(a) redesignated Title IX as Title V, which begins on p. 69.

B

National Nonprofit Resource Groups in Aging

Administration on Aging (AoA), Office of Human Development, U.S. Department of Health, Education, and Welfare, Washington, D.C. 20402; (202) 245-0213/0669 (National Clearinghouse on Aging).

Coordinates programs, services, and research to help older Americans. Administers and authorizes funds for major programs. Operates National Clearinghouse on Aging, which collects, stores, and disseminates information about the elderly. Responds to all inquires from the general public. State agencies and local Area Agencies on Aging offer consultation, grant application assistance, program information, and help to individuals.

AoA is the major starting point for all program information. As advocate for the elderly, AoA is committed to coordinated action of all federal agencies with programs and services involving older people and to the development of comprehensive information and referral programs. If you cannot locate your area agency in the phone directory, contact the mayor or local executive's office.

Publications: *Aging,* monthly magazine updating national, state, and local resources, legislation, and agency news, $9.25.

Other: *AoA Fact Sheets,* technical assistance documents, and other materials to meet the needs of the aged, general public, planners, and gerontologists. Publication list available.

Adapted and revised by permission from *Synagogue Aging,* January 1976, 3–5.

Special Committee on Aging, United States Senate, G-225 Dirksen Senate Office Building, Washington, D.C. 20510; (202) 224-5364 or 224-1467.

Studies and conducts hearings on all issues related to problems and opportunities for older people; sponsors appropriate legislation. Publishes findings and *Memorandum,* an occasional news sheet updating Congressional action on bills affecting the elderly and announcing future hearings. All public inquiries answered; written requests preferred.

Select Committee on Aging, United States Congress, 712 HOB Annex 1, Washington, D.C. 20515; (202) 225-9375.

Studies problems of older Americans, ways to encourage utilization of their skills and knowledge, policies for coordinating government and private programs. Holds hearings and publishes findings. Investigative body with no legislative jurisdiction; information resource for legislators and public. Phone or written inquiries answered; published reports available to public.

ACTION, 806 Connecticut Avenue, N.W., Washington, D.C. 20525; (800) 424-8580.

Federal volunteer agency administering Peace Corps, VISTA, and Older American Volunteer Programs: SCORE, which draws on the skills of retired business people; Foster Grandparents, volunteers who work with children on a one-to-one basis; Retired Senior Volunteers Program (RSVP), retirees who volunteer service to helping organizations; and Senior Companions, older people who serve older people with special needs.

Grants made available by 10 federal regional and 47 state offices to private nonprofit or public community organizations on a cost-sharing basis. For information on site sponsorship or volunteer participation, call toll-free number, local office on aging, or local RSVP program office.

Food & Nutrition Service (FNS), U.S. Department of Agriculture, Washington, D.C. 20036; (202) 447-8371.

Coordinates federal food stamp programs. Information available here or more directly from food stamp offices in most major cities. Six regional FNS offices: San Francisco, Dallas, Chicago, Atlanta, Princeton, Waltham; may provide consultation or speakers in areas of nutrition or food management. Surplus food for use by nonprofit, tax-exempt, residential institutions may be available from FNS; contact regional offices.

Editor's note: While food distribution for congregate dining programs may be coordinated by this office, the Nutrition Program for the Elderly is directed by AoA, and inquiries should be addressed to AoA or its area agencies. Meals delivered to homebound elderly as part of this program may be paid for with food stamps; contact food stamp offices for information.

Publications: *Cooking for Two,* large-print recipe book; U.S. Government Printing Office, PA-1043, $1.25.

Asociacion Nacional Por Personas Mayores (National Association for Spanish Speaking Elderly), 3875 Wilshire Boulevard, Suite 1401, Los Angeles, California 90010; (213) 487-1922.

The Asociacion Nacional is the only national Hispanic organization serving all segments of the Hispanic older population. Administers a five-state employment program for low-income persons 55 and over, a national needs assessment of the Hispanic elderly, and technical assistance to local regional and national organizations serving Hispanic elderly. National and local conferences on Hispanic elderly.

Publications: Newsletters and legislative bulletin for members.

National Caucus on the Black Aged, 1424 K Street, N.W., Suite 500, Washington, D.C. 20005; (202) 637-8400.

Advocates attention and programs for the black aged. Recommends public policies responsive to the needs of the older black American. Conducts research, curriculum development in the area of black aging, training of black professionals in gerontology, training of black elderly to assume leadership roles in services to black aged, and aids in participation of minority social organizations and businesses in service delivery to the elderly. Also conducts employment program for rural black elderly and operates elderly housing. National and local conferences on black aged.

Publications: Newsletters, $4.00; Job bank publications; reports on health, research, curriculum, and theoretical and policy perspectives on black aged.

National Council on the Aging (NCOA), 1828 L Street, N.W., Washington, D.C. 20036; (202) 223-6250.

Professional organization providing training, consultation and technical assistance, under contract, to public and private agencies working with older people. Maintains Center for Public Policy, which monitors legislation, research department, and extensive library containing books, journals, pamphlets, and local project reports. Library is open to public. Special projects include the Center for Older Americans and the Arts, the Media and the Aging, and National Voluntary Organizations (NVOILA).

National Institute of Industrial Gerontology provides analysis and information in the areas of age, employment policies, job design, and retirement. National Institute of Senior Centers (NISC) guides local center personnel in operations, community coordination, and upgrading services.

Publications: Free membership periodicals include: *Perspectives on Aging*, bimonthly magazine of general interest; *Current Literature on Aging*, quarterly summary of recent publications with brief annotations; *Senior Center Report*, NISC's monthly newsletter containing news of successful center programs, new resources; *NVOILA Newsletter*, irregular newsletter of voluntary groups concerned with the provision of alternates to institutional care.

Other: *Aging & Work*, quarterly journal by subscription. NCOA actively publishes in areas of interest to those working with or planning services for the elderly. Current publications list available.

National Indian Council on Aging, P.O. Box 2088, Albuquerque, New Mexico 87103; (506) 766-2276.

The overall purpose of the council is to bring about improved comprehensive services to the Indian and Alaskan Native elderly. Membership consists of 40 Indian and Alaskan Native individuals, of whom 12 constitute the board of directors. The council encourages legislative action, communication, and cooperation with service provider agencies, dissemination of information to the Indian communities, and supportive resources and, when necessary, intercedes with appropriate agencies to provide access to resources.

Publications: *National Indian Council on Aging NEWS*, $2.00.

Other: Conference reports: *Tribal Nursing Homes* and *State Regulations;* and *The Indian Elder: A Forgotten American* (1976), $4.00.

American Association of Retired Persons/National Retired Teachers Association (AARP/NRTA), 1909 K Street, N.W., Washington, D.C. 20006; (202) 872-4700.

National organization of older Americans with 2,000 local chapters. Services include legislative representation at the federal and state levels; mail-order pharmacy service for prescription medicine and other health needs; a well-developed preretirement education training program, Action for Independent Maturity (AIM); continuing education at the Institute of Lifetime Learning and its extensions; the Church Relations Office, which explores ways to expand services to older congregants; a travel service and insurance plan. Programs designed for chapter involvement: Health Education, Driver Improvement, Crime Prevention, Consumer Information, Senior Community Service Aides Project, and Widowhood Project.

Publications: *Modern Maturity,* bimonthly magazine of general interest and information for retired people; *News Bulletin,* practical monthly magazine; Better Retirement Series, individual booklets written for the older person: *Consumer, Food, Health, Hobby, Home, Job, Legal, Moving, Pet, Safety, Anti-Crime,* and *Psychology Guide,* single copies free.

Other: Booklets geared to retirement preparation and the older person to parallel the various program activities; *Dynamic Maturity,* AIM magazine for the preretirement years.

National Council of Senior Citizens (NCSC), 1511 K Street, N.W., Washington, D.C. 20005; (202) 783-6850.

Information service to strengthen grassroots-oriented social and legislative action programs. Prepares Congressional testimony on critical issues such as Medicare, age discrimination, improved housing, health care, and pension reform. Legal Research and Services to the Elderly (LRSE) works to improve state legislation. Membership open to individuals of all ages and to senior clubs and groups. Nonprofit services include a mail-order drug program, health insurance, and travel service.

Publications: *Senior Citizens News,* monthly legislative newspaper for members.

National Center for Voluntary Action (CVA), 1785 Massachusetts Avenue, N.W., Washington, D.C. 20036; (202) 797-7800.

Advocate for voluntary action. Prime source of information on successful programs involving volunteers; files on over 5,000 projects are updated regularly. Strengthens voluntary action movement through: leadership education in training volunteers and volunteer administrators; consultations and materials in the areas of public relations, fund development, community resources assessment, information systems development. Community impact through 31 state offices and local Voluntary Action Centers.

Publications: *Voluntary Action News,* bimonthly magazine for volunteers or organizations—includes program profiles, legislative updates, and book reviews—$4.00; *Voluntary Action Leadership,* quarterly forum for volunteer leaders and administrators, free.

Gray Panthers, 3700 Chestnut Street, Philadelphia, Pennsylvania 19104; (215) 382-6644.

Eschews special-interest focus; advocates change that will benefit people of all ages. Nationally, monitors issues of social justice and joins coalition groups speaking out on issues of health care, consumer fraud, nursing home reform, public transportation. Some 32 units in 18 states engage in community social action and legislative lobbying. Speakers bureau. Assists local groups to organize.

Publications: *Network: Age and Youth in Action,* newsletter, intermittent, $2.00; *Citizens Action Manual: Nursing Home Reform,* specific action guidelines based upon completed Long-Term Care Action Project.

Gerontological Society, 1835 K Street, N.W., Washington, D.C. 20006; (202) 466-6750.

Promotes scientific study of aging and application of research findings. Four areas of education stressed at annual meeting: biology; clinical medicine; behavioral and social sciences; social planning, research, and practice.

Publications: *Journal of Gerontology,* bimonthly journal of original scientific research (emphasis on data analysis, methodology); *Gerontologist,* bimonthly journal of applied research (interpretive).

National Interfaith Coalition on Aging (NICA), 220 South Hull Street, Athens, Georgia 30601; (404) 543-3513.

Relates Judeo-Christian values to the life conditions of the aging; stimulates cooperative action between religious and secular agencies; identifies programs and services best implemented by the religious sector. Special project—Survey of Aging Programs Under Religious Auspices—collects and catalogs data on service delivery, resources, training, and spiritual well-being concerns.

Publications: *Aging Persons in the Community of Faith: A Guidebook for Churches and Synagogues on Ministry to, for and with the Aging,* published for the Institute on Religion and Aging and distributed by NICA, P.O. Box 1986, Indianapolis, Indiana 46206, $1.00 single copy.

Legal Research and Services for the Elderly (David Marlin, Executive Director), 1511 K Street, N.W., Washington, D.C. 20005.

National Association of Area Agencies on Aging (Raymond Mastalish, Executive Director), 1828 L Street, N.W., Suite 400, Washington, D.C. 20036.

National Association of Retired Federal Employees (Michael C. Nave, President; Jack Goldberg, Vice-President), 1533 New Hampshire Avenue, N.W., Washington, D.C. 20036.

National Association of State Units on Aging (Daniel Quirk, Director), 1828 L Street, N.W., Suite 400, Washington, D.C. 20036.

Urban Elderly Coalition (Ruth Braver Director), 1828 L Street, N.W., Suite 505, Washington, D.C. 20036.

INDEX